PRACTICAL IMPLEMENTATION
OF SOFTWARE METRICS

PRACTICAL IMPLEMENTATION OF SOFTWARE METRICS

Paul Goodman

McGRAW-HILL BOOK COMPANY

London · New York · St Louis · San Francisco · Auckland · Bogotá
Caracas · Hamburg · Lisbon · Madrid · Mexico · Milan · Montreal
New Delhi · Panama · Paris · San Juan · São Paulo · Singapore
Sydney · Tokyo · Toronto

Published by
McGRAW-HILL Book Company Europe
SHOPPENHANGERS ROAD · MAIDENHEAD · BERKSHIRE · SL6 2QL · ENGLAND
TELEPHONE 0628 23432
FAX: 0628 770224

British Library Cataloguing in Publication Data

Goodman, Paul
    Practical Implementation of Software Metrics —
    (International Software Quality Assurance Series)
    I. Title II. Series
    005.1

    ISBN 0-07-707665-6

Libary of Congress Cataloging-in-Publication Data

Goodman, Paul
    Practical implementation of software metrics/Paul Goodman.
        p.   cm. — (The McGraw-Hill international software quality assurance series)
    Includes bibliographical references and index.
    ISBN 0-07-707665-6
    1. Software engineering. 2. Computer software — Evaluation.
I. Title. II. Series.
QA76.758.G66 1992   92-42989
005.1'4–dc20   CIP

1234 HWV 9543

Typeset by Alden Multimedia
and printed and bound in Great Britain by BPCC Hazell Books Ltd Member of BPCC Ltd

CONTENTS

ACKNOWLEDGEMENTS

This is the part of book writing that is both enjoyable and frustrating. Enjoyable, because it gives me a chance to thank publicly some of the people who have helped me over the years; frustrating, for various reasons. Firstly, I wonder how many people actually read them; secondly, there is nowhere near enough space to say what needs to be said; and, thirdly, I am bound to miss some people. Notwithstanding, I intend to indulge myself shamelessly — even if nobody ever reads this.

Where to start? It seems to me that I should start with Roger Betteridge and the team at the Inland Revenue in Telford. Roger started me off in the world of Software Metrics, so it is all his fault! With Roger and the rest of the team, plus help from Ian Drummond and Pat Middleton, I like to think that we actually achieved a few things.

Then came Frank Milsom and Andy Simpson, both of whom gave me more than enough rope, but always made sure that I didn't hang myself, and the many individuals I met at GPT in the UK and Stromberg Carlson in America.

I can also thank the gods for the opportunity I now have to work with the likes of Jim Hemsley, who lets me get on with it, Eric Trodd, Nick Ashley and Mike Berwick, who are usually involved in it and everyone else at Brameur, especially the support staff, who regularly work miracles. Life here is interesting, to say the least.

I also have to thank some other people. Darrel Ince and Phil Higham both reviewed this book, and helped to make it what it is, for good or bad. Both of them I have known for some time, both of them did me proud, as I knew they would. Jacqueline Holdsworth also reviewed this book, but I need to thank her not as a reviewer but as a friend, as a professional colleague of many years' standing, and as someone who has helped me crystallize so many ideas over the years I have known her.

I must also thank my copy editor who I do not even know yet but who will earn his or her keep tenfold and Jacqueline Harbor of McGraw-Hill who has helped nurture this book to fruition and has kept her cool doing it.

The list goes on, and could continue for many pages, but before I stop I do want to thank especially Keith Jackson and Mike Kelly — essentially for being themselves.

Finally, I need to thank Sharon, my wife, who puts up with too much, too often, with too little thanks and who, with my son Luke, make it all worthwhile. At least this gives me one opportunity to say thank you to them.

QUALITY ASSURANCE FORUM

The Quality Assurance Forum is pleased to publish jointly with McGraw-Hill this book which covers topics pertinent to software quality assurance.

The aim of the organization is 'to help the member organizations improve the quality of their computer services through the exchange of information between members and with other organizations with similar interests'.

The QA Forum has over 200 members, including organizations from all sectors of industry and commerce, as well as local and national government. While these organizations are predominantly based in the UK, this includes a growing number from other countries in Europe.

This series of books aims to provide an opportunity for authors to publish works which are both practical and state-of-the-art. In this way QA Forum members and other organizations will benefit from the exchange of information and the development of new ideas which will further the cause of quality in Information Technology.

The QA Forum publishes these books with the aim of stimulating discussion in the software community so that the industry as a whole will move forward to improved products and services. It is proud to be associated with the series while not endorsing every single point of view in every book.

If you would like to know more about the QA Forum, please contact:

Quality Assurance Forum
17 St Catherine's Rd
Ruislip
Middlesex HA4 7RX
UK
Tel: +44 (0) 895 635222
Fax: +44 (0) 895 679178

Section 1

1

WELCOME

Some twenty to twenty-five years ago Software Metrics was a curiosity confined to a few university researchers and one or two industrial or commercial organizations. Now it is a well-established discipline with a growing band of practitioners and adherents.

Today, it seems you cannot attend any software engineering conference or seminar without coming across at least one speaker who features the subject *Software Metrics*. We can find active user groups specializing in particular applications within the general domain of Software Metrics; there are research projects funded by the European Economic Community involving some of the largest industrial organizations in the world; and there are specialist international conferences and workshops that attract large audiences on a regular basis. In the UK, the Quality Assurance Forum operates three special interest groups that each meet three times a year. The Operations and the CASE groups are both effective forums for discussion, but by far the largest of these groups, normally with over a hundred delegates at each meeting, is the Software Metrics Special Interest Group.

However, despite the huge increase of interest in the use of Software Metrics within industry, and I include all types of commercial and engineering applications in the term 'industry', much of what we see is concerned with the definition of particular techniques. One of the problems facing the information technology (IT) industry today is the application of these techniques in a business environment. Little has been written about solving the very practical problems faced by organizations who wish to introduce the use of Software Metrics, and the aim of this book is to go some way towards correcting this situation.

The material in the book is based on four years' experience of implementing Software Metrics initiatives in two large organizations. This has been enhanced by experiences gained from acting in a consultancy role to a number of other organizations engaged in implementing similar programmes over a few more years. The suggestions and models presented in the text are the result of having to find pragmatic solutions to very real, business-related problems.

I do not claim that this book is the last word that will ever need to be said about the topic of implementing Software Metrics initiatives, it is not. What it does contain is a set of approaches and techniques, presented as a coherent whole, that have worked in those real business situations, together with discussions about specific aspects of Software Metrics based on those same experiences. Nor can I claim that all of the components that make up this book are my own. I have been privileged to meet some very talented people in many organizations across the world who have been willing to share ideas and concepts freely, so that everyone benefits. For this I thank them, and I have provided references to their work, whenever I could, throughout the body of this book.

This has not just been a sharing of successes, but also of failures and frustrations. I am able to contribute very easily when it comes to failures! I believe that one of the things this work has to recommend it is that it is based, in part, on learning from those failures, and the hope is that the reader can avoid the mistakes that I and others have made in the past.

Interestingly, I have found that there are great similarities in the mistakes we have made, and also in the successes we have had. It is this that makes me feel that a book like this which attempts to illustrate a generic approach to the implementation of Software Metrics programmes can work.

Turning from the background to the book itself, I hope that it will be found to be readable. To help in this, the material has been separated into three sections. The first defines exactly what I mean by the term *Software Metrics* and introduces the reader to the domain of Software Metrics by discussing the need for a measurement-based approach to the management of software engineering. This first section, then, for reasons which will become obvious, looks at a particular measurement technique, Function Point Analysis, before discussing specific areas of application for Software Metrics.

The second section is really the core of the book. This section describes an approach to the development and implementation of Software Metrics initiatives. Essentially, the approach centres around a model that breaks the work into a number of stages. This division of labour into phases is, of course, nothing more than the way in which most successful projects are handled; it is what makes up those stages that I hope will be found beneficial.

The third section is a collection of chapters that belong in this book, but do not sit naturally in either of the other two sections. Here we visit the topics that seem to be generating discussion today, and we will also look at some topics that may be key issues in the near future.

Appendices and references are also provided.

2

SOFTWARE METRICS — WHAT AND WHY?

In this chapter I would like to define what it is I mean by the term *Software Metrics*; to discuss in general terms the domain covered by that term according to my definition, and to discuss some of the reasons why an organization may consider the use of Software Metrics.

My introduction to Software Metrics came with a job move from a normal, commercial software engineering environment. The work had also involved some project management. The move required me to change location, and I arrived for my first day's work fully expecting to be put in charge of a development team — only to be offered something completely different. The work they wanted me to get involved in seemed to be dealing with some rather ill-defined problems, and I also had to figure out how to stop a spreadsheet package beeping at me every few minutes as I made yet another mistake with this new tool.

The first problem we considered concerned the question of change requests that went to make up an enhancement project, and, given that the scope of the release might have to be reduced, to identify those requests that could be most easily removed from the total package. My most abiding memory of those early days is of other people in the office walking up and asking what I was doing. My answer was invariably: 'I don't really know, but it's good fun'. And it was. I was making use of mathematical skills I thought had been consigned to the waste bin, I was meeting people and I had a good level of job satisfaction. What I did not have was a convenient handle by which I could describe my work.

However, we must have been doing something right, because the team grew quite quickly from two, myself and my manager, to the grand size of five staff. As we grew, we also started to hear of teams in other organizations who were involved in a new fad called *Software Metrics*. Well, not that new nor, perhaps, that much of a fad. The ideas we were hearing about had been around for twenty years or more, and some organizations had a significant investment in their use. Even more importantly, a few of these organizations seemed to be getting good returns on that investment. Yet it is true to say that the current widespread interest in Software Metrics only really started in about 1984. Since then, like Topsy, it has growed and growed!

This scenario, of my initial involvement with Software Metrics starting from the organization's almost total naïvety regarding the subject to the point where the topic becomes recognized as being important to the business, is not uncommon. It typifies the way in which Software Metrics programmes progress, and it is worth remembering that a good way to learn about any subject is to start working in that area.

DEFINITION OF SOFTWARE METRICS

So, our team now had a name that we could associate with our work, *Software Metrics*. But what are *Software Metrics*?

Software Metrics can be defined as:

> The continuous application of measurement-based techniques to the software development process and its products to supply meaningful and timely management information, together with the use of those techniques to improve that process and its products.

As will be seen, this definition covers quite a lot. Software Metrics is all about measurement which, in turn, involves numbers; the use of numbers to make things better, to improve the process of developing software and to improve all aspects of the management of that process. Software Metrics are applicable to the whole development lifecycle from initiation, when costs must be estimated, to monitoring the reliability of the end product in the field, and the way that product changes over time with enhancement. It covers engineers or programmers using techniques to spot error-prone components before they get as far as coding and controlling a project as it progresses, so that the fact that it is going to be six months late is recognized as early as possible rather than the day before delivery is due. It even covers organizations determining which of its software products are the cash cows and which are the dogs.

AREAS OF APPLICATION

There are many different ways in which Software Metrics can be used, some of which are almost specialities in their own right. There are also ways in which the domain of Software Metrics can be divided. The approach I prefer is to consider specific areas of application of Software Metrics.

The most established area of Software Metrics has to be cost and size estimation techniques. There are many proprietary packages on the market that will provide estimates of software system size, cost to develop a system, and the duration of a development or enhancement project. These packages are based on estimation models, the best known of these being the COnstructive COst MOdel, COCOMO, developed by Barry Boehm (1981). Various techniques that do not require the use of tools are also available.

There has been a great deal of research carried out in this area, and this research continues in the USA, Europe and elsewhere, with the Department of Defense in the USA, the Department of Trade and Industry in Britain, and the European Economic Community sponsoring much of it. One thing that does come across strongly from the results of this research work is that organizations cannot rely, solely, on the use of proprietary packages.

Controlling software development projects through measurement is an area that is generating a great deal of interest, both in Europe and the USA. This has become much more relevant with the increase in fixed-price contracts, and the use of penalty clauses by customers who deal with software developers.

The prediction of quality levels for software, often in terms of reliability, is another area where Software Metrics has an important role to play. Again, there are proprietary models on the market that can assist with this, but debate continues about their accuracy. The requirement is there, both from the customers' point of view and that of the developer, who needs to control testing and proving costs. Various techniques can be used now, and this area will become more and more important in the future.

The use of Software Metrics to provide quantitative checks on software designs is also a well-established area. Much research has been carried out, and some organizations have used such techniques to very good effect. This area of Software Metrics is also being used to control software products that are in place and that are subject to enhancement.

Recent applications of Software Metrics include research into the effect of soft or environmental factors on the effectiveness of the development process. This has prompted one large organization to build a development complex specifically designed with the needs of engineers or programmers in mind (McCue, 1978). This option is not open to most organizations, but there is usually a great deal that can be done to improve the development process by making changes to the environment in which that process operates.

Measurement can be used to identify where change should be concentrated. Just starting to measure soft factors can often lead to useful insights regarding the way in which a process operates, and this can lead to benefits to a business by improving performance in key areas such as lead time to market (Ahlgren, 1992).

Using measured quantities to compare one's own organization with others is an extremely popular area of Software Metrics. A number of consultancy firms including Butler Cox (now CSC-Index) in Europe and the DoD-sponsored Software Engineering Institute in the USA offer this type of service to the industry, and many organizations, large and small, make use of such services. It does, however, involve effort on the part of the organization, so the benefits must be weighed against the costs. One result of using such an approach is that we can actually discover that we were as bad as we thought, but that most other organizations are also as bad. This can be very useful information but, even more importantly, such a service can help identify who is 'best in class'. Once we have this information, we can learn from it.

Finally, we come to the most common use of Software Metrics, the provision of management information. This includes information about productivity, quality and process effectiveness. It is important to realize that this should be seen as an ongoing activity. Snapshots of the current situation have their place, but the most valuable information comes when we can see trends in data. Is productivity or quality getting better or worse over time? If so, then why is this happening? What can management do to improve things? The provision of management information is as much an art as a science. Statistical analysis is part of it, but the information must be presented in a way that managers find of use, at the right time and for the right reasons.

All this shows that Software Metrics is a big field! Recognizing this fact is an important step in that it presents a choice. You can probably see many of the areas identified above as having relevance to your business. Do you try to implement Software Metrics in these many forms or do you adopt a softly softly approach tackling one or perhaps two areas first? Both approaches have benefits and dangers associated with them. Resolving this issue within an organization brings us to the first principle of Software Metrics: implementation, pragmatism and compromise.

At this point, I would like to make a number of points regarding certain principles that, while I will attempt to justify them, I suggest are treated as axioms as far as this book is concerned. These are some of the concepts that form the foundation for the core of this book. I will also take the opportunity to discuss some of the inherent dangers if the approach taken to software engineering and its management excludes Software Metrics.

PRINCIPLE NUMBER ONE: PRAGMATISM AND COMPROMISE

The first principle of Software Metrics is that of pragmatism and compromise. Implementing Software Metrics in an organization of any size is difficult. There are many problems that have to be overcome and decisions that have to made, often with limited information to hand. One of the first decisions concerns the scope of the work. There is a rule in software development that we do not try something new on a large or critical system and this translates, in the Software Metrics area, to 'don't try to do too much'. On the other hand, there is evidence that concentrating on too small an area can result in such a limited pay back as to invalidate Software Metrics in an organization. As Darlene Brown, a long time metrics activist succinctly puts it: 'don't bet your career on a single metric'.

Metrics programmes that work seem to be a pragmatic compromise between these two extremes. Identifying the key requirements of the organization and satisfying these, while avoiding truly esoteric areas such as predicting the portability of new systems if this is not a key business requirement, is one approach that can be used to define the scope of a Software Metrics programme. The work of Basili and Rombach, among others, has been instrumental in formalizing this strategy (Rombach, 1990). Organizations such as Hewlett-Packard and Du Pont de Nemours who are recognized by many as having beneficial metrics programmes can show a portfolio of applied measurement techniques that form a multi-faceted programme. Organizations that introduce one metric, for example the software system sizing technique known as Function Point Analysis (FPA) which will be discussed later, and nothing else, often end up without a Software Metrics programme. This is truly unfortunate, because FPA can form the backbone of a successful programme, but alone it is not enough. So, help the programme to succeed by linking areas of work within the programme to specific business requirements in the organization.

This principle of pragmatism and compromise runs through successful Software Metrics programme implementations.

PRINCIPLE NUMBER TWO: MEASURING PEOPLE — DON'T!

Measuring the performance of individuals is extremely dangerous. I know of one organization which used individual productivity, in terms of functionality divided by effort, as a major determinant of salary increases. While this may appear attractive to some managers, the organization later stated that this was one of the worst mistakes it ever made. Using measurement in this way is counter-productive, divisive and simply ensures that engineers will rig the data they supply.

An associate of mine often says that management has one chance and one chance only. The first time that a manager uses data supplied by an individual against that individual is the last time that the manager will get accurate or true data from that person. The reasoning behind such a statement is simple, employees do not like upsetting the boss!

I do know of one organization that uses Software Metrics to measure individuals and who seems to do this effectively. A single measure is not used but, instead, productivity is combined with the quality of the items produced, and the environment of the individual is also considered. This information is used to benefit the individual by identifying training needs and ways that the environmental processes can be improved. Essentially, the information is used constructively rather than destructively.

Two points are worth noting about this second organization:

1. It has found that individuals with high productivity levels also tend to produce better quality products than individuals with lower productivity.
2. It is a Japanese organization.

My personal view is that most Western organizations are not mature enough to use the measurement of individuals constructively. Remember that, in the East, measurement is an integral part of life. In Japan, the kyu and dan grades are used to rank or measure many aspects of artistic life. I also believe that the culture in the West is such that any manager should be capable of assessing an individual's worth through knowledge of that individual. A good manager should not need measurement to know if an engineer is pulling his or her weight, and it is dangerous to use measurement in this way.

PRINCIPLE NUMBER THREE: MODELLING = SIMPLIFICATION

There is a great temptation in Software Metrics to seek the 'silver bullet', the single measure that tells all about the software development process. Currently, this does not exist.

Software Metrics depend upon the use of modelling and, by definition, this involves simplification. We may, for example, model reliability through *mean time to failure* or *defect density* (these are discussed later), but nobody really believes that these measures truly tell the whole story about reliability. Yet they can still be used to assess this attribute of a software system. In this way, they are a pragmatic attempt to satisfy a real requirement for information.

Models that simplify reality have a large role to play in any Software Metrics programme, but recognizing and accepting the limitations of these models is another major step forward towards making practical use of Software Metrics.

PRINCIPLE NUMBER FOUR:
ASK NOT FOR WHOM THE BELL TOLLS — ASK *WHY?*

At conferences and seminars that address the topic of Software Metrics, the question often posed is: 'what do I do with all this data now I've collected it'?

One glib answer with a great deal of truth behind it is to give it to a statistician. There is a very good reason for this. Statisticians are trained to interpret data, which is an art in itself but, more importantly, they realize that, for example, recognizing the presence of a trend is only the first step. The next thing to do is to find out why that trend is present. Why is something happening? Answer that question, and you have useful information.

Of course, the answer to the question 'why' may not be obvious from the data itself. Usually that data needs to be related back to the environment it came from. To illustrate this, imagine a trivial case where the number of defects found during testing suddenly rises from some norm. Let us also assume that the items being tested are essentially the same. In Fig. 2.1, each point could be an enhancement build on a generic software product where each build is of similar size and complexity.

What does our data tell us? Unless we relate it back to the environment, very little. Looking at that testing environment, we may find that at time t we changed our test strategy, perhaps introducing a new tool that automatically generates test cases, thus freeing up effort so that more testing could be carried out. An initial knee-jerk reaction that quality, in terms of the development deliverables to testing, had gone down would have been false.

Learning to ask 'why' is yet another important step towards making practical use of Software Metrics.

PRINCIPLE NUMBER FIVE:
'THE SUM OF THE WHOLE IS GREATER THAN THE CONSTITUENT PARTS'

This well-known axiom is often forgotten or ignored, yet it follows on from the previous principle. Consider again the situation outlined above. Also, imagine that additional information is available as shown in Fig. 2.2, i.e. field defects decreasing at t.

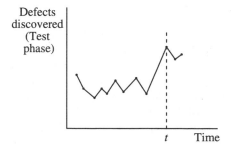

Figure 2.1 Test defects report.

Figure 2.2 Field defects report.

Putting the two pieces of information together may show that the new test strategy is discovering more bugs in testing before they are delivered to the customer. This information could be extremely useful, and may lead to the tool being made available to all test teams because of a demonstrable benefit.

Looking at the two items of information has given us much more than looking at each in isolation.

PRINCIPLE NUMBER SIX: CULTURE SHOCK!

This is more a fact of life than a principle. We must realize that implementing Software Metrics means changing the way in which people work and think.

The software engineering industry is maturing. Customers are no longer willing to accept poor quality and late deliveries. Management is no longer willing to pour money into the black hole of IT, and more management control is now a key business requirement. Competition is growing. We, as developers, have to change and mature as well, and this can be a painful experience as we find tenets of our beliefs being challenged and destroyed. Some simple statements that could be made by many in our industry together with my interpretation of current management trends will illustrate the point:

- *Software development is so complex, it cannot be managed like other parts of the organization.* Forget it, it will be or the business will find developers and managers who will manage that development.
- *I am only six months late with this project.* Fine, you are only out of a job.
- *But you can't put reliability constraints in the contract.* Then you don't get the contract.

The list is almost endless and the message is clear. We will grow up or we will cease to grow. Like any organism, no growth means no life.

Software Metrics cannot solve all our problems, but they can enable managers to improve their processes, to improve productivity and quality, to improve the probability of survival. But it is not an easy option. Many metrics programmes fail. One reason for this is that organizations and individuals who would never dream of introducing a new computer system without a structured approach ignore the problems of introducing change inherent in Software Metrics implementation. Only by treating the implementation of Software Metrics as a project or programme in its own right with plans, budgets, resources and management commitment can such an implementation succeed.

Some organizations have already bitten the bullet and now have Software Metrics programmes running successfully. From their experiences and my own, I have formed the opinion that the introduction of Software Metrics has a lifecycle not unlike that of other projects. It is that lifecycle model that we will investigate further in Section 2 of this book. Before that, we will look at some specific applications of Software Metrics in more detail.

SUMMARY

Software Metrics is simply the application of measurement-based techniques in a software environment. There are many, many ways in which such techniques can be applied, and I like to simplify things by considering four main application areas:

1. Cost estimation
2. Project control
3. The use of metrics in the design process
4. Management information

Some individuals still ask if the use of Software Metrics is justified. I would say to these people that not only is the use justified, but that it is actually inescapable. The reality today is that business managers are no longer willing to allow their IT departments or their software suppliers to operate without normal business controls. This is a new situation for the IT industry, the honeymoon is over. Either we will have such controls forced upon us, or we will grasp the nettle and start to put our house in order before the iron fist lands. Something of a mixed metaphor, but it makes the point!

We used to hear it said that the role of Software Metrics was to enable software engineers to understand the process in which they were involved. I claim today that the role of Software Metrics is to enable engineers and managers to survive in today's business environment. Of course, that means a greater understanding, but it also means that the pressure is on to start to get it right now!

This chapter is intended to give some meaning to the term *Software Metrics*. We have looked briefly at various areas where the techniques we collectively call *Software Metrics* can be applied, and we have looked at certain basic principles which, I would suggest, should underlie any measurement initiative. Finally, we have discussed some of the reasons why an organization may wish to invest in a Software Metrics programme, and in this respect the message is simple. *The use of Software Metrics does not ensure survival, but it improves the probability of survival.*

3

AN OVERVIEW OF FUNCTION POINT ANALYSIS

While this section of the book deals with areas of application of Software Metrics, I would like to spend some time discussing one particular measurement technique, Function Point Analysis or FPA. I have two reasons for doing this:

1. Of all the metrics that can form part of a measurement programme, FPA is one of the most widely used, at least within the data processing sector of the industry. Indeed, the use of FPA seems to grow exponentially year on year.
2. I wish to introduce the technique at this stage because it is very difficult to discuss modern Software Metrics, as we will be doing throughout the book, without making reference to FPA. Without some introduction to the technique those references could be confusing.

If you are already a user of FPA you may wish to miss this chapter, possibly returning to it later.

WHAT IS FUNCTION POINT ANALYSIS?

The concept of FPA was first presented to a joint SHARE/GUIDE/IBM conference in 1979 by the developer of the technique, Allan Albrecht, (Albrecht, 1979). Albrecht had required a long-term productivity measure for systems he was managing. The problem he faced was that his environment included different language types, and so he needed something that was technology-independent, or at least independent of the programming language used. That was the start.

Since then FPA has moved from being a locally used metric within one organization — in fact in just one part of an organization — to the situation we see today, which is that FPA is widely used in very many organizations in many parts of the world.

Supporting this use are a number of user groups, many consultancy organizations and many commercially available training courses. At times it seems as though there is a whole industry involved in promoting and supporting the use of FPA.

Given that FPA has been so successful in terms of widespread adoption, at least within the data processing environment, it is sometimes surprising to realize that FPA provides a very basic item of data. Function Point Analysis is simply a technique that can be used to derive a measure of the size of a software system.

The wide use of FPA and the fact that it has been in the public domain has led to some problems. For example, there are many variants of FPA. Some of these have been developed to address perceived limitations in the original technique, while others have been developed to extend the application domain of FPA beyond the data processing environment to the, so called, real time environment. For example, Charles Symons has developed a major variant of FPA, often called Mark II Function Point Analysis, which has been adopted by the British Civil Service as a standard, (Symons, 1991). Capers Jones (1988) has developed a variant of FPA known as Feature Points, which he sees as an experimental technique that could extend the use of FPA to real time applications. Don Reifer has also explored the application of FPA to real time environments, (Reifer, 1989). Being in the public domain has also meant that there have been numerous critical reviews of the technique, many of which have led to improvements in FPA or in its application.

Despite the wealth of information available, or perhaps because of it, many misconceptions exist about FPA. I would like to establish three basic ideas that should be appreciated by anyone before they start to use FPA. Before doing that I must stress that this chapter cannot fully explain or discuss the whole subject. To do that would take a book of its own, so please view the rest of this chapter simply as an introduction to the technique, and I would suggest that either the International, the European or the Netherlands Function Point User Groups are contacted for further information. Having said that, we can now consider three of what I consider to be key points regarding FPA:

1. *Function Point Analysis is a technique*, hence the use of the word 'analysis' in the name. It is not a simple count of specific characteristics, nor is it a totally de-skilled activity. Organizations that are seen as the most effective users of FPA often bring together an FPA expert and a system expert when they wish to size an application. To use FPA effectively requires training, may require support and will involve an investment of effort.
2. *Function Point Analysis produces a unitless answer or score*. This means that there is no such thing as a 'function point'. Appreciating this fact can save much confusion later. If this appears odd, then think of an FPA score as an index in the same form as the Dow Jones or Stock Market FTSE index. These are also unitless measures and once it is understood how the index behaves, use can be made of the information it provides.
3. *The number produced by FPA is a measure of system size*. Of itself this has little value, but it is a basic data element. I must stress that FPA is *not* an estimating technique, nor is it a device for productivity measurement. What FPA does is enable such activity by providing the basic data, size. Once you have a size value, this can feed into the estimation process for effort or cost. Size values are also used in basic productivity measures and, as will be seen later, in many other measures that provide meaningful information.

Having set the scene regarding some of the basics of FPA, we can consider the technique itself. This will involve a fair degree of technical detail and, if preferred, the following section can be omitted, in which case simply go on to the summary at the end of this chapter.

USING FUNCTION POINT ANALYSIS

At this point I would like to give a feel for what is involved in an FPA exercise. The variant used to describe an FPA exercise is the Albrecht form of FPA sanctioned by the International Function Point User Group (IFPUG). There is also a brief explanation of some of the main differences between the Albrecht variant and Mark II FPA.

Performing an FPA exercise

Function Point Analysis is a measure of system size. It is derived from an analysis of five basic, external, system parameters:

- Inputs;
- Outputs;
- Inquiries;
- Internal and
- External Logical Data Groups[1], or LDGs, operating within the *system boundary*.

Defining the system boundary

Defining the system boundary is the first step in FPA. The boundary is used to limit the scope of the sizing exercise and to help identify the other external parameters.

There are three views of the system boundary depending upon the type of FPA exercise that is being carried out.

1. The application or product boundary. This encompasses a full application, and this type of count is often done at the end of a development project when handing over to the maintenance group or when an organization first starts to use FPA. This type of FPA count can also be derived from a live system.
2. The initial development project boundary. This is a very similar kind of count to the previous one, the difference being that the count derives from requirements for which no system exists.
3. The enhancement project boundary. This situation arises where a system exists and further releases are made of that system. The enhancement project FPA approach differs from the previous situation in that added, changed and deleted functionality is considered rather than the totality of the system. Do not fall into the trap of counting the total system both before and after enhancement, and subtracting one total from the other. This is not a valid approach as can be seen if a project is considered that adds a certain amount of functionality and deletes the same amount in another part of the system. Subtracting the size of the system before the project from the size after the project will give a project size of zero!

---

[1] Logical Data Groups are often called Files.

There is a subjective element in determining the system boundary and, obviously, changing the system boundary will change the FP score. While this may seem an unscientific approach, in practice the guideline that the analyst should consider is to look at what is managed as a discrete whole. This enables most system boundaries to be defined easily. From this point, FPA is a more mechanistic process, but still demands skill unless a fully electronic design support system is in operation.

Defining the parameters

To be able to determine the parameter occurrences that will contribute to the *final FP score*, those parameters must be defined. The definitions presented below, which are partial quotes from the IFPUG *Counting Practices Manual* (1990a), will give an indication of what is required. Note that they are not full definitions.

External inputs: An external input causes the processing of data or control information which crosses the system boundary and, through a unique logical process, maintains an internal LDG. An external input is considered unique if data is maintained within an internal LDG and the input format is unique or the processing logic is unique.

External outputs: An external output results from the processing of data or control information that crosses the system boundary. An external output is considered unique if the format is unique or the processing logic that produces the output is unique.

Internal LDGs: An internal LDG, often called an internal file, is a user-identifiable group of logically related data or control information maintained and utilized within the system boundary. It is data that an experienced user would identify as fulfilling a specific user requirement of the application, and which the system being sized can write to.

External LDGs: An external LDG, often called an interface file, is a user-identifiable group of logically related data or control information utilized by the application, but maintained by another application. Essentially, the application being sized has only read access to the data.

Inquiries: An external inquiry is a unique input/output combination where an input causes an immediate output and an internal LDG is not updated. An input/output combination is considered unique if the input format is unique or the output format is unique.

The word *immediate* in this definition can cause problems. The key point to bear in mind is that, within an inquiry, data held by the system is not changed.

Identifying unique occurrences of parameters

Having defined parameters, we can now proceed to the next step, identifying all unique occurrences of parameters. When doing this, there are certain points that should be remembered:

- The expression *maintain* means to create, change or delete a record within a LDG.
- For all parameters, a logical rather than physical view should be taken. For example, if you consider a screen output, data may be presented on two physical screens, but if the second is a continuation of the first, then it is classed as one logical screen.

Also, if considering LDGs, it is the logical view of data as perceived by the user that should be taken rather than any physical storage view imposed by the technology or the implementation.

- For outputs, duplicate reports on different media or those sent to different locations are counted separately, as this should only be done to satisfy user requirements.
- Internal LDGs are often identifiable as singularly named data stores on a *data flow diagram*. Note that the system being sized must have the ability to add, change and delete data for it to be classed as an internal LDG.
- For all LDGs, temporary work files are not counted.
- LDGs maintained by more than one application are credited to each.
- No internal LDG is ever maintained by an inquiry.
- Logon screens that provide security functionality are counted as inquiries.

Remember also that a situation may arise, specific to a particular organization, which is not covered by advice in any set of counting guidelines. This simply reflects the fact that, as Albrecht has said at numerous venues, FPA is an evolutionary technique. In such cases it is up to the practitioner to make a decision or formulate a rule based on personal experience as well as that of others. The most important thing is to document that rule and to apply it consistently. For the benefit of other practitioners, it would be of great assistance if the relevant governing bodies, IFPUG, EFPUG etc are advised, so that they can ensure a consistent and standardized application of FPA across the industry.

Complexity assessment

The five basic parameters can be divided into two groups: *data function types* and *transactional function types* (see IFPUG *Counting Practices Manual* 3.0). This is done on the basis of how the complexity assessment is carried out.

Complexity assessment is carried out by considering two of three parameter characteristics depending upon the *function type*.

These characteristics are:

- Record types;
- Data element types;
- File types referenced.

If an LDG is considered to be a file, then a *record element type* can be thought of as a record. A *data element type* can be thought of as a field within a record.

Data element types should be viewed at the user recognizable level. If a date is stored as dd, mm, yy, i.e. as three separate fields for implementation reasons rather than to meet any customer requirement, then the three fields should be viewed as one for the purposes of FPA.

Fields that repeat, for example array elements, are counted once.

A *file type reference* is counted for each LDG accessed in any way during the processing of a *transactional function type*. Note that it is the number of LDGs referenced not the number of references made that is counted.

The complexity assessment is done by using standard assessment matrices. Note that inquiries are assessed at the level of their greatest constituent part. In other words, if the input part of the inquiry has the highest complexity assessment as an 'average', then the total inquiry is assessed as 'average'.

FPA sample counting form

Parameter	Complexity Count rating	×	Weight		Product
Inputs	Low	____ ×	3	=	_____
	Average	____ ×	4	=	_____
	High	____ ×	6	=	_____
Outputs	Low	____ ×	4	=	_____
	Average	____ ×	5	=	_____
	High	____ ×	7	=	_____
Internal LDGs	Low	____ ×	7	=	_____
	Average	____ ×	10	=	_____
	High	____ ×	15	=	_____
External LDGs	Low	____ ×	5	=	_____
	Average	____ ×	7	=	_____
	High	____ ×	10	=	_____
Inquiries	Low	____ ×	3	=	_____
	Average	____ ×	4	=	_____
	High	____ ×	6	=	_____
				Unadjusted FP score	_____

Counts of each parameter are then weighted and summed together to give the *unadjusted FP score*. These weights are shown on the sample counting form.

General system characteristic analysis

Having derived the *unadjusted function point score*, we now come to one of the more contentious areas of FPA. The technique generally used is to take an overall view of the system being sized via 14 *general system characteristics*.

The set of general system characteristics are each assessed on a scale of 0–5. The scores for each characteristic are then summed to derive the *total degree of influence figure*, the TDI.

Guidance on assessing each of the 14 general system characteristics is provided within the IFPUG *Counting Practices Manual*. These characteristics are listed below:

Data communication
Distributed function
Performance
Heavily used configuration
Transaction rates
On line data entry
Design for end user efficiency
On line update
Complex processing
Usable in other applications
Installation ease
Operational ease
Multiple sites
Facilitate change

Once the TDI value has been derived, it can be used in the following formula to arrive at the *value adjustment factor* or VAF.

$$VAF = (TDI \times 0.01) + 0.65$$

The *final FP score* can then be derived through the following formula:

$$Final\ FP\ score = Unadjusted\ FP\ score \times VAF$$

There is considerable debate within the FPA user community regarding the value of the *general system characteristics*. For one thing their assessment is somewhat subjective. It would also seem that there are dependencies between the various characteristics (Kitchenham, 1990), and, finally, in my experience for most systems the VAF is about 1 which, as a multiplier, has little effect. However, they do form part of the standard FPA technique, and the more experience that is gained in the use of FPA, the greater the probability that we will move towards a more scientific approach.

Differences between Albrecht's and Symons' variants of FPA

The Symons (1991) variant of FPA takes a slightly different view to that of Albrecht. The main differences are:

1. Counts are based around logical business transactions. This difference may be less significant than it seems at first, as I believe that this view is implied in the IFPUG definitions of inputs, outputs and inquiries that speak of unique processing.
2. A much more significant difference is that counts of inputs and outputs are based upon counts of data elements rather than of logical occurrences of, say, screens. This means that complexity does not have to be assessed independently of the occurrence.
3. Internal and external LDGs are not counted at the system level but instead data entity references are counted within a logical business transaction. This implies that an entity model may need to be derived for the system, but as the user view is maintained, this is generally not too difficult.
4. Symons defines 19 *system characteristics* and also allows for organizations to add more.

Overall, I believe that there is much to commend the Symons approach in that it has built on the landmark work done by Albrecht. The worst thing that could happen would be for the FPA community to split along political divisions based on method, and one can only hope that all FPA users will adopt the message of both Albrecht's and Symons' work for a harmonious, clearly defined approach to the sizing of software systems and projects. As both Albrecht and Symons have said more than once in public, we should expect to see Mark III, Mark IV and Mark V versions of FPA as the technique develops.

Finally, do not fall into the trap of looking upon FPA as the totality of a metrics initiative — it never is. Function Point Analysis is a very widely used technique, but all it provides is a measure of software system size. How that data is used to manage and improve a process is what really counts.

SUMMARY

Function Point Analysis is a measurement technique that has been adopted by a large number of data processing organizations, and some efforts have been made to apply FPA to real time environments. The technique consists of various steps, which together produce or derive a measure of system or project size.

Because of the widespread use of FPA, and the fact that it has been in the public domain for some time, there are many variants of FPA and numerous misconceptions. Used correctly, FPA can be a valuable component of a measurement initiative, but it should not be seen as the totality of such an initiative.

4

MANAGEMENT INFORMATION

Ask anyone to explain the meaning of the term *Software Metrics* and the chances are that it will be described as the provision of information through some form of statistical analysis applied to collected data, in other words, the furnishing of *management information*. This aspect of the subject is probably the most traditional form of Software Metrics.

What I hope to do in this chapter is consider why such information is wanted by managers, how it should, and perhaps more importantly should not, be collected and how such information should be presented.

WHAT IS 'MANAGEMENT INFORMATION'

Before we look at these aspects of management information, I would like to discuss some background issues that are quite important. Management information and the systems developed to supply that information (MIS), whether they are being developed as part of a Software Metrics initiative or not, are often thought of as single entities that service the in-house needs of a relatively small group of individuals, the management. This is a very dangerous viewpoint, because MIS applications are often large and complex in two dimensions. Firstly, they service, or should do, many different levels of customer from the MD or SEO to the team leader. Secondly, they have to satisfy a large number of different requirements within each customer set but still recognize the similarities that cross the set boundaries if they are to avoid massive data redundancy. Just to make life interesting, they may also have to deal with *ad hoc* requirements.

Now this may all sound as though it has little to do with a Software Metrics programme, but let me stress that such a programme is a Management Information System. Whether it operates through fancy computer systems or good old pen and paper, it still has to deal with all of the complexities outlined above.

The first dimension tends to be a function of your own organizational structure and it will be for you and your own management group to determine the levels at which your information system should operate. The second dimension has to do with the different requirements placed on that system by its users or customers. This implies that the use to which the information will be put is considered. There are many different, specific requirements that will be placed on the system, but they will all have something in common, or they should do! The aspect of a Software Metrics programme that concerns us is the provision of information. Output from the system should be related to a requirement for information, and should not be generated in any random way. One thing that should be noted is that requirements for information generally, if not always, should relate to an attribute of either a product or a process.

Managing an attribute

To make this clear, we can consider a couple of examples. A manager of a number of product teams may wish to know how those teams are performing and how that performance is changing over time. This is a basic information requirement if the teams are to be managed effectively. This requirement relates directly to the process attribute we call productivity, in other words, what do I get out for what I put in?

On the other hand, a product manager may wish to know how reliable his or her software system is during the first three months of live use across a number of releases. This information can be used as a direct quality measure of the product or as an indirect quality measure of the process that produces the product but, however it is used, it relates to the product attribute of reliability.

To manage an attribute means realizing that there are two information requirements associated with each of them:

1. The attribute be monitored. For example, if a manager feels that group productivity is important to him, then it needs to be measured and periodic reports fed back to the manager so that the information can be used. This is, traditionally, the type of requirement that Management Information Systems seek to satisfy.
2. The attribute be predicted. Now this can be much more difficult. For example, given a new product group within a division, how can we be confident that we can predict the productivity level for that group? But unless we can do this, we may find our business in danger, especially if we are operating in a fixed price environment.

Another example can be drawn from the area of quality. One of the biggest changes in the software industry over the last few years has been the rapid growth in maturity of our end users. They are much less willing now to accept loose specifications of quality and, to be honest, it is not only the fixed price contractors who are having to cope with the need to predict values for various attributes. For example, one of the largest organizations in the UK, an organization with a massive IT procurement budget, appears to be moving towards contractual specifications of reliability for software systems.

This means that we, as software developers, have to be much more capable than we have been in the past when it comes to being able to predict value levels for attributes.

How we do this needs to be given a great deal of thought. Should we attempt to use theoretical models of, say, reliability growth? Research by Bev Littlewood of City

University has shown that this can be very dangerous, (Littlewood, 1990). The problem is that while various reliability growth models may work for certain environments, it does not seem to be possible to identify the environment attributes that would enable a match to be made to a specific model with any degree of certainty. In my opinion, the only alternative is to use empirical models developed from data collected in-house. This would imply that our MIS should collect the data that would enable the derivation of such a model. Obviously, it is difficult to specify the requirements for data collection if we do not have the model defined which will use the data. However, a pragmatic and educated guess as to what will be required is often a valid starting point.

From the examples above, some of the problems that arise when moving into the area of predicting process or product attributes may be appreciated and it would seem that the provision of management information is not quite as simple as we may at first think. To summarize, requirements for information can be many, varied and complex. Attributes of both the process and the products of the process would seem to be fundamental to this aspect of Software Metrics. Attributes, once identified and defined, generate requirements of two types, the need to monitor and the need to predict values for the attribute.

Definitions of reliability

Before continuing and having mentioned reliability, I would like to digress slightly. As far as attribute definitions are concerned, watch out for *some* of the definitions of reliability that are still used.

These generally start by defining reliability as 'the probability that a software system will . . .'. This is not a definition of reliability because anything that is expressed in terms of a probability is, in fact, a prediction. The probability that a ten-year-old male child will grow to a height of six feet does not define the attribute height. This may seem a trivial point, but things like this do show the need for rigour in Software Metrics as such a definition can cost time and money. Imagine going to senior management with a reliability measurement proposal only to have it kicked out because the basic definition of reliability was seen to be flawed. If you think such a thing could never happen, then let me assure you that I have seen it happen.

WHY DO WE NEED MANAGEMENT INFORMATION?

Having discussed some of the background issues relating to Management Information, let us take a step back and consider something even more fundamental — why are we bothering anyway?

One of the most widely used, valid and succinct justifications for the collection of management information comes from Tom DeMarco (DeMarco and Lister, 1987), and says simply that if you don't measure it, you can't control it. I would also like to paraphrase a statement from Dieter Rombach, at the time working with the Software Engineering Laboratory in the USA. He said, at the Eurometrics '91 conference in Paris, that we no longer seem to be asking if we should measure, the question today is *how*? This is certainly true for some organizations and individuals, but it is still true to say that many still need to be convinced or even exposed to the idea of measurement within a software development or support environment. The next few paragraphs are included for those people who have the job of convincing such organizations or groups that management information is necessary.

Controlling the process

The verb 'to manage' is defined in my dictionary as *to control the movement or behaviour of*, which implies some form of control mechanism or loop. Control loops operate on a very simple principle. Measurements are taken of the process output, either by sampling or some other means, and these are fed into a comparator to relate attribute levels of the output to target or ideals. The difference between actual and optimum is then used to instigate corrective action if necessary. Such a control loop is easy to understand if you are a high-fi buff or think in mechanistic terms, but what about other processes? I suggest that the same control loop model can be applied to any process.

For instance, consider the situation where you have to move from point A to point B, 20 miles apart across open moorland or heath. You have with you a compass, and you know that B is due west of A. Assuming that you walk at four miles an hour, would you walk from A for five hours without checking your compass and expect to be at B?

What you would probably do is use your compass and bearings to check your course periodically and to make corrections to it. In other words you are sampling the process and, through measurement, initiating corrective action. This type of process control is epitomized by long-distance sailors who use celestial navigation, by means of compass, timepiece, sextant and chart to get from one coast to another.

It is worth noting that all of these examples include the concept of instrumentation, and this idea has been extended to the control of software development and support through the dashboard analogy put forward by Howard Rubin (1990), and others. This simply says that managers within the software industry need instrumentation if they are going to be able to control the processes they manage, and that part of Software Metrics is the discipline of supplying that instrumentation.

Another analogy that I use likens management in the software industry to the job of flying a plane. In the past, it was very similar to flying one of the old biplanes. It was new, exciting and there were few rules. Instrumentation was rudimentary; if you wanted to know how high you were, you looked over the side of the cockpit; if you got lost, you just followed a convenient road or railway track. Even a disaster like running out of fuel wasn't too bad — if you were lucky, you just set down in a convenient field.

Nowadays, things are different. Software development has increased in complexity and in importance to the core business of most organizations. We can think of management within the software industry of today as akin to flying a jumbo jet. We have to get there on time, we have to give 'good' service and we have to be reliable, because many others depend on us. And yet, for most organizations, their managers are flying that jumbo with the same instrumentation that they were using when they flew the old biplanes. Is it any wonder that we have so many disasters within the software industry! Do you still wonder why we need that instrumentation?

Having said all of that, let nobody think that putting in the right instruments guarantees success or removes the need for good management. Instruments in a jumbo jet do not remove the need for a pilot, nor will Software Metrics ever replace good managers. What Software Metrics can do is improve the probability that a good manager will succeed.

So one reason for installing a MIS concerns the control of the processes for which managers are responsible. If controlling the process for which you are responsible does not interest you, then perhaps you might like to think about protection.

Protection and fear as motivators

Protection and fear are two very emotive words, but they are starting to have real meaning within the IT industry. Everywhere we look today the unthinkable is happening — the Berlin Wall has crumbled, there is a McDonald's in Moscow, the policemen really do look young — and the management are thinking about shutting down the IT function!

What was that last one again? Well, you may think that it is unbelievable but, unless IT is your core business, you may be shocked to learn that this is a very real option open to managers. If you need convincing, I suggest you consider the following: a couple of years ago the whole team on a large UK Government project was disbanded and the work was handed over to a private contractor. Again in the UK, some Government departments have been converted into 'agencies', basically private companies owned by the Government, but managed under normal market forces. Almost invariably this has reduced job security. Finally, you need look no further than the growth in the facilities management sector of our industry.

Think about facilities management for a moment. An organization is going to come in, take over your IT function and for, let's say, the same amount of cash that you pay out now, will provide you with the same IT support. Why do they do this? Quite simply, they know that, for most organizations, the IT function is performing so badly that the facilities management company can make a significant profit just by improving working practices and, it must be said, by either redeploying some of the staff on to other work or by shedding some of those staff. Of course, it could never happen to you, or could it?

The one way to protect yourself from these kinds of threats is to be able to demonstrate that your IT function runs as a tight, lean machine, and that nobody could do IT better! Of course, you cannot do this without effective, quantitative management information.

Optimization — the Holy Grail

Fear can be a powerful motivator. Management through control is appealing. However, by far the most attractive reason for collecting and using management information has to be the concept of optimizing the process, actually using information about the process and its products — in our case the software development process and the systems that result to improve that process.

This fundamental concept underlies the Crosby (1985) and Deming (1986), quality models and Deming, in particular, points out that the concept cannot be applied without having the necessary information provided as part of the process itself. In fact, Deming uses various experiments to illustrate that tweaking the process, whatever it is, can actually make the results worse if this tweaking is done in a random and haphazard way. In other words, if we try to fix the process on gut feel rather than on the basis of quantitative information, we will probably make the process and the results worse. I would suggest that there is an exception to this. If we are so intimately involved with the process as to be a complete and integral part of it, then we probably can fix things on gut reaction and make it better. Equally, if we are that close to the process we probably do not have the power to change it. This is why engineers and programmers are very good people to ask if we think there are problems. They know many of the answers, but cannot do much about it. That is quite an indictment of our society.

Let us now assume that I have browbeaten you into accepting that there is a need for management information. We must now consider the typical requirements for management information, the problems of data collection and how we present results. I am going to do this in a slightly different order, looking at data collection first. The reason is that this is still the way many organizations approach the provision of management information and measurement in general. I hope to show that this is not the way to do things!

COLLECTING THE DATA

'Yes', shouts the MD or CEO 'we want information' — thus giving the required management commitment. What do we do next? Unfortunately, many groups and organizations who have started an initiative to provide management information have gone out 'data hunting'. The average dedicated data hunter is nothing if not thorough. He or she has two guiding principles: if it does not move, measure it; and if it does move, pin it down — then measure it!

The average data hunter is also something of a fanatic who wants to involve everyone else in his (or her) abiding interest. The data hunter will lay traps with forms and procedures seeking to include everyone in his passion. Only when everyone is spending great chunks of time and effort supplying information to the data hunter will he be truly happy.

And what is the result of all this happy hunting? Well, the first thing to realize is that it tends to be costly. Since one thing about the average data hunter is that he is impatient. Not only does he want lots of information, he wants it now. This means that teams of people are often required to sift through old data or even possible sources of old data. Joy to a data hunter is a 50 000 line COBOL listing. There are so many ways the data can be cut. Sorting through any form of old documentation, except code, which is at least available electronically, so that the hunter can get lots of data quickly, takes time and effort. Lots of it. This costs money.

Now having got the data, what do you do with it? Obviously, you analyse it! Do you know how much raw data you can get from a 50 000 line COBOL listing? Let me put it this way, do you have a spare room? All of this data needs to be analysed but, despite the advances in electronic data analysis support, working with more than about 10 variables, (the number of subjects the preconscious brain can handle), is pushing your luck. You need huge amounts of effort to carry out the analysis of all this data, which increases the cost again. In fact, some organizations have rooms full of data that they have neither the time nor, to be honest, the inclination to analyse. Such organizations fell into the hands of data hunters.

Even if you do manage the data analysis, the results may cause you even more heartache. If you have lots of data and lots of variables, something is almost bound to relate to something else, just by chance. And, by the way, do not fall into the trap of believing that the laws of probability apply in anything but their fullest sense. This means, as proposed by Murphy's most important rule, that: 'if event E has a probability P of occurring on a specific day, this means that event E will occur when it can do the most damage or on the first day after counting begins, whichever has the greater disaster potential'. In other words, the probability of two data items relating to one another through chance may be mathematically small, but this means you will probably go into your senior managers' meeting and state that programmers who keep hamsters make good testers, because that's what the data shows! Chance got you again.

I can vouch for the final problem of the data hunting approach from painful experience. As someone who did once dabble with data hunting and someone who also believes that data, somehow, must be of some use if only one had the time to .... As I was saying, the final problem is that you will always miss the most important variable. Murphy's laws again.

More seriously, organizations who do operate under a data hunting regimen tend to have very disgruntled employees, because all they see is bureaucracy and yet more bureaucracy!

But if data hunting is not the answer, then what is? One of the key points that I hope this book can get across is that measurements should only be made to satisfy specific requirements for information which, in turn, should be linked to business objectives. Management information is no exception to this rule, data is collected because the modelling process indicates that the collection of that data will satisfy an information requirement.

REQUIREMENTS FOR INFORMATION

Before I go any further I do need to talk about models and measures. We are going to be discussing requirements during the next few paragraphs, and it is very possible that some 'solutions' to those requirements may creep into the text. Now some people will immediately get annoyed about this, claiming that 'off-the-shelf solutions' never work. Let me put my case very clearly. I suggest that business objectives across organizations are very similar. At their most basic, these objectives resolve into maximizing output while minimizing cost and waste. The problems faced by organizations, especially in the IT industry are also, I will suggest, effectively the same, cost estimation and project control being examples.

The question is, are the solutions to these problems also the same, or at least similar across organizations? Solutions tend to be detailed and are often specific to specific organizations.

However, I believe that what are truly portable in many cases are solution models. Metrics or measures, as will be discussed in more detail in Section 2, are derived from models, and will probably be different between different organizations. If I offer a solution to any requirement talked about in this chapter, it is a model. If you decide to use any of these, you still have some work to do to turn the model into a metric, and an approach to this is also described in Section 2, when I talk about the Goal/Question/Metric paradigm of Basili and Rombach (1990).

Productivity

To illustrate a requirements-based approach to management information, let us look at some of the typical requirements managers have for information. One of the most common requirements for management information is to have productivity figures available. Productivity measures are seen, in many industries other than IT, as performance indicators. Export performance is often expressed in terms of sales over units of time, the implication being that the cost over time is constant. The car industry uses cars produced per workday or month as a measure of factory performance.

Productivity can be defined as the work product divided by the cost to produce that product, and in the IT industry productivity is usually expressed in terms of *lines of code* or *function points* produced divided by effort, in terms of engineering days or months.

These types of measures do not tell us everything we wish to know about performance, but they do give us a high level indicator of performance provided you remember one very important fact. Absolute productivity values, in any terms, do not provide much in the way of useful information. To get any real value out of productivity measures we need to consider the trend over time and what we want to see, of course, is an improvement over time.

The other thing to remember is that productivity should not be considered in terms of good or bad, only higher or lower values. For example, I would expect a small in-house development team who work within very loose documentation constraints to achieve much higher productivity values than a team developing safety critical applications in, say, the defence sector of the industry, where documentation control is extremely stringent. This does not mean that the small in-house team is performing better or that the defence application team is performing worse. What I would want to see, over time, is both teams improving their productivity rates.

This does mean that we need to be very careful when comparing productivity across teams or organizations. Not only can the simple productivity measures lead to erroneous comparisons, but we also need to be very aware of differences in terms of the definitions used for the base data elements. There are, for instance, many perfectly justifiable ways of defining a *line of code*. There are also many variants of Function Point Analysis around, almost as many as there are users of FPA. As if this wasn't bad enough, it is often instructive to ask how the cost element of the productivity function is defined. My idea of an engineering day can be very different from yours. Now it may be that someday we will have recognized standards in these areas, but they do not exist today. This means that such comparisons can give totally false impressions. Having said this, such comparisons can be useful if used sensibly, with great care and always in the presence of a large salt cellar from which to take the occasional pinch.

Finally, never measure productivity at the personnel level. This has been said before, but I make no excuse for repeating myself. I know that it can be tempting to do this, but individual differences and circumstances will probably swamp any meaningful interpretation of the results. For example, I once knew a programmer analyst who was superb at her job. Yet her productivity rate over anything other than a carefully selected short period of time was abysmal for the simple fact that she was used to train and assist the less able team members. This was actually an excellent use of this lady as a resource, because she was not only excellent at her official job, she was also an excellent teacher. Now, we may feel that we would always be sure to take that kind of circumstance into account, but can we be sure that everyone else would all of the time? Anyway, measuring at the individual level and, even worse, using that data as part of assessment activities, leads to demotivated staff, lousy team spirit and an abdication of responsibility by management. A decent team leader should never need that kind of individual measure to assess performance.

Productivity measures have their place. If we use them wisely, we can get hold of a great deal of useful information that enables us to assess process performance, provided we avoid the traps!

Certain other requirements, like productivity measurement, seem to crop up time and again. Getting a handle on the effectiveness of cost estimation within the organization is an example of such a requirement. This is a relatively simple requirement to satisfy since all that is necessary is to compare the accuracy of estimates to the actual results. Few things in Software Metrics are that simple, and this is no exception. Very often such a request hides the real requirement, which is for the implementation of a cost estimation strategy, but more about that later.

Quality assessment

Another basic requirement for management information is in the area of quality assessment. This can really be fun.

If you ever want to waste half an hour or so, get a group of IT professionals together and ask them to define what is meant by 'quality'. Even after the introduction of *Total Quality Management* initiatives by many IT organizations, this continues to trouble the industry. After the half hour is over, you will still not have a definition of 'quality', but you will have seen the whole range of human emotion expressed by normally reasonable men and women. In fact, the best example I ever saw of this type of discussion was among a group of about half-a-dozen quality managers. I leave you to draw your own conclusions!

Of course, the problem is not with the definition of quality, it is with the application of that definition in any sensible way. I am quite happy to accept the Crosby (1985) definition that quality is *the satisfaction of user or customer requirements*. I fully accept that a small hatchback can be a quality car, and that this accolade is not reserved for the best of the super cars. I agree that a quality service is one that meets, or exceeds where cost effective, customer expectations. Does this help me measure quality? Well, it is a start, but that is all. I believe that one must go further than this and that the concept of 'quality' must be further subdivided into a number of quality attributes.

Quality attributes

Identified quality attributes apply to specific applications and to specific deliverables from the development process, such as designs, to a greater or lesser extent. This is well worth remembering.

Typical quality attributes for IT products include, and I apologize in advance for the number of words that end in 'ity', but that seems to be the nature of the beast — reliability, maintainability, testability, usability, portability, etc. The list can go on and on and on and on .... Defining product or process attributes and then relating these to the quality requirements for the process or product is a very effective start when we need to measure 'quality'.

Again, there are certain points that should be borne in mind. Not all attributes apply to all applications. For an embedded application required for a single mission, such as the Voyager satellite, portability may not be a concern. The level of quality required by specific applications may vary according to the attribute being considered and the application type. For instance, the reliability required in a piece of games software is likely to be lower than that for a life support system.

Defining quality in terms of specific attributes may seem a difficult task, but fortunately most managers are very clear in their requirements when asked to state the kinds of information that they would find beneficial. A good beginning, I would suggest, is given in *Software Product Evaluation, Quality Characteristics and Guidelines for their Use*, coded IS 9126 (1990) which is available from the International Standards Organization (ISO). The ISO and the (IEC) have been working on standards for quality attributes for some time now, and this document is the result of their work. Their definitions of the various quality attributes that they have deemed to be important are certainly a valid starting point, although some tailoring may be required to suit the needs of individual organizations.

My only major disagreement with the ISO attribute definitions is in the area of *maintainability*. Within the IT industry there is a great tendency to use maintenance, and hence maintainability, as a catch-all for corrective, adaptive and perfective maintenance as defined by Swanson (1976).

While this made sense at the time, when applications were somewhat simpler, it does seem to cause us problems now. Based on research carried out by the Inland Revenue, and supported by discussions with many IT managers, most IT functions seem to devote about 60–70 per cent of their overall effort to maintenance according to Swanson's definition, but most of this effort is expended on enhancing existing systems in line with new or additional user requirements. This is a direct result of the IT industry adopting, almost universally, a strategy of sequential builds or releases against a generic product or system. The production of these new builds or releases involves all the stages of most of the standard lifecycle models used for development of new systems with, of course, the added complication of integrating new and changed functionality with the core system.

This being the case, it would seem to make sense to treat enhancements to a system separately to 'bug fixing' or corrective maintenance, and I feel that maintainability and enhanceability should both be considered as top-level quality attributes in terms of management information requirements. Of course, maintainability is now defined in terms of corrective maintenance. Perfective maintenance should be included under enhanceability, as it is generally carried out as part of a release development project rather than being part of any patching work.

SOME PORTABLE MODELS

I now intend to provide a small number of models that I believe can be used as the basis of a set of management information measures within an organization. These are my own personal choice and have resulted from applying the metrics derivation procedures described later in Section 2. I have used them successfully in a number of organizations but, let me stress, they are models not specific measures, and they will need additional work before they can be used as metrics for any particular organization. Also, I do not guarantee universal applicability, all I can say is that they have worked for me, so far, in a number of environments.

Measuring reliability

For measuring reliability I suggest a simple defect density measure, i.e. defects reported from the field or customer divided by the size of the product. If you need to compare applications that are used at different rates, say in terms of the number of site installations, then I suggest you build in a usage metric to the denominator, multiplying not adding. I prefer defect density to the common Mean Time Between Failure (MTBF) measure for two reasons. Firstly, I am always wary of using means within software data sets which tend to be skewed, so that the mean is not a suitable level indicator and, secondly, I have never found it easy to collect failure data for the environments in which I have worked. One other minor point is that failures are the really visible defects, the showstoppers. Many users get very fed up with the less critical defects that do not cause the system to fail but which are, none the less, defects or faults.

It is also possible to classify defects according to their severity, but we should beware of introducing sophistication before the basics are in place. Incidentally, defect, error or fault reports used in this measure should be reduced to include only validated and non-duplicated reports. That means that only defects that are found to be the result of genuine faults should be included in the reliability measure, and that if a defect is reported by more than one source, i.e. user, it should be treated as a single defect from the point of view of this measure.

Measuring usability

Usability is a difficult measurement area, so much so that the EC has been funding a research project called MUSiC targeted at just this topic since 1991. However, as a starting point you could do worse than looking at the number of user complaints, defect, fault or error reports, from the field where the root cause is not related to the reliability of the software. Here I intend that you should consider all such reports and not reduce the set by considering only validated non-duplicates. The reason for this is that you are looking for the 'pain' level felt by the customer as a result of you not providing sufficiently good documentation, training or support to that customer. This is an incredibly simplistic approach to usability measurement, and I would accept that it ignores the ergonomic aspect of systems. In defence of this measure, I would say again that it is a 'pain' measure, and that pain is really the inverse of usability.

Measuring maintainability

Maintainability, as I consider it as corrective maintenance, results in the most complex of the suggested models. I find that there are three parameters that affect managers' and users' views of the system maintainability. These are:

- The number of defects fixed, d;
- The time it takes to fix a defect, t;
- The number of defects outstanding, i.e. not fixed, n.

Combining these, I suggest that a maintainability metric can be derived from the following model:

For a given time period, say one calendar month, consider the average time taken to fix a defect multiplied by the sum of the defects fixed and the defects outstanding, i.e.:

Maintainability $= t \times (d + n)$

In this model, if any parameter worsens, the overall result also worsens and the source data, the three parameters, can be investigated to identify the cause of this. Simply recording the parameters separately can cause you to miss a problem developing, specially when the three parameters all start to get slightly worse at the same time. You do not see a problem, but the user does.

Measuring enhanceability

Finally, for enhanceability, the ease by which requested changes can be made to a system, you can consider the number of components affected by a change divided by the total number of components in the system. The reasoning behind this model is that systems do degrade as more and more enhancements are made, and the system level cohesion and coupling properties worsen. In other words, the mix of functionality within a given system component tends to increase, and the number of links between components increases. This tends to reduce enhanceability. This model reflects those effects, and enables corrective action, such as strategic rewrites — namely work that adds no functionality to the system but which is intended to improve enhanceability — to be carried out.

Again, these models are presented as suggestions or starting points. I do not claim that they are perfect models, or even the best available, simply that they have worked for me. What you use in your organization is up to you.

FEEDBACK

Of course, having the models, defining the measures, collecting the data and even analysing that data is not the end of the story. You now have to present or feedback the information to managers. This is an art in itself, and there are some classic examples around of how it should not be done, which I am sure everyone with any management experience has come across. It is an area where a trained statistician can be worth his or her weight in gold, and much of what follows is the result of assistance given to me by such individuals over the years.

The first thing to remember is what is required from such feedback, what does your customer, a manager, want? Well, what is not required is an example of how clever you have been collecting all this data and collating it into nice tables, pages long! Managers are, by definition, simple folk, otherwise they would still be programmers or technical designers. They are also busy, or believe they are — which amounts to the same thing, and as a result of this have only a limited amount of time available. Do not expect them to analyse data sets or to develop relationships between results. That, as the presenter of this information, is your job.

Remember also that different people relate to different styles of presentation, and as you may not know everybody who will see your feedback of information, you will not know whether or not they relate to pictures or words. For this reason, I advocate the use of pictures, in the form of graphs, which I will talk about later, and text. Use the text briefly to summarize what the graphs are saying, but also use a separate section or paragraph to point out any points and relationships that you feel are important. Simply presenting the summarized data is seldom enough.

I favour a management summary at the front of any report that summarizes the summaries in both words and pictures, and I try to use this to point out potential problems. Do not be afraid of doing this. Provided you maintain a reasonable tone to the presentation, and do not insist that your interpretation is the only one, most managers quite like to be told what is happening. It makes a change for them to get usable information, and they like to be told things.

There are some important points to note about management information that relate to feedback or presentation. Some people lay great store by the idea of *Statistical Process Control*. This is an extremely useful concept and approach, but it does depend upon a process or product attribute being statistically stable. By this I mean that most variation is predictable. For example, assuming I was any good at archery, the process of firing an arrow at a target would probably be statistically stable in that my arrows would normally be clustered within a certain circumference away from the gold. If I then shot an arrow and it hit the target rim, it would be exceptional, in statistical terms an *outlier*, and I should ask why it happened. I may investigate and find that the arrow was warped, so I could improve the process of firing by not using that arrow again.

For a software system I may also observe statistical stability when, say, reliability values in terms of defect density for each three monthly release remain within a certain range for a given space of time. Once I have this stability, I can set two bounds around the norm. If I am using defect density as a reliability measure then, if the value increases, it is bad, but remember that, if statistically stable, just because the current value is worse than the previous value, it is not a cause for concern provided the current value is within the expected range. I should set a control bound at some value greater than the highest expected and acceptable value. You will find references to two or three sigma, usually defined as standard deviation from the mean, for this control bound, but I believe that common sense and specific business constraints are a much better guide. If a value exceeds the control bound, then it should trigger investigation and, potentially, corrective action.

The other bound I can set is a target for the attribute value. Using our reliability example, I would set a target at some value lower than the least expected value. I assume that the target is reached when the values for reliability over some period of time, not just for one data point, or the associated trend values are lower than the target value.

Of course, norms and control bounds should be periodically reassessed. Target levels should be changed once the target has been met, but do ensure that everyone concerned knows the target has been reached, and also make sure that they all get a pat on the back.

SUMMARY

Management information is a major topic in most Software Metrics programmes. It concerns the collection of information which can be combined through measurement models, so that meaningful information can be conveyed to managers. It also involves the presentation of that data and, ultimately, its use to improve the process that supplied the data in the first place. Do not fall into the trap of believing that simply supplying information will bring about change — the metrics programme also has to enable change.

This brings us to the end of the discussion on management information as part of a Software Metrics programme. Much of this chapter is simply an expression of common sense and good practice, but then metrics, like most enabling disciplines, is just that.

5

COST ESTIMATION

While many people see traditional Software Metrics as the provision of management information, it is the area of estimating, and especially estimating the cost of software development or enhancement projects, that has received the most attention over the years. Given the amount of work that has been done in this area, and a history of over 20 years for commercial IT, it is somewhat surprising that the industry has such a terrible, and often well deserved, reputation for poor cost estimation. Basically, we still cannot get it right. Even if a project is delivered 'on time', the amount of functionality that is delivered on that date is often a drastic reduction over what was 'contracted' to be delivered.

COST MODELS AND BEYOND

Why are we still getting it wrong? Part of the answer lies in the type of work that has been done. For many years, cost estimation has been seen in the context of parametric or mathematical models derived from sets of collected data. Examples of such models include COCOMO (Boehm, 1981), and SLIM (Putnam, 1979). The premise has been that such models can be applied to different organizations and project types without any loss of accuracy, provided, of course, we calibrate. Unfortunately, the term 'calibration' is often misunderstood or the process of calibration is misapplied. I will discuss calibration in more detail later.

Another problem with the various cost models is that they have been driven, mainly, by a size estimate in terms of *lines of code*. However, more than one project manager has said to me that they find it as difficult to estimate the *lines of code* to drive a cost model as it is to estimate the effort directly. Despite this, cost models are widely used and many find them beneficial.

Within the industry, we are starting to realize that cost estimation is a process in its own right, and that optimizing that process depends on more than simply adopting a model or cost estimating tool.

Of course, the attraction of the model-based approach is obvious. To derive a cost estimate from a mathematical model is inherently satisfying, as it smacks of a scientific approach. Such models are also mechanistic in use and their application is repeatable. These are two of the criterion for the automation of a process, hence many people quickly realized that such models could be packaged within software and an industry has grown up around this idea.

I am loath to list a set of cost estimation packages, as it may be seen as a recommendation when, in truth, I only have experience of some half dozen such tools. It is also true to say that there is little to choose between the various tools in terms of accuracy. Also, any such listing would be out of date before this material is published, so frequently do new packages arrive in the market-place.

The cost estimation industry has even established specialized user groups who stage large international conferences for both the initiates and newcomers to the field. The best known of these is probably the COCOMO User Group, based in both the USA and Europe. A contact address is provided in Appendix A.

The underlying theme of this chapter is to take a different viewpoint. I claim that cost estimation is a discipline and a process in its own right, and I hope to give a coherent view of that process. I firmly believe that the commercially available cost estimation tools have a place within that process, and I also hope to show where that place is.

WHY DO WE ESTIMATE?

I wish to start by stating what, for some people, will be the obvious. I am going to discuss why we in the IT industry need a cost estimation process within our installations and why, from a business viewpoint, that process can be vital to our success and, in some cases, to our survival.

Software development and enhancement centres around a project view of work. That is, around components of work that are managed as discrete elements with a defined end-point and, if we are lucky, also a defined start point. The management of these elements is documented in the project plan in the sense that it is this plan that guides management activity. For example, if we are failing to meet the milestones described within the project plan, we would hopefully instigate some form of corrective action to identify and deal with, or at least to contain, the problem that was causing the slip.

The foundation of the project plan is the estimate of cost or duration for the work items within the plan. The plan, in another form, may also be used to 'bid' for the work in the first place. Based upon an initial statement of requirement from a potential customer, information is prepared that tells the customer what the cost of that work and its duration is likely to be, and this can form the basis of a contractual agreement between the customer and the supplier.

So we can already see a process beginning to evolve around the 'estimates'. An estimate can form the basis of a bid for work, and it can also feed into the more detailed planning process, including plans for risk management when the work is won.

I remember attending a project planning course some years ago that most certainly did not live up to the expectations of some of the audience. Although the course was presented in an exceptionally clear and professional manner, it concentrated on the techniques of project planning, such as critical path analysis and earned value reporting. As such, it did not address the problems that some of the audience wanted to have resolved which was ways of answering two questions: 'What will this work cost me' and 'How long will it take'? Project planning, as presented, seemed to consist of applying very clear techniques to a very basic item of data, the estimate. What the individuals who felt somewhat cheated required was, obviously, a course that taught them how to estimate, or was it? As will be seen, my belief is that estimation and project planning are so closely related that you cannot totally separate the two and make either work.

Of course, once an estimate and a planning process is used to produce cost and duration figures, we are effectively making a promise. 'This work will be done for this cost and it will be delivered to you, the customer, at this point in time.' If the organization, be it the organization as a whole or an internal IT function, intends to operate a policy of 'quality service', then, by definition, those promises must be met. This implies that the estimation process, and I now include planning in that process, had better produce figures that can be met. We cannot deliver a quality service if our projects arrive late and cost more than originally stated.

This should always be seen as a success factor for any business, but it becomes a truly critical success factor if we operate in a fixed price environment. Such an environment has no mercy on the poor software supplier. If the project we have bid on and won costs more than was thought, then we have no contractual right to cover those costs. Get those estimates wrong, and we will suffer the consequences — totally!

SOME BASIC PRINCIPLES

Given that cost estimation is important from a business viewpoint, we need to consider how effective cost estimation can be obtained. To do this, we need to consider, as a first step or starting point, some basic rules or principles of estimation. Most of these are common sense, but I make no apology for stating them here as they are so often forgotten or ignored. Most of these principles are also generally accepted within the world of cost estimation. That is to say that if you attend a conference on cost estimation or one of the user groups mentioned earlier, you will hear the same points made there as I will make here. Notice the use of the word 'most' two sentences back. I have taken the liberty of sliding one or two of my own 'principles', based on experience, in with the others. Those of you who have been to cost estimation conferences can have fun spotting the interlopers.

The first point I would like to make is more a statement of fact than a principle. It is simply to point out that life is a harsh, but fair, task mistress. If we give nothing, we should expect nothing. So why is it that many of us expect to be able to use some magic approach that enables accurate cost estimation at the very start of the initiation stage when we have practically no information or understanding of the work to be done?

Imagine a similar situation in another environment.

'Good morning sir,' says the friendly travel agent, 'and what can I do for you?'

At this point please imagine a John Cleese or Peter Sellers character. 'Oh hello. I would like to know how much it would cost for a two-week, foreign holiday please.'

'Of course sir, let me just check the price chart. Yes, that would be three hundred and twenty-two pounds.'

'Guaranteed price?' — which is simply the equivalent of fixed price.

'Of course, sir.'

Away goes our customer wondering how this agent can manage to send him to Hong Kong, Thailand, Bali and Australia — all for three hundred pounds!

Obviously, this situation is ludicrous, but it happens every day in the IT world. In fact, I can almost guarantee that, as you read this, someone, somewhere is making a promise to deliver on a system requirement that they know very little about.

Of course, there is an easy answer to this problem. Organizations that initially commit only to a requirements definition activity, often at fixed price, and who, as the final part of this work, carry out an estimation process that leads to a formal quotation for doing the actual implementation often find that they operate more effectively. It is easy to understand why. Requirements definition can be managed effectively on a fixed price basis, because it can be constrained within a set of identified viewpoints. The implementation estimate is then only performed when the requirement is well understood. Is it strange that this leads to more accurate estimates?

There are two points to bear in mind about this approach. Firstly, it does not guarantee success or accuracy. Requirements can change, things can go wrong on the project or the estimate may simply have been wrong. The chances of getting it wrong, however, are reduced.

Secondly, there can be a great deal of resistance to this approach. Interestingly, this resistance tends to come from the IT professionals rather than the customers. Customers quite like the idea of getting delivery by the promised date.

However, this approach is not ideal for every environment. In a fixed price, competitive scenario, you may have to bid for the whole job. If you are close to the prospective customer though, you could ask why they were doing it in this way. You may get an interesting reply like, 'because that's the way we've always done it, but now you come to mention it ...'.

Presentation of estimates

The next point concerns the presentation of estimates and, again, impinges upon the maturity of our industry. An estimate is an estimate, not an actual. Obviously, this is true — but what does it imply? The implication is that an estimate will contain a degree of error. As such, estimates should not be presented as absolute figures. We all know that when a project manager presents a cost estimate as, for example, twelve engineering months, what is actually being said is that the most likely estimate for this work is twelve engineering months give or take x per cent. It is the x that causes the problems. The project manager may be thinking in terms of give or take *three* engineering months, but the more senior manager or, worse, the customer, may be thinking in terms of give or take *one* month!

A cornerstone of our industry is communication. We should take our own medicine and start to communicate estimates clearly as bounded intervals. We should also realize that such intervals can be severely skewed. For instance, an estimate that is presented as:

'This work will cost at least six engineering months' effort, but the most likely estimate is eight. Note that because of various risks associated with this project, consideration of the worst case scenario produces an estimate of fourteen engineering months',

should be perfectly acceptable. I was amazed to find that this kind of bid estimate is even being adopted in one fixed-price arena. The idea is that the customer and the supplier communicate more honestly, and share benefits if the project is delivered early, but share risk and cost if the project is delivered later up to some predetermined limit. Much as I would like to, I cannot name the organization involved, because the supplier sees this as a major competitive advantage.

Again, there can be resistance to this idea of presenting estimates as bounded intervals but, really, it is only a recognition and application of common sense.

Contents of estimates

The next point concerns what should be estimated. Size and cost are valid candidates for estimation. Duration, which is often estimated, should, in fact, be planned. Size is driven by the functional requirement, and cost is driven by the functional requirement, possibly expressed in terms of size, and the development environment including the productivity rate that applies within that environment. Duration is very heavily influenced by the organizational environment. Duration depends on so many things that are outside of the functional requirement that it can rarely be estimated effectively, and this is one of the most common complaints from estimators. Even teams that are very good at estimating cost or size find it difficult to estimate duration, which in many ways makes sense. If I size a decorating job up as having to paint four walls and I know that I can paint two walls in three hours, effectively an evening's work, am I right to say that the duration of that job will be six hours or two evenings? This is true only if I use the term 'duration' to mean cost, as many planners do. To my mind, duration is more to do with calendar time than with cost. For this decorating job, I may plan to do two walls on Monday evening, but then I am away from home Tuesday, I am out on Wednesday and there is a film I want to see on Thursday. If I plan to finish the job on Friday, then the duration of the decorating project will be five days. This is because I have planned it that way, not because of an estimate. This is certainly how my wife sees it when she, as the customer in this case, finds that she cannot use that room for five days.

The same is true of a software development or enhancement project. I may estimate that it will take nine engineering months, within bounds of course, but the duration it will take depends upon its priority, how I ramp up staff, who I put on to the project and many other factors.

This may be one reason why cost estimation tools tend to produce acceptable cost estimates, after calibration, but tend to perform less effectively for duration estimates.

Reassessing the estimates

Next I would like to consider our view of the estimates themselves. How often do we come across a project that is missing milestones, or about which there are serious concerns, only to find that management is still working with the very first set of estimates that were made? Estimates should be seen as dynamic entities, and they should be reassessed whenever a significant milestone is completed, in other words when we have gained significantly more information or when there is a change in the requirements we are seeking to satisfy.

Yet again, this is simply the application of common sense. For most projects, the estimates to which the project team are working should be reassessed at the end of the design and implementation or coding stages as a minimum. This assumes that the approach of estimating development *after the requirements definition* was used. For short-term projects of up to six months' duration, it is probably more practical to assess the estimates at the end of each month, because of the degree of phase overlap common on smaller projects, re-estimating if necessary.

Long-term projects of more than two years' duration, and that is from initiation to first delivery, will probably have a greater number of milestones identified. Typically, these will include the end of requirements specification; high-, intermediate- and low-level design; and delivery to the test group of major functional items or subsystems. Estimates should be reassessed at each of these points.

These are simply ideas about suitable points in the development lifecycle at which re-estimation makes sense. The main point to understand is that re-estimation is not only acceptable, but it should be seen as desirable, because a great deal more is known about the project and the work involved at the end of the design stage than at the project's initiation. When a re-estimate is made will depend upon the particular environment and development methodology, but there should be clearly defined points within the project plan at which re-estimation will occur.

The other trigger that should cause a re-estimate is when the requirements change significantly. How big a change is 'significant' is a moot point, but most project managers know when this type of volatility is going to cause them problems.

If a sizing technique like *Function Point Analysis* or even estimated *lines of code* is used, then I would suggest, as a rule of thumb, that a 10 per cent change in the size of the project as a result of requirements change should trigger the re-estimation process.

Incidentally, have you noticed how requirements changes always make the project grow rather than shrink? Remember, one of the aims of re-estimation is to ensure that probable delays are identified and discussed with the customer early, so that they do not come as a total shock. At the very least, the project manager should be aware of these potential problems, and not have to report a six month delay, one week prior to delivery.

The estimators

What about the estimators themselves? How do they fit into the estimation process. I will have more to say about this later but, for now, I would like to make two points. Firstly, the techniques that are made available to estimators, for example cost models, are there to assist the estimator. They do not remove the responsibility for the estimates from the estimator.

Secondly, estimators should use the techniques in a sensible way. If two or more techniques are applicable at a given point in the development lifecycle, then two or more techniques should be used. There is a very simple reason for this. Estimation is always going to be something of an art and, at the end of the day, it relies upon the judgement of one or more individuals. To assist in this judgemental activity, the maximum amount of information should be made available and, as each technique can possibly provide more information, or at least a different view of the same information, it makes sense to use as many techniques as is practical. At the very least, an estimator should not rely upon only one technique to produce an estimate.

You should also be aware of an interesting phenomena in the area we are discussing. When it comes to making an estimate, people tend to produce optimistic predictions. I am tempted to say that people always underestimate, but there is one case where this is not true, namely when estimating productivity. This does not apply only to software projects. My wife has the endearing habit of always expecting me to finish a DIY job in half the time I estimate it will take, and I always underestimate anyway!

We also come across this aberration when asking people how long it will take to get from one place to another. An ex-colleague of mine, when asked how long it would take him to get from his house to an airport, quoted a time that would require a mean speed of 155 miles an hour. But, as he said, he was not going to be travelling during the rush hour! Another ex-colleague arranged to meet me at the end of a meeting that: 'will take no more than two hours, so I will see you at two o'clock.' At four-thirty I was still waiting for him to finish that meeting. And I think he put his finger on it when he did finally emerge: 'Yes I remember now,' he said, 'we only ever actually finished at two o'clock on one occasion.'

People tend to remember good times or successes, and try to ignore memories of failures or problems. This is why, when you ask someone to estimate, say, the cost of a job, they will give you an answer based on the best case scenario. The organization that asks four project managers for an estimate, then doubles or triples the average result, would probably survive in a fixed price environment! It is worth remembering that this phenomenon exists next time you have to accept or produce an estimate.

Old data — look in the bin

Now if all of this is good advice and you take it on board, you should expect to see an improvement in estimation effectiveness. Could you prove it?

You may remember earlier that I said there is a 20-year-plus history of software development in some organizations. You would expect to be able to get hold of some data from these organizations. Think how likely you would be to find a similar project to the one you have to estimate today, if you had 20 years' worth of data to fall back on. You will be lucky if that data is available. Well OK, 10 years' worth would be good enough, in fact, 5 years' worth would probably be better, as it is probably closer to what we do today.

You may like to go into a project team and ask them if they have data, even just estimation data, from their last project. If the answer is yes, then you are in luck. Most teams do not even keep the past estimates for their current projects!

Keeping data about itself and its work is not something the IT industry does well, which is ironic when we think what 'IT' stands for. If you wish to do something practical, then you should insist that your projects start to keep some basic data about themselves. It does not have to be a sophisticated or complete system of measurement. Raw data, such as size of project, estimated cost and planned duration and the updates to these figures, together with the actuals, can be a good starting point. Get really clever by asking the project manager to summarize his or her feelings about the project. What made this one different to the others that the manager had been involved in? Keep this summary short, no more than one page of A4, and you have a very useful source of information, even if it is somewhat subjective.

To summarize, there are certain basic principles that appear to apply to the estimation process no matter what environment we consider. These principles can be listed as:

• The first estimate is likely to be an underestimate. Act accordingly.
• Estimates are estimates, so use bounds not absolutes.
• Cost is estimated, duration is planned.

- Estimates are dynamic, re-estimate when milestones are completed and additional information becomes available or when the requirements change.
- The estimate is the responsibility of the estimator, not the tools or techniques.
- Keep previous estimates.

MODELS AND TOOLS REVISITED

To apply a set of principles, which operate at the conceptual level, we have to develop an operational process model and that should be founded upon a logical view of the process. This is a very high-falutin way of saying that we start with a set of ideas, the principles — we use these to put together an approach, and we build a set of mechanisms that we can use on a day-to-day basis within that approach.

There are basically two strategies for cost estimation that are generally seen as competitive. Fortunately, more and more people are realizing that the two strategies can work harmoniously within a cost estimation process. The two strategies can be termed *model-based* and *technique-based*.

MODEL-BASED STRATEGY

Looking first at the model-based approach, we find a profusion of models to choose from, and we may be forgiven for asking: 'where did they all come from' or perhaps 'why are there so many?'

Models are really a scientific answer to the problem of cost estimation, and they appeal to many individuals within the IT industry. The size of the potential market is one reason why there are so many models — basically everyone would like a chunk of what is going. It is also true that most, if not all, of the models are really nothing more than a variation on a theme. So how does a model come about? There are two approaches that can be adopted, both well recognized and accepted within the world of mathematical modelling, which is what we are really talking about.

1. This goes something like this:
   (a) Go and collect a lot of data about a lot of projects.
   (b) Investigate the relationships between input and output variables, for example size and complexity as inputs, cost and duration as outputs, and use these relationships to construct a model.
   (c) Finally, validate your model on a different set of data by comparing actuals to the model predictions.

2. This is only slightly different:
   (a) Produce a hypothesis that models the reality. This will usually be in the form of an input–output model.
   (b) Next apply your model to a data set to test the hypothesis it contains. Modify the model in the light of these experimental results.
   (c) Validate the revised model on a different set of data, again comparing actuals to

predictions. That final validation step is often missed out, which is one reason why these models need such careful calibration.

What we do when we have our model then depends upon our own personality and preferences. Some people take the very admirable step of placing their models in the public domain. The best known of these are Barry Boehm, (COCOMO) (Boehm, 1981) and Larry Putnam, (SLIM) (Putnam, 1979). Of course, once a model is in the public domain, then it becomes fair game for everyone to adopt, package, or shoot down in flames.

Another approach is to package the model personally and then to present it as a black box solution to the cost estimation problem. I would say the best-known individual in this category is Capers Jones (Checkpoint, USA or Checkmark, UK). This really irritates some people, but I must admit that I can see the commercial sense of this approach. After all, the individuals who do go public come in for a great deal of criticism. Sometimes unjustified, sometimes justified.

This leads me to an interesting point. Within Software Metrics there are a number of gurus, some of whom are best known for their work in the cost modelling area, and I have heard most of them speak at some time. One thing has impressed me. They are fanatical only about improving processes that they see as needing improvement. They are not fanatical about their own particular ideas, ideas which they have very often moved on from. Barry Boehm, Putnam, Jones and the others in their league all recognize that they have only provided partial solutions, and they actively welcome constructive criticism that can be used to enhance their own original ideas. It is in this direction that we should be focusing our activities and energies rather than the rather pointless arguments about whose model is best — arguments that the developers of the models studiously avoid.

Having made my plea for sanity, I think we should get back to the topic and think about the basic construction of these models.

Basic construction of models

Essentially, the models apply mathematical operations such as multiplication by a constant, to an estimated size, usually in terms of *lines of code*, although at least one model derived from and driven by size in terms of *function point* scores is now available. Note that many of the packages that claim to be driven by *function point* scores are, in fact, only converting those scores to *lines of code* values using in built tables.

I would like to talk a little bit more about the COCOMO cost estimation model, as I find this to be the most widely used of such models. In my opinion, COCOMO is also a very typical cost estimation model, but in some aspects is also one of the more sophisticated.

There are three levels of COCOMO model, but I would like to consider the basic model. This takes the form of a formula:

$$\text{Effort} = a \times \text{Size} \char`\^ b$$

where Size takes the form of thousands of delivered source instructions or KDSI with a and b as constants. COCOMO being quite sophisticated recognizes three types of development environment and provides different variations of the basic model for each environment.

1. The *organic environment* is essentially that of a small scale, non-bureaucratic project and for this environment the model takes the form:

$$Effort = 2.4 \times Size \char`\^ 1.05$$

2. The *embedded environment* is the opposite of the *organic* in that it relates to a very bureaucratic, tightly controlled and formal organization. For this environment the model takes the form:

$$Effort = 3.6 \times Size \char`\^ 1.2$$

3. The so-called *semi-detached environment* is one that falls between the two extremes, and for this the model takes the form:

$$Effort = 3.0 \times Size \char`\^ 1.12$$

Various other elements of the model can then be used to modify the basic result. These elements are often termed *cost drivers*. For further information the reader is referred to Boehm (1981) and to Rook (1990).

There is a great deal of debate currently about the validity and usefulness of these cost drivers which can range from the experience of the project team to the layout of the office. There are two easily identified camps that can be identified with respect to cost drivers. One feels that the basic set of cost drivers that come with most models are insufficient; the other believes that there are too many cost drivers being considered. Personally, I feel more affinity for the second view, and this seems to be borne out by research that has been done as part of the ESPRIT MERMAID project (Kitchenham, 1991). The results of this research, which is based upon a statistical analysis of both newly collected data from a number of sources and the data sets originally used by the developers of some of the better known cost models, indicates that the drivers are not orthogonal. In simple terms, the same thing is being addressed by more than one driver. When we use the drivers to adjust the base estimate, we are effectively double counting or perhaps cancelling out effects depending upon how we answer specific questions.

It is also interesting to note that locally developed cost models, that is models developed from data within a single environment or installation, tend to have no more than five or six adjusting drivers, and these are often different to the drivers provided by the publicly or commercially available models, which I will call 'generalized cost models'.

This may indicate why there is a group that seems to be looking for more drivers. My feeling is that there is a level of dissatisfaction with the drivers already identified within the generalized models. This dissatisfaction exists because users feel that other drivers are needed for their sites or application environments. It is not so much that more drivers are needed, it is that different drivers are needed.

Calibration

If there is debate about the number of cost drivers that are required within a cost model, there is, however, one point that just about everyone agrees about as far as generalized cost models are concerned. They need to be 'calibrated'.

Checking my dictionary again, I find that to calibrate means, 'to fix or correct the scale'. How is this done for a cost model? Calibration is more than simply redefining the questions that a package implementation of a cost model asks so that the questions have meaning in particular circumstances. This is necessary because, while people tend to underestimate, they do tend to present worst case scenarios when asked certain types of question. Ask a team leader how complex an application is, and I guarantee that the answer will be 'very complex', even if it is the most simple of batch processes.

So what is meant, in the practical sense, by this term 'calibration'? I think that I can best illustrate the answer by example. Part of the work that I do includes assisting with the evaluation, and often the introduction, of generalized cost models. The evaluation goes something like this:

> For a number of projects that have been completed, data is put through the cost model and the predicted effort, and often the predicted duration, is recorded. The actuals are also obtained from historical data held by the installation. Obviously, if the organization does not record effort data or the start and end dates of projects, then I have a problem with this approach, but such an organization may not be ready to use generalized cost models as it cannot calibrate them. An alternative that is sometimes viable within an enhancement environment is to use one project across, perhaps, a six month period as the calibration vehicle.

> The next step is to compare the predicted values with the actuals, at which point we usually find glaring discrepancies. It is now that people fling their hands up in horror and prepare to throw in the towel, but why? Do we really expect a model that was derived from a specific set of data in a specific installation to be immediately applicable to another installation? Of course not.

Some tools salesmen will also throw their hands up in horror and then patiently explain that it is the 'actuals' that are inaccurate, not the predictions. All I can say to this is that, time and time again, I have found locally collected cost data to be perfectly acceptable. Not accurate to decimal places, but accurate enough. In fact, one piece of research in which I was involved, albeit to a limited extent, found that cost data extracted from a particular time recording mechanism on a specific site was very inaccurate, but it was consistently inaccurate. Think about that. Because, of course, that is the key factor to look for when comparing predictions to actuals. We should expect to see inaccuracy, but we should hope for consistent inaccuracy. For instance, one such evaluation found that two of the commonly used cost models were consistently underestimating effort by 40 per cent, give or take a percentage point or two either way. Interestingly enough, I found that one of the models, when used within a different organization, was overestimating effort by about 80 per cent, consistently. That certainly illustrates the need for calibration!

But what do we do if we find that there is not even consistent inaccuracy? Faced with that situation on one occasion, I very nearly did throw in the towel until a consultant with one of the companies, which sold the tool we were evaluating, suggested that we look at the hot buttons — the drivers that really affected the results significantly.

Well, we went further than that, we reduced the information input to the tool to:

1. Size.
2. Class of work, i.e. enhancement or new development.
3. Class of system, i.e. commercial, telecommunications or systems software

The result was within class of system and class of work. Inaccuracy was still there, but it was consistent. This illustrates the care with which cost drivers should be treated.

There are three further points to make about these calibration exercises:

1. I have found that calibrating for effort or cost predictions takes a lot less data than

calibrating for duration. This is one reason why I feel that duration should be planned rather than estimated.

2. While most, if not all, cost estimation tools will break the overall estimate down into the cost associated with specific phases of the project, I am still wary about using this. Again, a significant amount of data is needed to calibrate these to a particular environment, and I believe that few organizations are able to do any more than treat these as more than ballpark figures. Anyway, most organizations would be quite happy if they could get accurate project estimates let alone, for example, accurate design phase estimates.

3. These types of calibration exercises do tend to use actual size figures as the input to the models. If estimates are available, try running the models with that data, but there may be problems in variability of size estimate accuracy. If we were simply to introduce the tools or models and expect them to solve our estimation problems then we may be in for a shock. I hope to show that there is a place for these types of tools, but only as part of an overall estimating strategy or process. That strategy must address the question of estimating project size, which is then used as input to the models.

A final point about calibration. If you are operating within an environment that develops products over a long period of time, and by that I mean about five years from initiation to first delivery, then you will have a problem with calibration. For all sorts of reasons, you will probably not have historical data available and you, obviously, cannot calibrate in real time the way, say, a group producing new builds every three months can. The best you can probably hope for from generalized cost models is to use them as a stimulus for practical and sensible discussion. The great value of cost drivers, and one case where the-more-the-merrier principle applies, is that they are excellent vehicles for getting project managers to think about the factors that can effect the cost and duration of their projects.

TECHNIQUE-BASED STRATEGY

Having discussed the model-based approach to cost estimation, we should now consider a different and, I believe, complementary approach. I call this approach technique-based and think of it as 'people orientated' and as will be seen when I discuss specific techniques in the context of the estimation process, some elements of the model-based approach also creep in. The difference is that here we are really considering estimation as a people-driven activity, that is as a slightly technical art, rather than as a formal, repeatable, scientifically based activity.

The points to note about the people-orientated approach are that they take more time than simply cranking parameters through a model, and that the techniques used often appear to be very simplistic, almost trivial. The most important point to note is that they also work.

The people-orientated approach together with the techniques it encompasses have two main aims:

1. To make estimators think about what they are doing and introduce some degree of

discipline to the estimation activity.
2. To encourage communication by encouraging estimators to seek assistance from other people rather than leaving them to estimate in isolation.

That is all I will say about this approach to estimation for now. As will be seen, it is this approach that forms the backbone of the estimation process template, which is where all this talk is leading us.

Local cost models

Before we go on to discuss the estimation process template in more detail, I would briefly like to mention again local cost models, which is one of the main thrusts of the ESPRIT MERMAID project (Mermaid, 1989). Local cost models are simply mathematical models derived and used within a specific organization or organizational environment. They are there to make estimation more effective within your specific environment, they are not global solutions.

Many pundits claim that it can take ten, fifteen or twenty years for an organization to develop such models, because it takes that long to get sufficient data. Experience within a few organizations suggests that this is not so. One retail organization, J C Penney (IFPUG, 1990b), in the USA took three years to develop a cost estimation model, to validate that model and to go public with the statement, supported by statistical data, that it gave them as accurate a set of predictions as those claimed by the leading generalized cost models.

Another organization, again in the USA, claimed in passing at another IFPUG conference that their local cost estimation model, which included factors for requirements growth, gave them an accuracy of plus or minus five per cent against actuals for predictions made at the end of requirements specification. It only took them five years to get this good.

What was common to those models? They were local, they both used Function Point Analysis (FPA) as the size parameter and they both had a limited set of cost drivers. The other factors that they shared is that they worked; they also took a lot less than ten years to develop and they both fitted into an estimation strategy that went beyond the models.

A strategic template for cost estimation

Estimation is a process. To control estimation, to improve its effectiveness within our own organization, we must stop treating it as a black box activity and remove the air of formula-driven magic so often promoted by IT staff. Do this and the process can be defined, managed, modified and optimized.

Definition of estimation

What I want to do now is present a template definition of that process which I hope can be tailored to your organization. This will give you the process definition and you can then get on with managing that process.

Overview: We start with an overview of the estimation process. If you imagine the development process as a V model with requirements definition and high- and low-level design as the components of the left leg of that V, coding or implementation as the apex and the various testing activities — unit, subsystem or link and system testing — forming the right leg, you may ask where the estimation activities fit. I suggest that you think of a second V model paralleling the development V. The components of the second V include work consolidation to form the basic project, estimation at different stages of development, project control and project, rather than technical, reviews. This chapter concentrates upon the estimation activities.

You can think of the various techniques used to help estimators as 'bricks' out of which we build the estimating process. You can select from those presented here and, from the various commercial tools to form your own organizational estimating strategy. All of the techniques mentioned here are described in other technical books that deal with the subject, and one of the best collections of such descriptions can be found in the appendices of the *Software Reliability Handbook* (Rook, 1990).

In fact, so much has been written about estimating techniques that I do not intend to repeat the very detailed technical discussions here. If you are interested, then I suggest you use the sources quoted in the bibliography, and form your own opinion. Here, you will only find a brief discussion of technical aspects.

Interaction with environment: The estimation process must interact with its environment, and you may wonder if this template can apply to both enhancement projects and to new development work. I will state quite categorically that the template does apply to both environments. Corrective maintenance, that is fixing bugs in the current release of the system, is better considered as support. This type of work needs to be managed, and that management depends upon the collection of relevant management statistics that will allow you to estimate the likely support costs for a given release for your own environment. However, it is not feasible to produce estimates from some formal mechanism when you have a red priority defect that has to be fixed a.s.a.p.

The most important impact that the environment has is that things tend to be easier in a maintenance environment where more than one release is made during a financial year. The reason is simply that the data is available to you on a regular basis, and this data can be used to manage and assess your estimation process.

The role of people: Given that estimation is a process that involves people, we should now consider the different roles that those people can play. This brings us to an interesting point. There is considerable debate as to whether estimation should be the responsibility of individual project managers or of a centralized estimating group. The arguments go something like this:

> If my IT group is regularly required to produce estimates, then I am tying up valuable project resources by diverting them on to this type of work, which would seem to suggest that we could improve effectiveness by establishing a centralized function that took on the responsibility for estimate production. Furthermore, a group of individuals whose main role is to make estimates will quickly develop expertise in that work. Essentially, this approach would produce an experience centre.

The counter argument is:

> People do not react well to imposed estimates whether they come from management or from an estimating group. In fact, presenting a project manager with an estimate and then expecting him or her to deliver against

that estimate is almost certainly going to lead to projects that do not deliver on time and in budget. Of course, if every project manager is going to be expected to take responsibility for estimation then this does increase the scale and complexity of the job if you try to improve your own organizational estimation process.

So, what is the answer if, as it appears, both approaches have positive and negative aspects? A wise man once said that, when placed on the twin horns of a dilemma, you should seek the middle. In other words, there are more than two ways to skin a cat!

The primary estimator: I believe that ownership of the estimates by the project manager is vital, and I suggest that the primary estimator be the project manager. The primary estimator is the person who has the final say over which estimate is submitted to the estimate recipient. Assuming that the estimate is accepted, the project manager cannot then claim that the estimate was imposed on him. Your own organization will have to define the level of project or projects for which there will be a primary estimator.

The primary estimator should not be expected to do the work in isolation. Your organization should define the role of assistant estimator. Assistant estimators help the primary estimator by providing additional views of the project, by providing different levels and types of experience and by providing sounding boards against which the primary estimator can bounce ideas of cost and duration.

Estimation support group: Additionally, you should, in my opinion, establish an estimation support group. This group can develop into the experience centre mentioned earlier, the main difference is that it acts in a consultative role rather than in a prescriptive role and its position in respect of the primary estimator is clearly defined. It also has another role. In most organizations, the estimation process can be classified as '*ad hoc*'. This is a polite way of saying chaotic! Changing this situation so that the organization boasts a defined, managed and optimizing estimation process will not happen overnight, and somebody must be there to facilitate this evolution. The estimation support group can provide training, can cross-check estimates from managers to assess their feasibility, and can monitor the process to identify improvement and areas that need improving.

While such a group represents an additional overhead, it must be realized that change does not happen automatically or without cost. To rephrase a common quotation from the Quality guru Crosby, Quality is free — eventually!

The estimate recipient: The final role that needs to be defined is that of the estimate recipient. This can be a real customer, especially in a bid situation, a planner, marketing or a manager. I often remember a tale told to me by a technical director of his project manager days. He went in with an estimate, which was then cut by his boss. Needless to say, the project manager's estimate proved to be much more accurate even though, he assured me, he tried to do the job as quickly as possible. I sometimes wonder how he treats his project managers now that the shoe is on the other foot. This tale raises an important question — what happens when the estimate recipient questions that estimate?

In reality, this situation will be constantly present and the estimation process must identify and facilitate a subprocess of negotiation and reconciliation. Obviously, personalities will have an impact on this activity, but I feel that it is safe to assume that most individuals involved in project management, and hence in the estimation process, are actively committed to making sure that a project succeeds. There should be a formal, minuted meeting between the primary estimator and the estimate recipient which is structured around the concept of the project management triangle.

This model simply states that there are three, high-level parameters that affect projects: duration, cost and content. Only one of these parameters can be fixed. For example, if I have to decorate a house, then the content may appear to be fixed. I can only do the work faster if I load resources on to the job, increasing cost, in other words if I fix content, then duration and cost trade off. But, of course, the content, even in this job, is not necessarily fixed. I may reduce content by specifying one coat of paint instead of two, and in this way I may work to a fixed duration by trading off content and cost.

Such a discussion assumes that my estimates of cost, content and duration are true and, in software engineering projects, it is impossible to be sure of this. What I can do is increase my confidence in those estimates by recording past performance and, most importantly, by recording the assumptions that lie behind my estimates. It is much easier to discuss, or argue, about assumptions than about estimates, because my ownership of the assumptions is less solid.

Of course, if a manager insists that my estimate be reduced, then he should expect to have to justify that reduction by recording and stating the underlying assumptions that apply. This acceptance of responsibility should form part of your estimating procedures or strategy and should be accepted and endorsed by your organization. Implementing such a strategy is not easy, and this is one area where the estimation support group can help, because they should be responsible for auditing the process and its application. The manager who insists that an estimate be reduced records the reasons why, and the support group ensures that this is done.

The worst case scenario, where a project manager has to accept estimates imposed from above that are lower than those he or she believes apply, needs careful management. What has happened is that a risk has been associated with the project and two things should occur. The project manager should be allowed to record the fact that the estimates are imposed, and the resulting project should receive management attention to a greater extent than normal during the whole of its life, or until the risk is resolved through re-estimation.

If your organization has a central project control office, then this risk management action should be their responsibility. However, you may be in for a pleasant surprise. It does seem that when estimation processes are defined along the lines described so far, the perception of imposition concerning estimates reduces, because the project manager will be more involved in the estimation process than may otherwise happen. Why is this? It may be the fact that everyone is now working within a defined procedure that, in part at least, demystifies the estimation process, and that sets out clear responsibilities with lines of communication. This results in clearer understanding and a depersonalization of that process and, hence, a reduction in conflict. After all, none of us wants a project to fail, but sometimes we don't talk about the problems. Which is fine in theory, but what about the estimation template? Let us start with some of the possible building bricks that we can use, the estimating techniques I have mentioned. Again let me mention the *Software Reliability Handbook* (Rook, 1990), for a fuller description of these techniques in their pure form. What follows is a description of those techniques as I have helped implement them in more than one organization.

The Modified Delphi technique

I will start with something called the Modified Delphi technique. This is based on the *wideband Delphi technique* that is fully described in *Software Engineering Economics*

(Boehm, 1981), and it is nothing more that a slightly formalized approach to using expert opinion.

The Modified Delphi technique is a way of eliciting and reconciling the opinions of a group of individuals. It can be used, as can all of these techniques except the use of models, to derive cost or size estimates and, because it relies on opinion, it can be used at any time during the development lifecycle, but I feel it is best used from initiation to the end of high-level design.

The first thing the primary estimator should do is to form an estimating group consisting of him or herself and at least two other assistant estimators. One individual should be nominated as the Coordinator. In reality, these groups usually exist permanently within product groups and are activated as necessary. In this way, they act as good training grounds for estimators. The group should not exceed seven individuals even for large projects, as larger groups often become unmanageable.

Next, each group member is given access to any material about the new project, typically this will be a customer request document or a requirements specification. They should be given sufficient time to study this material bearing in mind their other work and, typically, we are talking about a week of elapsed time. They should also be notified of a date when a reconciliation meeting will be held.

Each group member makes his or her estimate and submits this to the Coordinator at least two days before the reconciliation meeting. The Coordinator calculates the median or mid-point of the estimates received, and returns this value to the estimator together with his/her own estimate. Optionally, the estimator can submit a revised estimate to the Coordinator.

The reconciliation meeting starts with each estimator being made aware of the latest median value. The purpose of this meeting is to reach a consensus regarding the estimate value. The ownership of particular estimates should remain confidential during the meeting unless someone owns up, but other than using this confidentiality to avoid embarrassing particular individuals, open discussion should be encouraged. If the Coordinator feels that new estimates should be made because an important point has been agreed, for example that everyone is now convinced that it is a more complex system than they originally thought, then this is perfectly acceptable.

A consensus level should be prespecified, for example it could be said that consensus has been reached when the extreme estimates are no more than 30 per cent either side of the median, if this was a session at the initiation stage of a fairly large project.

The value of the Delphi approach is that it involves more than one individual, and it encourages discussion. It also tends to produce more accurate estimates than most organizations enjoy today.

Ranking functional entities

The next technique has been formed by taking elements of Bozoki's ranking technique and concepts from Putnam's Program Estimating and Reporting Tool, PERT. It can be combined with a Delphi session or can be done by individual estimators, and applies once functional entities of the system have been identified, so it should be used during high-level and intermediate design stages. You should also have data from earlier projects relating to at least two similar functional entities that are similar in size and in development environment. Do not use more than seven of these reference points or it becomes confusing.

The first thing to do is rank the functional entities (FEs), that is the discrete and identified system components, such as programs, for the new project in respect of those of the known or reference entities (REs). For example, my first FE may be smaller than one of the REs but larger than the second. My second FE may fall into the same category, but be larger than the first FE.

What I am doing through this technique is reducing the scope of the problem. Rather than having to think about where an entity fits, in terms of the whole project or system, I am now relating it to the known reference points, and to where I have placed my other FEs.

Expert opinion is then used to assign three estimates to each of my functional entities. These estimates are a smallest, a most likely and a largest estimate. Note that these are seldom distributed evenly about the most likely. For instance, I may say that for one of the entities, if all goes really well and we face no problems, the minimum cost is going to be three engineering months. However, I know what things are like on most projects and, being honest, it will probably take us four engineering months. But, if things really hit the fan and that sneaking suspicion I have about the message switching function turns out to be right, then this component could take us eight engineering months. Hang on, if I am right, then the only person who has experience of that is Jane, and she is on leave for a month just at the time when we will need her — so make that nine engineering months, because she will need time to get back into it. Notice the skew — when things go wrong they really go wrong!

Once you have your three estimates, you draw them together by multiplying the most likely by four, adding the smallest and largest and then dividing the total by six. To get the total cost or size for the whole system, you add the results for each of the individual entities.

Let us work through a very simplistic example of this technique

Let us assume that I have a simple development project that consists of two functional entities, F1 and F2. Further, assume that I have data from a previous project of a similar type relating to two functional entities that have been delivered, R1 and R2. The data for these is given below.

Entity	Cost
R1	50 person days
R2	100 person days

I now consider the work I have to do in terms of the reference entities. Let us say that, in my opinion, F2 is a bigger component than R2, and that F1 is bigger than R1, but smaller than R2. So ranking gives me:

R1

F1

R2

F2

In this case the ranking exercise is trivial as we are dealing with so few components but, in real-life projects of many units, it is a worthwhile exercise.

The next step is to produce estimates for the two components that have to be developed. To do this, I may use Delphi or analogy or simply expert opinion. The key is to provide the three types of estimates already mentioned, a minimum (Min), most likely (ML) and maximum (Max) estimate.

So:

	Min	ML	Max
F1	40	60	90
F2	100	140	200

Notice that the ML estimate does not necessarily fall half-way between the Min and Max estimates. To calculate the estimates for F1 and F2 I apply the formula:

$$\text{Estimate}(Fn) = [\text{Min}(Fn) + \text{ML}(Fn) \times 4 + \text{Max}(Fn)]/6$$

So:

$$\text{Estimate}(F1) = 40 + (60 \times 4) + 90/6 = 62$$

$$\text{Estimate}(F2) = 100 + (140 \times 4) + 200/6 = 143$$

$$\text{Estimate (Total Cost)} = 62 + 143 = 205$$

One word of warning, watch out for the accumulation of rounding errors on projects of many functional entities. I suggest you work to four decimal places and then round your final answer to whole days, or months for very large projects.

There are other statistical techniques that you can apply but most practitioners are wary of these, as the basis for the whole thing is still subjective opinion, and you can convince yourself of 'certainties' that, in reality, are built on very weak foundations.

Functional decomposition

The next technique is one of my favourites because it is less dependent on personal opinion, and it can be applied and improved very quickly. It depends on historical data, but one project gives you enough to start with. It is also conceptually very simple. This is always a good point.

Often known as 'bottom up' estimating or functional decomposition, it is applied during intermediate and low-level design. This is quite late in the development lifecycle, but given the high cost of testing, estimation is still necessary at these points.

You start with identified low-level components. Typically, low-level components are C functions or COBOL sections or paragraphs. Looking to historical data, you determine the average effort or size associated with these components (note: average indicates mean, median or mode, whichever is most suitable for the distribution), and then all you do is multiply total project components by the average. To illustrate this with a simple example: if we have a new development that is adding 50 new low-level components, and we know that it takes on average 10 person days to develop a 'typical' component, then our estimate would be $10 \times 50 = 500$ person days. So simple as to be trivial, but there is power in simplicity.

Looking at your historical data, you can also use standard deviations or percentiles to associate risk, in other words bounds, to your estimates.

As you get more historical data, you can get more sophisticated by classifying components by size or even by functional type, for example by looking at average costs for input, output and processing functions. You could get really smart by looking for an association between high-level designs and the number of low-level components, but it must be said that this has rarely been done so far. It would involve analysis of historical data to determine what elements of a high-level design were related to the number of low-level components finally produced as the implementation of that high-level design.

Analogy estimation

The last two techniques I want to identify as potential candidates for a cost estimation strategy can be applied at any time during the development lifecycle. The first is estimation by analogy.

If a group of software developers is asked how they estimate, this will be the technique most will claim to use, except the honest ones, who usually answer by sticking a wet finger in the air. Estimation by analogy is a simple approach that asks you to look at your project in terms of what it is expected to deliver, what is the function of the product, and how you expect to achieve that not in design terms, but in terms of the development environment. Then you simply find a project that has already been done which is similar to yours, and you use data from the completed project to help you estimate for yours.

For most organizations it is reasonably easy to find a project that was similar in terms of functionality. It is also very easy to forget about the soft factors or the development environment. It is no good finding a perfect functional match, where the completed project was done with a top-flight team using tried and tested techniques, and then expecting to deliver in the same time and at the same cost with a team consisting of mainly new graduates using tools never employed before.

However, while these concepts are simple, there is one major sticking point as far as estimation by analogy is concerned. The technique depends upon having an accessible history file of projects, but most organizations, as I have said earlier, fail to keep much data on current projects, let alone past work.

Given this situation, you should concentrate on establishing that history file. It does not need to be complex. Record data such as size, actual effort, actual duration, type of project through a simple classification scheme, team size and composition. You can add other elements to your records, such as effort per phase, but remember that it is better to get something simple going than to have a detailed procedure that is never used.

Also remember that you will seldom find a perfect match for your new project — so once more expert opinion is needed to guide judgement. Again, in a maintenance environment where new releases occur regularly, building up a usable history file does not take long.

Generalized cost models and associated tools

The final component I wish to discuss are the generalized cost models and the associated tools that were discussed earlier. The tools can be used at any time during the development lifecycle provided that you have a size estimate with which to drive them. This estimate can come from any of the other techniques described so far and, in this way, the tools can provide a good confidence check provided that they have been correctly calibrated.

The other great benefit that can come from using these types of tool is that they can get project managers thinking about the different factors that can affect projects. One organization, a large UK clearing bank, has integrated an estimation tool with Delphi sessions using the tool to stimulate discussion with interesting and beneficial results.

Interaction between estimating techniques and the development lifecycle

We now have a variety of bricks, but we really need to put them firmly within a template

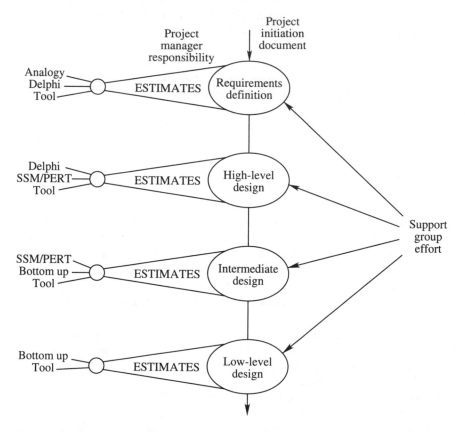

Figure 5.1 Estimation template.

by considering the channels of communication between bricks and the development lifecycle, and the management of that lifecycle. Figure 5.1 presents one such view and is offered as an estimation template that could be tailored to your organization. It shows how the various techniques fit against a typical development lifecycle. There is overlap and this is quite deliberate, as you will realize from our earlier discussions regarding the basic principles of estimation.

The diagram shows a set of bricks or estimating techniques associated with certain lifecycle phases for just the 'development' arm of the V, but not for testing, together with a link from the project manager to the estimation support group. Notice that in the expansion of the estimation support group's role in Fig. 5.2, there is a commitment to training, checking and to the development of local models. This model is presented as a strategy for a typical software engineering organization of today, and will apply, I suspect, for some years. It is not presented as the final solution. We will only have fully solved the estimation process when organizations tie effective estimation to the project management process. This will take effort and time, but will provide rich dividends in terms of customer satisfaction.

Figure 5.3 shows a typical process diagram of a first-stage estimation process as implemented in a number of organizations. Notice the use of FPA to size individual work requests and the final project. This two-stage sizing is used because economies of scale can

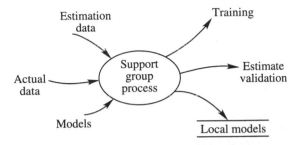

Figure 5.2 Role of the support group.

sometimes be realized at the project level. Function Point Analysis is also used to drive the negotiation with the customer, sometimes in conjunction with cost estimates against individual work requests. One weakness in this approach is the need to convert *function point* scores to *lines of code* counts using standard tables. The risk associated with this has been reduced by using data from within the organization rather than industry standards.

Monitoring the effectiveness of estimates

Finally, there is one element of estimation that has not been discussed, how do we monitor the effectiveness of the process? In essence, this is simply a comparison of estimates made at specific lifecycle points to actual results within projects. In practice, this data needs to be collected, analysed and presented to management to demonstrate an improvement over time. Again, this will not happen automatically, and this responsibility should fall to the estimation support group from the very start.

The following three suggestions may help to get you started as far as presenting this type of effectiveness measure is concerned. All three charts are simply based on collection of actuals versus estimates. The first, Fig. 5.4, plots the estimate against the actual so that the

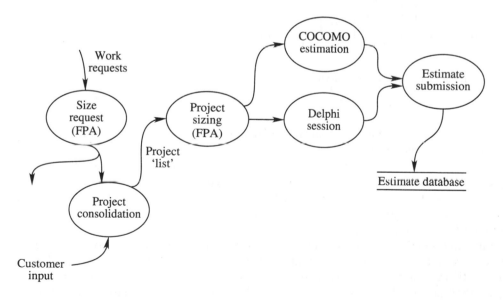

Figure 5.3 Typical process diagram.

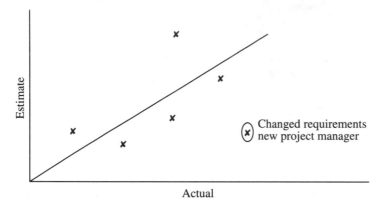

Figure 5.4 Monitoring and feedback (actual vs estimates).

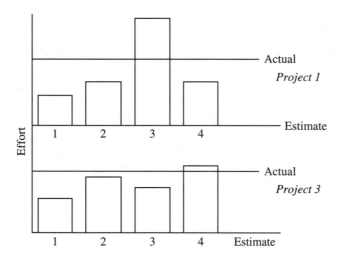

Figure 5.5 Monitoring and feedback (estimate vs effort).

distance from the 45° line indicates the level of estimate accuracy. A plot on the line means that the estimator got it spot on!

Figure 5.5 shows four estimates taken during the course of two separate development projects. An actual line is included and the variance against the actual is apparent. As this is based on real data, notice the way the estimation process has become more sensible by the time the third project is reached. This should be compared against the wild variances experienced on the first project.

Figure 5.6 takes the absolute variance, that is ignoring the fact that it may be an over or underestimate, between the estimate and the actual, and plots this for a number of projects. In this case, we are using the initial estimates, and we have data from four projects that have used an estimation strategy. This type of diagram enables the benefits of such an approach to be represented to managers and to customers.

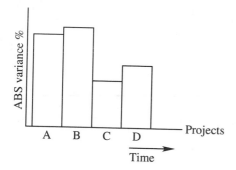

Figure 5.6 Monitoring and feedback — initial project estimates.

What about the leading edge, big projects?

One final point. I am often asked what can be done to help with the cost estimation problem in very large projects, possibly developing for 10 years before the first delivery of software is made, and where the systems being developed are at the leading edge. This is a very difficult question to answer as proving the effectiveness of the answer takes so long. The best suggestions I can give are that you ensure sufficient contingency to cover the many risks associated with this project, that you base your initial estimates on the Delphi method, and that you apply rigorous project management to control the project. The reality, of course, is that if you are at the leading edge of technology and you are dealing with big projects, then you are unlikely to have much chance to develop the historical data upon which so many estimation techniques depend.

SUMMARY

This chapter has discussed estimation within the software engineering environment. We have looked at the need for effective estimation and the effect that poor estimates can have on a business. For most organizations, effective estimation is a critical factor for success and for customer satisfaction. Remember also that you may appear to be delivering on time, but if you are only achieving this through significant reductions in the amount of functionality that is delivered, compared to what was agreed for delivery, your customers will not be very happy.

We have considered estimation as a process, and we have looked at various techniques that can be used to populate that process. We have also discussed the use of tools within a cost estimation process or strategy. Remember, cost estimation is not simply about tools or fancy techniques, they alone will not solve your problems. You need to have a strategy or process for cost estimation.

If the estimation principles in this chapter strike you as nothing more than common sense, and if you are singularly unimpressed with the complexity of the estimation techniques presented here, then I make no apologies. Estimation like most areas of Software Metrics relies heavily on common sense, and simple solutions often work best, especially when the starting point is an *ad hoc*, undefined process that many view as close to magic, or blind chance. Managers and customers tend to dislike magic.

6

APPLIED DESIGN METRICS

Now we come to an area that always strikes me as the poor relation in the use of metrics. This is a great shame, because the techniques are easy to apply; they cost very little in terms of additional effort; they are used by engineers or programmers; and they are a form of Software Metrics that can have a very real impact on the quality of the product delivered to the customer.

So what are these new wonder cures? Well, firstly, they are not new — in fact the concepts are as old as systems theory itself and, secondly, as with all Software Metrics, they are not a panacea. Put simply, I am referring to a set of techniques, firmly based upon measurement, that are applied to designs at different levels to assess the complexity of those designs — hence the name that I have chosen to describe the collection of such techniques: Applied Design Metrics (ADM). The basic premise behind such metrics is that *designs exhibiting higher levels of complexity will also exhibit poorer reliability and maintainability characteristics.*

The wording of that last statement demonstrates that I view the results of using these techniques as indicators of quality. I will not claim that a design with a high complexity rating will always produce a system that is unreliable and unmaintainable, but I do claim that such a system is potentially more likely to exhibit those characteristics. Applied Design Metrics provide indicators or pointers to likely problem areas *within* systems and, at the highest level, to potentially troublesome systems. While these metrics are generally indicators, there is one example, discussed later, which has boundary values associated with it. Beyond there it can be dangerous to travel.

Of course, it is easy to talk in terms of complexity, but it is not always so easy to pin down such a term. Towards the end of this chapter, I will discuss aspects of complexity in more detail but, for now, I present a working definition:

Complexity — The degree of entanglement within a system or its components.

Before we look at specific examples of ADM, I would like to stress one other point. These techniques are not *management metrics* in the sense that the latter are used to assess performance at any level, and they are in no way related to the normal productivity and quality metrics we looked at when discussing management statistics. Applied Design Metrics are used by engineers or programmers on a daily basis. They should form part of the basic training and then become the tool-kit of every competent engineer working on software development or maintenance, because more and more evidence is being presented that shows their use directly affecting delivered quality.

As with many aspects of Software Metrics there are several variations on the theme of ADM, one common classification being that of the inter and intra measures. *Inter* measures are concerned with the way in which modules or components connect, while the *intra* measures are more concerned with assessing what goes on within a module. While this classification can be useful, I believe that it is important to consider the application of any measurement-based technique in terms of its business benefit. For this reason, I would like to concentrate on what are possibly the two most widely used and accepted design metrics, and I wish to discuss them in terms of their business application. In fairness, I should add that these techniques are not universally accepted by the software engineering community and are often the subject of discussion. However, my belief is that they offer a clear route to rapid payback of the investment necessary to implement them in a business environment.

McCABE METRICS

The first of the techniques I would like to discuss are the McCabe metrics. McCabe measures are among the more established Software Metrics in use today, and they do seem to be going through a revival after a somewhat troublesome time when numerous individuals criticized their effectiveness. I was also among the doubters until I had the good fortune, some years ago, to hear their originator, Tom McCabe, present a paper at a conference. This taught me two lessons:

1. Any Software Metric will be criticized, not least because so many people are looking for the silver bullet, the one metric to solve all our problems and, frankly, this will not be seen during our lifetime. Many of the criticisms of McCabe metrics stemmed from them being put to uses for which they were never intended.
2. If you want to learn about something, then, if possible, go to the source.

That presentation, coupled with the opportunity to talk to some individuals who were making use of McCabe metrics in the way that was intended, induced me to try them. I can honestly report that the results I have had with their application convinces me that they are a very powerful tool.

So, what are McCabe metrics? There are two measures commonly known as McCabe metrics: cyclomatic complexity and essential complexity, both founded upon graph theory. I am going to concentrate on describing Cyclomatic Complexity, because Essential Complexity, as will be seen, is very similar in its application.

Cyclomatic Complexity

This whole subject is somewhat complex, but bear with me, because the basic concepts are very simple to use. McCabe metrics are applied against 'flowgraphs' which are simplified flowcharts, all 'boxes' being represented as simple, unmarked nodes. I am tempted to leave it there, but for a recent salutary experience when a young engineer told me that he had never been taught how to use flowcharts — 'after all, they went out with the ark!' So for those young enough never to have had the pleasure of flowcharting, and anyone who has forgotten the basic principles, let me try to explain what a flowgraph is in more technical terms.

Flowgraphs

If you look at Fig. 6.1, we will see a fragment of code that contains an example of sequence, selection and iteration. By representing each statement as a simple bubble or node, and each control flow between statements as a connecting line or edge, we can present that code fragment as a flowgraph, i.e. simply a collection of nodes and edges. For the code fragment in Fig. 6.1, an associated flowgraph is shown.

Now a flowgraph can be constructed for any code fragment that can be seen to have a single entry and exit point. Generally speaking, McCabe metrics are applied to low-level system components such as COBOL paragraphs or sections, C functions, etc. Flowgraphs can also be derived from most pseudo-English design notations so that we do not have to wait for code before using these techniques. Even so, McCabe metrics do come into play relatively late in the development lifecycle, but consider — how late is too late? Even if I were at the point of producing code, it is still cheaper for me to make changes rather than

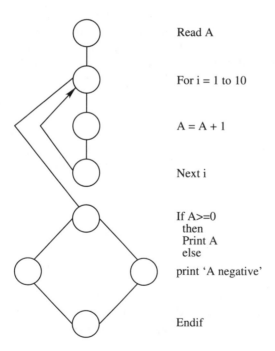

Figure 6.1 McCabe metrics background theory — example of flowgraph (1).

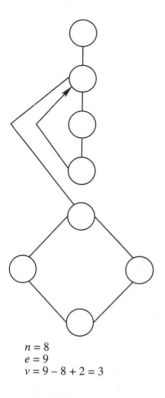

$n = 8$
$e = 9$
$v = 9 - 8 + 2 = 3$

Figure 6.2 McCabe metrics background theory — example of flowgraph (2).

produce and deliver system components that are prone to defects and maintenance problems. Equally important, by using McCabe metrics, I can identify potential hot spots in my system, and advise the test people that these should be even more rigorously tested than the rest of the system surely will be.

Having got the flowgraph, we count the number of edges e, and the number of nodes n, then simply apply the formula below to calculate the McCabe Cyclomatic Complexity value, v:

$$v = e - n + 2$$

A simple example is provided in Fig. 6.2 to illustrate the use of this formula.

There are other ways to calculate the value v. Perhaps the most useful is, given code or a good pseudo-English approximation, to count the number of IF statements and add one, remembering to treat compound conditionals as multiple IFs. This basic algorithm can be used to produce a very simple automated tool that will calculate the value v once it has code to work on.

McCabe's *cyclomatic* metric is a measure of how complex a specific realization of a design is. Basically, if my code or low-level design is seen as a black box that exists to do something, how complex have I made the inner workings of that black box?

Essential Complexity

Essential Complexity is a much more simple concept to explain in that it is a measure of

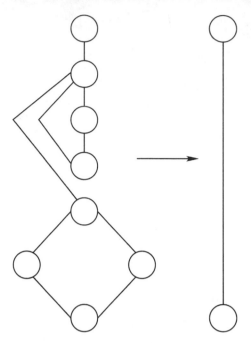

Figure 6.3 McCabe metrics background theory — example of reduced flowgraph (1).

'structuredness'. If we look at a piece of code, or the low-level pseudo-English that is one step away from code, we will find standard constructs within it. These are sequence, selection and iteration constructs. If we look at the flowgraph representation, we will find that we can reduce it to the essential flowgraph by replacing these constructs by single nodes.

When we cannot do this, because the basic rules of sequencing, selection and iteration have been broken, usually through the use of 'GOTO' commands, the degree of structuredness is reduced. Figures 6.3 and 6.4 show the reduction for a flowgraph that is (a) well structured and (b) one that contains illegal constructs.

Calculating Essential Complexity

Calculating Essential Complexity is simply a case of applying the same formula as that used for Cyclomatic Complexity, but with counts taken from the reduced flowgraph, thus:

$$vr = er - nr + 2$$

where *vr* is Essential Complexity and *er* and *nr* are the edge and node counts from the reduced flowgraph.

The meaning and use of numbers

But, of course, all we have so far are some numbers. What do they mean and how do we use them?

Let me start to answer that question by putting forward some very concrete guidelines, and I will then discuss a slightly less pedantic approach.

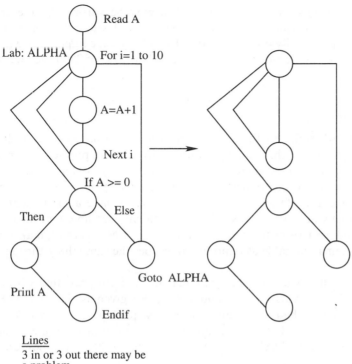

Read A

Lab: ALPHA — For i=1 to 10

A=A+1

Next i

If A >= 0

Then   Else

Print A

Endif   Goto ALPHA

Lines
3 in or 3 out there may be
a problem

Figure 6.4 McCabe metrics background theory — example of reduced flowgraph (2).

According to followers of McCabe, and as always I stress the word 'followers', the rules are quite straightforward. If we are working on a new development or an enhancement project that is adding functionality then, for any single low-level component, the value for v, Cyclomatic Complexity, should not exceed ten and the value for vr, Essential Complexity, should not exceed two.

One project in the USA that applied these rules did achieve zero defects for at least 12 months after delivery. Think about that.

Now let us talk about the more common reality. Most of us do not have the pleasure of working on new developments, and any additional functionality that can add to systems as part of an enhancement project tends to be swamped by straight changes to the base system. Also, if we are managing a system, we may feel it to be slightly over the top suddenly to insist that everyone start bringing things in line with the ten/two rule.

In a maintenance environment, a good guideline is to do a McCabe analysis before a change is made and then do another one after you have designed the changes. If the values for v and vr are the same, or a little bit better, then implement the change. If they are worse, then go back and redo it, because otherwise trouble is in store.

If you are in the situation of developing new systems or adding low-level components then, in all honesty, you could do a lot worse than apply the ten/two rule. In a maintenance environment, this may be a bit much for people who have not come across these ideas before. In this situation, do an analysis of the system for which you are responsible, either by analysing the whole system through a tool that uses code as its source, or by sampling components from the system. You may be surprised, or even shocked, to find components with *cyclomatic* values of 500+. Yes, I know the guideline was 10, but that is not a mistype, I really do mean 500+! I regularly see components with values like this. I have even been told about one component with a value of 2800! Believe it and weep.

Problems and problem solving

Now we do have to take a deep breath here for two reasons. Firstly, we have to accept the fact that there are modules around like that, and we wonder why we have problems in this industry. Secondly, we must realize that there is one very easy way to bump up the Cyclomatic Complexity value of a component without destroying its reliability or maintainability. How? Use a CASE statement — which is where I have a fundamental difference with some individuals in our industry. CASE statements are fine, and have a role to play in designs and coding. However, there is a limit which, when reached, makes a CASE heavy component as unmaintainable as a module that does the same thing through multiple IFs.

It may upset the fundamentalist structured programmer, but if I am presented with a design that goes over a *cyclomatic* value of 50, and the excuse given is that a CASE statement has been used, somebody had better find cover very quickly! Complex CASE statements are difficult to understand. I say this as an ex-maintenance programmer who regularly had to attempt to decipher CASE statements that went to 20 or 30 lines, and were not easy to comprehend.

Enough of the problems, what can be done about them?

If it is thought desirable to introduce the use of McCabe metrics, use a sampling exercise like the one I have outlined to set short-term targets. For example, looking at our current system; the average McCabe values are 25 and 5 for Cyclomatic and Essential Complexity respectively. From now on, the rule will be that no design solution gets through a review, and it would be sensible to say it does not even go for review, unless it makes the McCabe values better than they were before or, if new functionality, has values of 20 and 4. Given the environment, these targets are reasonable and the situation can always be reassessed in six months' time and the targets made tighter.

Effectively, I suggest that McCabe metrics be used as control gates. The actual values used for those gates are less important than the fact that the engineers are asked to think about the results of their actions.

The benefits of McCabe metrics

But do such approaches work? Are McCabe metrics worth anything? I have already mentioned the experience of one organization that achieved zero defects when it piloted these techniques. I also know that Hewlett-Packard have published data which shows a 0.9 correlation between Cyclomatic Complexity and defect reports across a large number of applications. That is pretty impressive no matter what reservations there are about correlation statistics.

The best example I have come across to support the use of McCabe metrics is somewhat back to front. A while ago, I was asked to pilot *complexity metrics* in an organization as part of a quality improvement programme. I was given a particular application and work team and initial discussions indicated that McCabe metrics would be the best approach. I asked what the current quality levels were in terms of defects, only to be told that this application did not have defects, at least so few that it was almost zero. Needless to say I asked for proof, and this was not available. Being something of a cynic, I suggested that we put in a defect reporting mechanism on the current project, a fairly straightforward 5000 line enhancement job.

This was done, and I returned expecting to find a good few defect reports awaiting me from the link tests and from the user acceptance or system tests. There were three defect reports. Two of these were due to data, and could not be blamed on the programming team. This meant I had a system that appeared to be exhibiting a reliability level better than 0.001 defects per thousand lines of code changed. Bear in mind that the best norms we have to work with suggest four defects per thousand lines for USA and European software.

Why was this? Well, the team was not large, consisting of three individuals who were quality staff to their toenails. As the team leader said, those three defects should not have got through, and she meant it! They had a very close and good relationship with their user. Obviously, it all helped, but the thing that really battened it down was that most of their system components conformed to the ten/two rule. They were applying McCabe concepts automatically, and they were getting the results.

Incidentally, this team had one individual who manually analysed all the components associated with that 5K project and it took him three days. I would not recommend that McCabe analysis was regularly carried out by hand, but it shows that it can be done.

Of course, everything is not perfect, even with these metrics. There can be problems with recursion, when sections of code call themselves, and with fall through, where one component passes control down to another and so on, so that there is no single entry/exit point. However, most managers steer clear of recursion, wisely I believe, and fall through is fortunately quite rare, so I tend to ignore these concerns. More important are the people worries that sometimes arise. Some managers are very concerned about the use of such metrics, because they see their use adding to development time. In my mind, the results speak clearly in favour of their use, but it should be remembered that a McCabe analysis, when done as part and parcel of the day-to-day work, adds about five or ten minutes to a component change that typically takes a minimum of an engineering day when due allowance is made for familiarization, redocumentation, and all the rest of IT processes.

McCabe metrics do also seem to open some other interesting doors.

Spin-offs

There are a number of tools around that support McCabe metrics. These include ACT and Battlemap from McCabe Associates in the USA, TESTBED from Program Analysers Ltd in Newbury, England, and a large number of other static and dynamic analysers. Some of these tools also enable the automatic production of unit test cases. This can offer a significant saving on testing effort.

Even more interesting are some of the reports that have been coming from the USA during recent months. It seems that some people have been using McCabe metrics and the automatic generation of test cases to identify redundant code within systems. By redundant code, we simply mean modules that do the same job as other modules in the same system. For example, you may need a sort routine and so may I. Assuming you write yours for release 1, is it very likely that I will check things out before writing my own for release 2 or 3? The answer seems to be, no. I will write my own in any case. For further information about this experimental technique see McCabe (1990). Based on the work done so far, it seems that we could expect systems to exhibit about a 30 per cent level of redundancy, which is an awful lot of code to exist unnecessarily.

To summarize, McCabe metrics are a well-established, well-proven foundation for techniques to manage complexity and, hence, reliability and maintainability. Like them or not, many people have found that they work.

INFORMATION FLOW METRICS

The other set of metrics I would like to place under the ADM umbrella are generally known as 'Information Flow' (IF) metrics. At the conceptual level, IF metrics are not difficult to understand — it is when you come to apply them that the fun can start. Having said that, a pragmatic approach, as always, works wonders.

The basis of IF metrics is founded upon the following premise. All but the most simple systems consist of components, and it is the work that these components do and how they are fitted together that influence the complexity of a system. If a component has to do numerous discrete tasks, it is said to lack 'cohesion'. If it passes information to, and/or accepts information from many other components within the system, it is said to be highly 'coupled'. Systems theory tells us that components that are highly coupled and that lack cohesion tend to be less reliable and less maintainable than those that are loosely coupled and that are cohesive.

Sometimes definitions of terms like cohesion and coupling help, so I present the following as working definitions of those terms:

- *Cohesion* — The degree to which a component performs a single function.
- *Coupling* — The term used to describe the degree of linkage between one component and others in the same system.

Now, what is a 'component'?

- *Component* — Any element identified by decomposing a (software) system into its constituent parts.

This systems-view maps to software systems extremely easily as most engineers today use, or are at least familiar with, top down design techniques that produce a hierarchical view of system components. Even the more modern 'middle out' design approaches produce this structured type of deliverable, and here again IF metrics can be used.

Information Flow metrics model the degree of cohesion and coupling for a particular system component. How that model is constructed can justifiably range from the simple to the complex. I intend to start with the most simple representation of IF metrics to illustrate the basic concepts, how to derive information using the metrics and how to use that information. I will then expand this basic IF model.

Workers in Information Flow metrics

Just before I do this, I would like to acknowledge the credit for these metrics and the approaches I outline here where it is due. In terms of applying IF metrics to software systems, the pioneering work was done by Henry and Kafura (Henry, 1981). They looked at the UNIX operating system, and found a strong association between the IF metrics and the level of maintainability ascribed to components by programmers. Other individuals who tried to apply these principles found difficulties in using the Henry and Kafura approach. Further work was done in the UK by Professor Darrell Ince and Martin Shepperd (Ince and Shepperd, 1989), among others, which resulted in a more practical IF model. This work was complimented by Barbara Kitchenham (1990), who addressed the same problem, and who also presented a clear approach to the question of interpretation.

I had the good fortune of having the assistance of Ince, Shepperd and Kitchenham when I was first attempting to use these metrics. What is presented here is a distillation of that assistance.

The basic Information Flow model

Information Flow metrics are applied to the components of a system design. Figure 6.5 shows a fragment of such a design, and for component A we can define three measures, but remember that these are the most simple models of IF:

1. 'FAN IN'. This is simply a count of the number of other components that can call, or pass control, to component A.
2. 'FAN OUT'. This is the number of components that are called by component A.
3. This is derived from the first two by using the following formula. We will call this measure the INFORMATION FLOW index of module A, abbreviated to IF(A).

$$IF(A) = [FAN\ IN(A) \times FAN\ OUT(A)]\ \hat{}\ 2$$

The formula includes a power component to 'model the non-linear nature of complexity' as most texts on IF metrics describe it. The assumption is that if something is more complex than something else, then it is much more complex rather than just a little bit more complex. Given that assumption, we could raise to a power three or four or whatever we want but, on the principle that the simpler the model the better, then two is a good enough choice. From my point of view, raising to two makes it easier, as will be seen, to pick out the potential bad guys. That is a good enough reason, and I will leave it to the purists to worry about the finer detail.

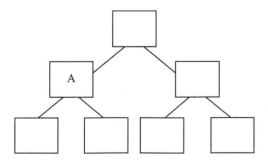

Figure 6.5 Aspects of complexity.

Information Flow metrics can be applied to any functional decomposition of a software system. Examples of these include structure charts, Dataflow diagrams and SDL block diagrams. Obviously we may have to tailor our terminology to suit the notation being used. For example, in a Dataflow diagram we do not have 'calls', instead we have data flows between processes. The principle is the same. One of the easiest applications I have come across is to use IF metrics on the hierarchical tree that forms a basis of some configuration management systems. This is a good example of the synergy that can sometimes be found to operate within software engineering.

Given that IF metrics apply to these forms of functional decomposition, they come into play from as early as the high-level design stage, and serve a useful purpose right the way down to low-level design when you can start to use McCabe metrics.

Given functional decomposition it will be seen that there is one additional attribute possessed by each component, namely its level in the decomposition. The following is a step-by-step guide to deriving these most simple of IF metrics.

1. Note the level of each component in the system design.
2. For each component, count the number of calls to that component — this is the FAN IN of that component. Some organizations allow more than one component at the highest level in the design, so for components at the highest level which should have a FAN IN of zero, assign a FAN IN of one. Also note that a simple model of FAN IN can penalize reused components. As a pragmatic rule, if a component calls no components, its FAN IN is greater than seven, and it is deemed to be 'small'. This last point requires the discretion of the designer. Then assign a FAN IN of one.
3. For each component, count the number of calls from that component. For components that call no other, assign a FAN OUT value of one.
4. Calculate the IF value for each component using the formula above.
5. Sum the IF value for all components within each level. I will call this the LEVEL SUM.
6. Sum the IF values for the total system design. I will call this the SYSTEM SUM, which brings us to the analysis phase — so to continue:
7. For each level, rank the components in that level according to FAN IN, FAN OUT and IF values. Three histograms or line plots should be prepared for each level.
8. Plot the LEVEL SUM values for each level using a histogram or line plot.

This may sound like a great deal of work, but for most commercial systems that I have encountered, provided the documentation exists, this data can be derived and the analysis done within one engineering day. If the systems are larger than the ones I have seen, then it will obviously take longer, but remember that once done, it is very easy to keep up-to-date. Depending upon the environment it may even be possible to automate the calculations.

Having got the information, we now need to utilize it. It must be realized that, for IF metrics, there are no absolute values of good or bad. Information Flow metrics are relative indicators. This means that the value for your system may be higher than for my system, but this does not mean that your system is worse. Nor does a high metric value guarantee that a component will be unreliable and unmaintainable. It is only that it will probably be less reliable and maintainable than its fellows.

The rub is that, in most systems, less reliable and less maintainable means that it is potentially going to cost significant amounts of money to fix and enhance. Potentially, it could even be a nightmare component.

A nightmare component is the one that the system administrator has nightmares about, because he or she knows that if anyone touches that component, the whole system is going to crash, and it will take weeks to fix because Fred designed it and Fred was weird. Fred also left five years ago!

So the strength of IF metrics is not in the numbers themselves, but in how the information is used. As a guide, the 25 per cent of components with the highest scores for FAN IN, FAN OUT and IF values should be investigated. Now in practice it may well be that a certain number of modules stick out like a sore thumb, especially on the IF values. If this group is more or less than the 25 per cent guide, then do not worry about it, concentrate on those that seem to be odd according to the metric values rather than following any 25 per cent rule slavishly.

High FAN IN values indicate modules that lack cohesion. It may well be that the functions have not been broken out to a great enough degree. Basically, these components are often called because they are doing more than one job.

High levels of FAN OUT also indicate a lack of cohesion or missed levels of abstraction. Here design was stopped before it was finished, and this is reflected in the high number of calls from the component.

Generally speaking, FAN OUT appears to be a better indicator of problem modules than FAN IN, but it is early days yet and I would not wish to discount FAN IN.

High IF values indicate highly coupled components. These components need to be looked at in terms of FAN IN and FAN OUT to see how to reduce the complexity level. Sometimes a 'traffic centre' may be hit. This is a component where, for whatever reasons, there is a high IF value, but things cannot be improved. Switching components often exhibit this. Here there is a potential problem area which, if it is also a large component, may be very error prone. If the complexity cannot be reduced, then at least make sure that that component is thoroughly tested.

Looking at the LEVEL SUM plot of values, we should see a fairly smooth curve showing controlled growth in IF across the levels. Sudden increases in these values across levels can indicate a missed level of abstraction within the general design. For systems where the design has less than ten levels, then a simple count of components at each level seems to work equally well.

The final item of information is the SYSTEM SUM value. This gives an overall complexity rating for the design in terms of IF metrics. Most presentations on this topic will say that this number can be used to assess alternative design proposals. At which point there are often wry chuckles from the practitioners in the audience, who feel they never have enough time to develop one design, let alone alternatives. My sympathies have always been with the practitioners, but let me just state that I have recently come across two teams in different organizations who do prepare alternative designs at this kind of level for enhancement projects. Information Flow metrics gives them the opportunity to increase confidence in the choice they eventually make by quantifying aspects of complexity. Score one for the so-called academics!

A more sophisticated Information Flow model

We have looked at the most simple form of IF metrics, but the original proposals put forward by Henry and Kafura (1981) were more sophisticated than the control flow-based variant discussed above. As I said earlier, Ince and Shepperd (1989) and Kitchenham (1990) have done a great deal of work to help in the practical application of Henry and Kafura's pioneering proposals, and it is a distillation of that work that I will now summarize into the more sophisticated IF model. It should, however, be realized that this is a *model*, and it will need to be tailored to your own organization's design mechanisms if it is to be used. Such a tailoring process should not take more than two days for counting rule derivation and documentation of these rules, provided a well-defined design notation is used together with a competent engineer who knows that notation.

The only difference between the simple and the sophisticated IF models lies in the definition of FAN IN and FAN OUT.

For a component A let:

a = the number of components that call A;
b = the number of parameters passed to A from components higher in the hierarchy;
c = the number of parameters passed to A from components lower in the hierarchy;
d = the number of data elements read by component A.

Then:

$$\text{FAN IN}(A) = a + b + c + d$$

Also let:

e = the number of components called by A;
f = the number of parameters passed from A to components higher in the hierarchy;
g = the number of parameters passed from A to components lower in the hierarchy;
h = the number of data elements written to by A.

Then:

$$\text{FAN OUT}(A) = e + f + g + h$$

Other than those changes to the basic definitions, the derivation, analysis and interpretation remain the same. I must say that my advice to any organization starting to apply IF metrics would be to build up confidence by using the simpler form. If these work, then leave it at that. If, and only if, the simpler form fails in your environment, in other words you are confident that no significant relationship exists between the simple measures and the levels of reliability and maintainability, then spend the effort to tailor and pilot the more sophisticated form.

It is encouraging to know that there have been a number of experimental validations of IF metrics that seem to support the claims made for them. Programming groups that have been introduced to IF metrics have been able to make use of them and they also report benefits in the area of design quality control and system management. They seem to work, but there appears to be some reluctance in the industry as a whole to make use of IF metrics. Perhaps one reason is because managers feel they are a bit 'techie'. Perhaps others feel that they are not yet ready to use sophisticated techniques like IF metrics. I hope that this brief explanation of the measures has shown that they are a practical and pragmatic method of ensuring quality.

SUMMARY

This chapter is based on the assumption that avoidable complexity costs our industry a great deal of money. If we can design avoidable complexity out of our systems before we deliver them to testing groups or, worse, to the end customer, then we will save much of that money. The simple metrics-based techniques offer an opportunity for organizations to start that designing out process.

What is complexity?

You may ask if the models behind these techniques are complete and the answer would be no. Complexity itself is complex as it operates in at least four dimensions:

1. The complexity that results from the way systems components are connected, which we can call 'coupling' complexity.
2. The complexity that results from the black box view of a component, basically how cohesive is it.
3. Complexity also derives from the white box level. How does a component do what it is supposed to?

We can use IF metrics to model the first two dimensions and McCabe Cyclomatic and Essential Complexity metrics to model the third. None of these models are a totally accurate representation of a complexity dimension.

We have also completely ignored the fourth complexity dimension — data complexity which itself can cause major problems with live systems. Complexity is almost certainly a function of these four variables and there may be others, one candidate being the degree of concurrency in a system. Unfortunately, very little work seems to have been done in this area, and we can only hope that further research into the different aspects of complexity and how they relate to one another will be undertaken in the near future.

The metrics and the associated techniques in this chapter do not give a total solution to the problem of complexity, but they provide a start, which does not cost an arm and a leg to put to good use.

7

PROJECT CONTROL

The final chapter of this section looks at the topic of project control. This is often seen as being outside the scope of a metrics initiative, or it may not even be considered during the requirements analysis stage of implementing a metrics programme.

If the reason for this is that the organization has projects under control, then I have no argument with the position that this is not part of the remit for a metrics programme. If, however, the organization has a requirement for project control that is not being addressed by another part of that organization, then it makes sense to me to put project control within the programme's terms of reference. I believe that I can justify this position with one sentence. Software Metrics initiatives are there to improve the quality of products and *processes*, and if that means enhancing the project control mechanisms then so be it. This concern merely demonstrates the difficulties we face in defining clear functional boundaries for 'metrics'.

Talking of boundaries, perhaps I should define what I mean by project control. Consider the following situation:

You receive a customer's statement of requirements, the wish list, and you carry out your initial estimation and submit the bid. Notice that you still have not managed to convince the customer or your own organization that you should actually bid for the requirements definition phase first, but you are working on it! Now, despite all expectations to the contrary, you get the contract.

What happens next? Usually a whole group of people start beavering away on that requirements definition. Hopefully, you also get some sort of a project plan together with the obligatory milestones. Oh yes, this is a 'Quality Organization' now, because the top man said so a couple of months ago, so you had better have a quality plan. OK, that has got the overheads sorted out, now let's get those people cutting code! Let's just hope things go better than last time. Remember what happened? Two weeks before delivery, you had to tell the customer there was a six month delay. That was embarrassing. Especially as you had spent two years on the project!

The chances are that you do not have a situation that is as bad as that, do you? Let us now run a slightly different scenario.

> You have won the bid, and have got first-cut project plans which will be refined after you get more information from the requirements definition stage. The first-cut plans have been through a feasibility check and the refined plans will also be checked in this way. You have also pulled in the standard quality plan for this class of project and made any necessary modifications. Of course, these have been checked and agreed by your project control people and, perhaps, the customer. After all you do talk to the customer more these days, since the quality initiative made everyone realize there was such a thing as a customer. You have also put together your risk management plans, and prepared contingency plans and, of course, all of the team leaders know how progress is going to be monitored across the life of the project. Now, you have increased overheads, but you have also increased the probability of delivering on time.

This is a scenario in which project control is operating. Looking at the components that go to make up the picture, we see the following. There is project planning and feasibility checking of those plans, quality plans, risk management and progress checking.

Project planning is a well-established discipline, and I do not intend to address it here. There are many good reference books that deal with work breakdown, scheduling, logical task linkage and critical path analysis, for example *Project Management, A Managerial Approach* by Meredith and Mantel published by Wiley and *Critical Path Planning* by Barnetson, published by Newnes Books. Your own organization may well have standard approaches to these areas. There are also numerous commercially available project planning tools.

Quality planning is also an area that is relatively well established, especially in organizations operating a Total Quality Management policy. If not fully established, at least the concepts are well understood, and I could do no better than to recommend (Humphrey, 1991).

The areas I would like to discuss, quite briefly, because each is a subject in its own right, are feasibility checking, risk management and progress checking. However, before we go any further, I would like to touch on the implementation of the techniques we are about to discuss, because a common reaction is to throw one's hands up in horror at the additional costs implied. If an organization effectively operates one project at a time over long durations, typically between five and ten years, then these techniques are certainly applicable and justifiable. In fact, they are almost mandatory. However, this type of environment is very rare outside defence work.

More commonly, the work is in a mixed environment of maintenance, which includes enhancement, and development. New developments typically take no more than two years elapsed time, but the majority of the available effort is spent enhancing existing products through new releases once or twice a year. Within the IT function there could easily be 100 projects on the go at any one time.

The wheel is not reinvented every time a new project is started. Standard approaches to feasibility checking, risk management and progress checking should be implemented and, after a bedding-in period, the deviations from these standard approaches should be minimal. Note that justifiable deviations should be allowed, and are the responsibility of the project manager.

FEASIBILITY CHECKING

Feasibility checking is a very close relation to cost estimation, but in this case the cost has been estimated and the planned duration contained in the project plans, and the probability of achieving those estimates now needs to be assessed.

Given the relationship to cost estimation, it should come as no surprise to find that it is possible to manipulate the public domain models to get this kind of feasibility check. In its most simple form, the check is performed by plotting effort or duration against size, holding all other variables such as programmer skills constant, and then seeing if the estimates for the project at its given estimated size lie above the plotted line. If they do, then we are, according to the model used, in the feasible region. If the estimates lie below the line, there is a problem. Putting it diplomatically, we plan to do the project more effectively than the model predicts we will. Remember that we need to use a model calibrated to the environment.

More sophisticated models can be set up, based on industry data or our own experiences, and there is an obvious potential here for automating those models. One organization has already done this. Quantitative Software Management in the USA and Europe market a tool called Slim Control which is, as far as I am aware at the time of writing, the only tool that is focused on this feasibility aspect of project control, although other cost estimation packages can be adapted.

Of course, we may wish to apply a more humanistic approach to feasibility checking. There is no reason why project plans should not be reviewed or inspected just like any other deliverable. These plans should satisfy two requirements: they should be complete in that everything that is expected is present, for example, the *critical path*, if that is normally used; they should also be, in the opinion of the reviewers, feasible. This may mean discussing the assumptions that underlie the estimates, and also implies that the review team should have project management experience.

So it can be seen that both simple and sophisticated techniques do exist to administer this aspect of project control, but if we have a plan that looks good, what about when things go wrong? That brings us to Risk Management.

RISK MANAGEMENT

Risk Management is a topic that really does require a book in its own right and, like many other topics, it is one that has strong links to Software Metrics. All that can be done in the space available heré is to give a brief overview of the subject, and to demonstrate those linkages between Risk Management and Software Metrics.

The process of Risk Management starts, as we might expect, with an identification of those factors that could cause problems for the project, identifying the 'risks' themselves. These can range from the possibility of key individuals going sick to the satisfaction of requirements being more complex than was originally thought. Basically, we should identify anything that our experience, and that of others, tells us could cause problems and, by problems, we mean factors that could result in missing milestones and delivery, or exceeding cost budget.

Each risk factor should now have a probability of occurring assigned to it. This brings us to the first link between Risk Management and Software Metrics. In an ideal world, we would look back at the collection of project data, all partitioned by class of project and, within the relevant class, we would identify each time that particular factor made its presence felt. Is it too much to ask how many of the last 100 projects reported absence due to illness of a key individual? Of course it is. As stated earlier, we probably do not have decent data on the last project, let alone the last 100.

So what do we do? Well one thing that we can consider is to use a Delphi approach to probability assignment. Get some of the team together and ask them how likely is it that they are going to suffer from sickness? Alternatively, make a guess. This is not a perfect or even good solution, but at least we are starting to think about managing the project rather than letting it manage us. Managers who let their projects control them rather than vice versa often state that they spend most of their time fire fighting. The trick is not to let the fire start.

Of course, there is something else that can be done. Start collecting information on risk factors. But what about the fact that every project is different? Let us see if some of the commonly identified risk factors ring any bells with you:

* Milestones being missed;
* Requirements volatility and growth;
* Staff loss and turnover, resulting in a lowering of application knowledge;
* Customer or management pressure on delivery dates;
* Morale loss due to external events such as a reorganization;
* Unanticipated complexity, sometimes called the 'how did I get into this mess' syndrome.

If these do ring bells, then we probably know projects where they have occurred. The chances are, unfortunately, that we will work on projects in the future where they will also occur. Most managers will agree that these are probably risk factors on their projects wherever they are. That being the case, we should be able to collect information from projects where those risks become problems and, equally, from those projects where they don't. This enables us, at some time in the future, to derive probabilities based on more than pure guess work.

But why bother? We want those probabilities for a very pragmatic reason. There are only so many hours in the day, and we do not want to spend time managing a risk that has a 1 per cent probability of occurring as a problem. Much better to concentrate our efforts on those that are likely to become problems.

As a personal guideline, I believe that Risk Management principles should be applied to any risk factor with a 25 per cent or more probability of occurring — but, I am a great believer in Sod's Law that says that anything that can go wrong will, at the worst possible moment!

Having decided what risk factors are probable, or at least more probable, to be the problems of tomorrow, we should decide what to do about them if and when they occur. In other words, we should prepare contingency plans. Personally, I prefer two levels of contingency planning — what I call amber plans and crisis plans. My amber plans usually reflect the belief that I can still contain the problem, perhaps by working a little overtime or shifting a couple of priorities. The crisis plan is something else again. When a crisis plan kicks in, the bells go off, lifeboats are readied, extra strong coffee is brewed and leave is cancelled until we get it licked.

Never try to run a crisis plan for long. No team can work at the pitch a crisis demands for long. If we try, the chances are we will make the situation worse!

To illustrate the two different types of plan, let us look at a greatly simplified situation:

I notice that morale is dropping because of concerns about a reorganization. The first thing to do is 'go public'. A memo goes off to my manager saying that the lack of information is causing me problems. I might also decide to take everyone out for an extended lunch, the idea being to get them off the battlefield where they can talk more freely. I may also start to run a 'happy hour' for the last couple of hours on a Friday.

Now what if things still go from bad to worse? The situation is that people feel so browned off that work is not getting done. What is getting done is shoddy and, because of an increase in rework, it really looks as if this project is going to miss delivery, exceed its budget and be seen as a failure. Assume I also *know* that the cause of this is the way the reorganization is being handled. First rule again, go public. Start banging the drum so hard that someone has to take notice. Advise the most senior available director, advise the customer, at least of the effect if not the cause. Run a containment action. Perhaps we should stop work, get the team off site for a couple of days and talk it through as a group. Maybe nothing can be done to fix the problem, but we can certainly start to feel better about the way we handle the problem.

Now you may not agree with the way I dealt with the particular problem in the above scenarios, but one thing should be realized — none of the reactions outlined was a spur of the moment thing. They were all planned in advance and were there ready and waiting to be called into play when needed. This approach means that we are able to worry about containing the effects of the problem rather than worrying about how we are going to achieve that containment.

The trick, of course, is to know when to kick in those contingency plans, and this brings us to the next link between Risk Management and Software Metrics. The risk factors must have measures associated with them, and these measures must be monitored. Additionally, there should be predetermined levels at which the contingency plans, amber or crisis, come into play.

PROGRESS CHECKING

How we measure the risk factors is an area of great interest to those in the metrics discipline, but what it really involves is the positioning of monitors with which we can comfortably work. In many cases, these will be subjective, but it should be remembered that there is nothing intrinsically wrong with subjective measures. Certainly, the last time I purchased a car, a not insignificant personal investment, the only hard measure involved was that of price. The rest of the decision was purely subjective.

Looking at a couple of the risk factors I claimed were fairly common across projects, we might decide to measure morale by having the project team fill in a questionnaire each month. When I first ran this as an experiment to see if it was feasible to collect soft or environmental data in this way, I was pleasantly surprised that I was able to detect changes in morale across the team by asking about things like promotion prospects and training. I was also surprised at how happy the team were to take part in the exercise. They felt it gave them a chance to point out the good things and the bad things in their working environment and, hopefully, to have an effect on that environment.

Complexity could be handled in much the same way. Each of the designers could be asked simply to state if they thought recognized complexity was less than it was last month, the same, or greater than last month. Add in a couple more options to give them more scope and if 50 per cent or more of them say it has grown, there could be a problem. Watch out for creeping growth. If there is a small increase each month, you can end up with a big increase over the life of the project.

Wherever possible, it is best to use hard measures, and this is certainly possible for some risk factors. The occurrence of many risk factors shows itself in a reduction in progress, and monitoring progress against plan is one of the most effective ways of controlling a project, especially when this is tied into an effective Risk Management strategy.

Various approaches to progress monitoring

There are a number of ways that progress can be monitored.

Milestone monitoring

If the milestones operate at a fairly low level, which normally means that they are being passed with no more than a fortnight's gap on each major plan stream, then milestone monitoring can be an effective progress check. All that is needed is to monitor the milestones that should be achieved during a particular timeslice against what has actually been achieved.

Earned value analysis

Another, somewhat more complicated, approach is to use *earned value* analysis. This is well described in most project planning books, but the basic principle is that, by the time it is delivered, a project will have spent a certain amount, say in terms of engineering hours. At a particular point in time, a comparison is made between what has been spent to what should have been spent, also building in how much is still to be spent. The formulas become a bit messy, but most project planning tools which allow for the recording of actual effort spent will calculate *earned value*. *Earned value* is fine as far as it goes, but it does assume that the plan is realistic. This is not always the case.

RAG technique

An approach I particularly like is known by the inauspicious name of the RAG technique. RAG stands for *Red*, *Amber* and *Green* which gives a good clue as to how this approach works. The principle is one of project classification, and one of the major benefits of the approach is that it allows managers to concentrate their efforts where they will be most beneficial. The technique works where there are a number of projects running simultaneously or where a large project can be subdivided into smaller elements or subprojects.

Each project should have a project manager, and this individual is tasked with filling in a questionnaire each month, or perhaps fortnightly. The questionnaire can be as long and complex as it need be, but remember that someone has to spend time filling it in. Personally, I believe ten or twelve questions should be ample for most environments.

Question and answer pairs are of the multiple choice variety, and the responses are run through a very simple scoring algorithm. If, for example, there was a question that related to resource usage, the picture might look like this:

Q Compared to planned budget expenditure for this project, how much has actually been spent to date:

	Possible score	Actual score
> 20% Underspend	5	
< 10% Underspend	3	
As planned	0	
< 10% Overspend	1	
> 20% Overspend	5	

and the score is added to a running total.

The final score is then simply used to classify each project as being at status *green*, *amber* or *red*.

The nice touches in this technique are that *green* projects are allowed to go on their merry way because, after all, everything seems to be fine with them. They are hitting milestones on time, spending what they said they would, and the project manager is happy. Why should a more senior manager waste time formally reviewing a project that is running well. Of course, that manager should make sure that the truth is being told.

Amber projects do not have serious problems, but should be watched. The easiest way to do this is to have a rule that says projects at *amber* for two months out of three will go to *red* status. Again, the system can be abused, but what system can't.

Red projects receive special attention. Where this approach works is when the project manager whose project has gone *red* is not hit over the knuckles like a naughty boy. The chances are that the problems are totally beyond his or her control, as they may stem from another department or they may be the fault of, for example, more senior managers. Having recognized that a problem exists it is necessary to contain and remove it, not to make someone feel bad. To do this, the project manager, his manager and someone from the project control office who administers the RAG system should get together. Of course, if someone continually has projects that perform poorly, and the fault seems to lie with them, then that is a particular type of senior management failure — the wrong person may have been put in the wrong job.

It should also be noted that a project manager should always be given the option of asking for the project to be made *red* even if everything currently looks OK. Typically, RAG questions relate to progress and could include the following examples:

- What percentage of milestones due have been achieved?
- Are any deliverables due from external sources behind schedule?

This technique was presented at an ESPRIT project user panel a couple of years ago by British Telecom which is the largest private business operating within the UK, and it would be foolish to say that RAG is used in every part of the organization. However, that presentation did put up some interesting claims for the success of RAG, including dramatic reductions in replans and late deliveries. GTE, another telecommunications organization, in the USA also make use of the RAG technique.

One of the best things about RAG is its simplicity. It costs little to administer and can really provide a handle on project control.

SUMMARY

The topic of project control illustrates the wide range of areas that include, and benefit from, an element of measurement. It is a fact that projects that are not controlled, not managed, have a high probability of failure in terms of over-running on cost and duration budgets. Control cannot function effectively if it depends upon gut feel. This is, in microcosm, the problem faced by all managers. The particular problem facing managers in the software engineering industry is that managing by gut feel or flying by the seat of your pants is the norm. This is one reason we have so many problems, and they will not go away unless we do something about them.

The other thing to remember about project control is that it is already seen as a necessary piece of bureaucratic control by most engineers. This means that devices, such as questionnaires, can be introduced into this area with a lot less controversy than in some others. If, however, some time is also spent talking to the engineers, involving them and getting them to help shape the bureaucracy, they start to own it. People are generally more careful of things they own than they are of things they do not.

Section 2

8

A LIFECYCLE FOR METRICATION

This chapter introduces the second section of this book. The section discusses the development and implementation of Software Metrics initiatives or programmes within business organizations and the intention is to provide a route map that will take a practitioner from the initiation of such a programme all the way through to its first stage of implementation. At that point, it is a question of expansion and further implementation, and all the points that will have been discussed by then apply for the future.

The framework upon which this section is built is a lifecycle model, and I would like to spend some time discussing that model. I appreciate that you may be very familiar with the concept of lifecycle models and, if this is the case, you may wish simply to skim this chapter to familiarize yourself with my use of various terms or pass over it completely. The following chapters put the meat on the bones by discussing each of the lifecycle stages in more detail. The work involved in each stage, the problems that may be encountered and, most importantly, some possible ways of overcoming those problems will be described.

THE LIFECYCLE MODEL

The lifecycle is a generic model. This means that you may need to tailor it to your own specific environment by adding a further level of detail. You may also need to add some additional activities that are specific to the way in which your organization operates. The most likely area where this will be necessary is in the budget approval tasks. You may even be able to miss out some of the specific tasks described later.

The model is described by means of a dataflow diagram type of notation used to describe a process rather than to model a computer systems behaviour. I have found this to be an extremely useful way of modelling processes. As will be seen, the notation is quite straightforward.

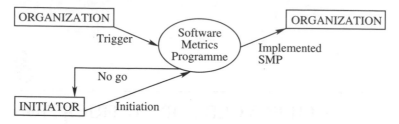

Figure 8.1 Software metrics initiative context diagram.

Circles represent processes, tasks or activities. Essentially these show elements of work that need to be carried out by people. Directed lines show the inputs or outputs of processes. These are objects, resources or deliverables consumed or produced by the processes. Parallel lines indicate stores of information. Conventionally, these are files or database entities within a computer system but, in our model, they have a wider meaning. They can be electronic stores, but they are also used to indicate paper files, any type of repository and even generic stores such as 'literature'. Rectangles retain the conventional dataflow diagram (DFD) meaning of terminators. In this model, they represent objects or entities with which the Software Metrics implementation process must interact.

The model is layered with greater detail being added to each layer. We start with the highest level of the model, the context diagram of Fig. 8.1. Notice that I will use the term 'Software Metrics programme' (SMP) to describe the development and implementation of a measurement initiative.

This diagram describes the system boundary of our implementation programme. It shows that the programme is a process in its own right that takes, as input, some trigger from the organization and delivers, some time later, the results of the implementation back to the organization. I have deliberately shown the initiator of the SMP, separately, because this individual or group of people is a major element in determining the scope of the programme, as will be seen in the next chapter.

The context diagram is useful at the conceptual level because it recognizes that the trigger, the situation or situations that give rise to a need for a measurement initiative, the initiator and the eventual customer or recipient of the SMP are external to the process of developing and implementing that programme. The key word is 'customer' and this theme of the programme serving the needs of customers will recur many times.

Something else we need to note is that a decision not to proceed with the SMP is possible. We will try to avoid this situation, but forewarned is forearmed.

If we move down one level and explode the SMP process bubble we see that the lifecycle model looks familiar (Fig. 8.2). It bears a close resemblance to simplistic system design lifecycles common in the computing industry. This is quite deliberate.

Introducing the use of Software Metrics to an organization demands the same approach as any other project whose aim is to develop a system. Ignoring this fact, or missing out one or more of these high-level stages, probably accounts for more failed SMPs than any other single mistake.

Initiation stage

Everything starts somewhere, so we recognize this with an initiation stage. Decisions taken

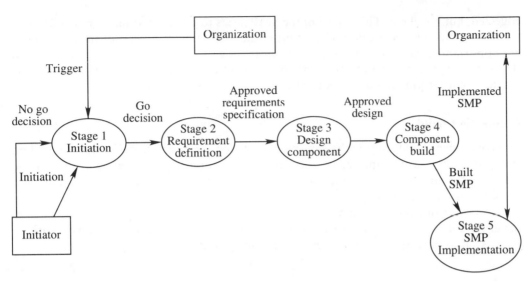

Figure 8.2 Level 1 lifecycle model.

during this stage set the scene for the rest of the programme, and can form the foundation of a successful programme or sound its death knell before it ever really gets going. It is a question of designing for success rather than designing for failure, and we probably all have experience of projects where the latter was the case.

Requirements definition

Requirements gathering and specification, which I have referred to as *requirements definition*, is the next stage and is so often ignored. It is not enough simply to read the literature and then blindly to impose a programme on the organization. It is very easy to define and develop an SMP that addresses productivity measurement only to find that the most senior customer for that programme is concerned about user satisfaction and not productivity. The SMP needs to address the problems of the organization, and we cannot do this unless we know what those problems are. Please remember that one person's view of those problems will never give the total picture. There are always different viewpoints within an organization, and these will have different problems and different requirements. I will talk more about this later, but let me stress the importance of this by saying that recognition of these different viewpoints is another important step towards a successful measurement initiative.

Component design

Design is also necessary. This stage encompasses both the choice of specific metrics, and notice that it is only now that this is considered, together with the design of the infrastructure that will support the use of those metrics. Many programmes fail because they concentrate on the metrics at the expense of this infrastructure and one of the areas that seems to let many such programmes down is in the area of feedback. Many programmes seem to assume that this will happen automatically once data has been collected, but it will not. This aspect of the SMP needs to be addressed in as much detail as the derivation and specification of the metrics themselves. Both aspects of the programme are important. I have used the term *component design* to indicate that there are different streams within the programme, perhaps concentrating on cost estimation and on management information as an example.

Component build

The component build stage is the easy part. Provided the design is right, and is based on effective requirements capture, the design stage is equivalent to coding from a good software design, this stage is mechanistic. That is not to say that there will not be a considerable amount of work to do. You will not only have to do the equivalent of coding in terms of writing operational procedures, you will also have to build the full system from the ground up, from welding the case together to writing the user guides! A job of work — so make it as easy as possible by getting the earlier stages right.

Implementation

Implementation is where it gets difficult again. This is where you will be putting your theories into practice. You will meet many problems that have not been anticipated. You will be working closely with other people who may not immediately see the benefits of your proposals — you will be changing the culture. Anyone who has been involved in the introduction of a new computer system will be only too aware of the vagaries and upsets that can occur during this stage, but will also be aware of the satisfaction that comes with success.

And if you succeed, well then you do it all again expanding the system across more of the organization tackling the requirements you put off until the 'second build'. Do you really want all this grief?

If you do, if you become responsible for the introduction of Software Metrics to your organization, be prepared for a roller-coaster ride. Like a roller-coaster, you will find things start off slowly as you climb the first slope, but once you pass the summit of that first slope, you will be moving so fast through the ups and downs that you will often feel things are out of control. You may well experience real fear at some of the things that happen and the things that you see, but you will also see a lot more than those on the ground. The trick is to keep control of yourself and the programme. When you finally get off the roller-coaster, you will have a real sense of achievement. Welcome aboard!

9

STAGE 1 — INITIATION

As the developers and implementors of a measurement programme, initiation is the first point of contact with the customers whom we will have to serve. This orientation, almost fixation, on the customer angle that runs through this section has its basis in reality. Too often, measurement initiatives fail because they are developed in ivory towers that are totally removed from the software engineering environment, or the people involved in that development pay lip service to the concept of customer service, and then proceed to ignore that interface.

If we remember nothing else, then remember that we, in this part of our life, exist to make things better for others within our organization. The organization, with its many facets, is our customer. The organization does not exist for our benefit.

Having said all that, this is also the first point that we begin to realize what we may have let ourselves in for. I have a theory that people are appointed to Software Metrics teams when they are ill, on leave, or absent from work for some other reason. Surely nobody actually asks to join this bunch of mad people who, for some strange reason, actually seem to enjoy trying to do the impossible, for the ungrateful, with practically no resources.

It all starts with the initiation stage of the process. Figure 9.1 contains some information about this; the format I will adopt is to set the scene early, and we can then discuss details in the text. As the diagram shows, everything starts somewhere, even Software Metrics programmes (SMPs).

THE FIRST STEPS

The initial management decision

Two factors lie behind the start of an SMP, an organizational trigger and an initiator. The

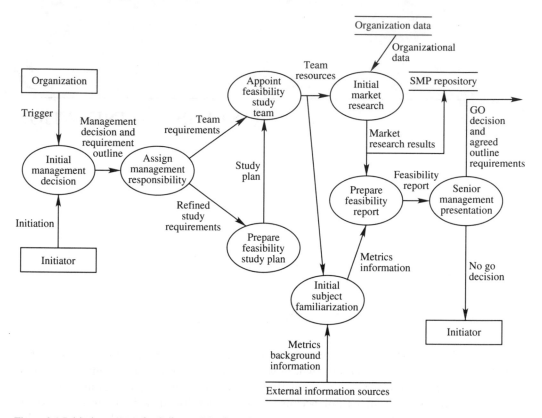

Figure 9.1 Initiation stage of a Software Metrics programme.

trigger comes from some need within the organization. The initiator realizes that the need exists, and seeks to satisfy that need.

The trigger

Software Metrics programmes can be triggered by many different situations or events such as:

- General quality or productivity concerns;
- Concern about customer complaints;
- Customers' requirements for increased information;
- Knowledge of competitors' activity in the metrics area;
- Quality programmes;
- A cost-cutting environment;
- Management pressure for more information;
- A consultancy recommendation;
- New awareness of the possibility of measurement, perhaps as a result of someone attending a conference or seminar.

One point that should be recognized is that it is rarely possible to attribute a single trigger to an SMP. The reality is that there tend to be multiple triggers for such an initiative. This can be both a blessing and a curse. A blessing in that it tends to widen the scope of the work, so that difficulties, and even failures in one area, can be outweighed by successes in others. A curse because widening the scope of the work can slow things down, and one problem with any metrics programme is that the lead time, as it were 'the time to market', can be seen as a liability by an organization.

This problem is often a result of limited understanding of Software Metrics within the organization.

> After all, we are only talking about putting in a bit of measurement, aren't we? Other industries measure, so it can't really be that difficult. We should be able to get something going by next month.

Well, of course, we can. It will not work, will probably cost money, and will also probably result in at least part of the organization being turned against metrics for the foreseeable future!

It is vitally important that an SMP is not seen as a quick fix. In terms that anyone involved with a Crosby (1985) or Deming (1986) style quality programme will understand, Software Metrics is about fixing the process rather than patching to fix the fault.

For example, it will take a certain amount of time to develop and implement a productivity measurement programme, some time to collect data, and a small amount of time to interpret that data. This is not a rapidly deployed defence against the threat of outsourcing within the next two weeks. Depending on the scope of the programme and the size of the organization, there will be a minimum elapsed time necessary before the programme can be implemented, and the lifecycle that is described in this section will enable a manager to assess that minimum time for his or her organization. After all, if we know what needs to be done, we stand a much better chance of estimating how long it will take.

Recognizing the trigger or triggers is important, because they can affect the SMP by driving it down a particular road. For example, it is no good advising people how to measure software usability, if the sole trigger is concern over productivity levels. When you start to plan your own SMP, it is a useful exercise to list the triggers acting within your organization, as you see them. This gives you your initial focus, but bear in mind that this is not cast in stone. You will be gathering specific requirements as you progress through the lifecycle, and these can broaden the scope of the programme.

The initiator

We can now consider the initiator of the programme. I view the initiator as someone who is external to the SMP, but who will still interact with that process, especially during the earlier stages of its lifecycle. Generally, an initiator identifies a need for measurement, determines that something will be done to satisfy that need, and then promptly delegates the responsibility for development and implementation to someone else. This is generally known as management! Seriously, such delegation makes sense. Initiators tend to be in positions where they are affecting strategic positioning, whereas the developers and implementors function at the tactical and operational levels.

The initiator sets out the scope of the work, and will often obtain or even give the initial authorization for that work. The initiator's role is important, because he or she sets out the boundary of the eventual system — thus bringing in the first set of constraints. At the same time, the initiator will not be a Software Metrics expert, and so should not aim to constrain the programme too tightly. In many ways, the initiator's role is akin to the

Table 9.1 Requirements clarity

Initiator	Too rigorous	Too vague
Chief Executive or Director		×
QA function		×
R&D group		×
Customers or users	×	
A technocrat	×	
Management consultant		×
Auditors	×	

person who chooses a site for a new building. Picking rocky terrain will mean that the builders will have their work made more difficult by external constraints — they will have to cut through solid rock; pick shifting sand, by giving no guidance on the initial direction; and there will be many false starts.

The initiator must draw a balance between constraining or tightly-defined requirements, and a vague problem definition that is liable to drastic changes. Different initiators tend to lean one way or the other as illustrated by Table 9.1.

As a guideline, it is better during the initiation stage to tend towards vagueness rather than rigour. After all, at this stage we do not really know what we are getting into, so a rigorous definition will probably be incorrect anyway. Notice that I said 'tend towards vagueness'. Make sure that you, as the initiator, do not put your people on shifting sand by at least giving them the space to define their own terms of reference. These can then be reviewed by you to ensure that they meet business goals.

The people responsible for the development and implementation of the SMP will probably have little to do with the early part of the initiation stage, so let us now assume that a decision has been taken within the organization to do something about Software Metrics. Now we get down to the real work.

Assign management responsibility

Somebody has to take responsibility for the work being done. Ideally, this will not be the people doing the work, but rather somebody with authority within the organization and someone with access to senior management. Access to senior management is important, because the final activity within the initiation stage concerns a proposal for further work. This further work will involve a cost, and will need to be authorized. Many programmes flounder because they cannot get a fair hearing from senior management, who control the purse-strings. As you are going to face enough problems anyway, design to succeed from the start, by making sure that you can get that fair hearing.

There are many terms used to describe the individual who takes on responsibility for a work item; the sponsor, the champion and the customer authority are some common examples. Personally, I prefer the third choice, as sponsors and champions can lack involvement, merely lending their name to the project, while the term 'customer authority' implies someone with a specific role, namely to act as the final arbiter for the project when decisions have to be made. Whatever term is used, and an organization will have its own preferences, a relatively senior individual should be appointed as the sponsor or customer authority for the SMP. As a general guideline, the more senior the customer authority the better, provided the involvement of that person can be assured. Do not go for seniority at the expense of involvement.

One other point, it is generally advised that the customer authority should not change during the lifetime of a project. Reality often means that such a change will happen, possibly more than once. We all know the pain that severe changes to requirements can cause a project so, if your customer authority does change, endeavour to ensure that the new sponsor accepts and agrees the requirements, designs, etc., that have already been signed off. This can involve some effort, but it more than pays for itself. Notice that this implies that such things are documented and retained. It is no good having the terms of reference in people's heads.

Appoint feasibility study team

The initiation stage involves the concept of a feasibility study. The organization has demonstrated an awareness of Software Metrics by initiating the implementation project, but it may well need to be convinced that the effort will pay back the cost. At the very least, there will be some senior managers who have doubts about whether it is possible to control the software development process through measurement. They will need to be convinced that there is some merit in going forward, and this should be done as early as possible. This is one of the things we hope to achieve at the end of the initiation stage. Now, who is going to do this work and convince these doubters?

The feasibility team should be small. Even in a very large organization, it should not consist of more than three or four people. For most organizations one or two people, reporting functionally to the assigned customer authority, should be sufficient. Although there is considerable debate about whether metrics team staff should be full or part time, I firmly believe that the team should be assigned its responsibility on a full-time basis, or the work will be patchy, shallow and will take too long.

It is unlikely that an organization will possess a 'metrics expert'. It is also true to say that Software Metrics is not yet so well established that recruiting the services of someone who is experienced in the area will be easy. The use of consultants can help overcome this, but it is important that any consultant be employed on the understanding that one of his/her main tasks is to transfer knowledge to the organization. At the risk of offending some people, I have found consultants to be like little boys. When they are good, they are very, very good, but when they are bad, they are awful! Remember, even good consultants will need help from someone who understands the business of the organization.

This brings us to the skills we need in the feasibility team. We cannot expect to get an SMP that works well for the organization, if we do not understand the business, so we need someone who knows the business or who can get that knowledge quickly. We will also need someone who can get valid and useful information from other people, so we need an effective interviewer. A good systems analyst can often supply these first two skills, and is a godsend to any Software Metrics team. We also need to be able to present our ideas to other people, so a good presenter, both in terms of writing skills and the ability to talk to different types of audience is important.

Finally, measurement is about numbers, so a good understanding of mathematics is desirable. We are really talking about applied rather than pure mathematics because, in many cases, it is the application of mathematical techniques to new and different areas that is necessary to make Software Metrics work.

The initiator and the customer authority should ensure that they appoint good people to the feasibility team. Do not be tempted to assign dead wood to this group. Once again, design to succeed, do not design to fail, or you will!

Prepare feasibility study plan

The feasibility team will also need to be given an initial direction. In other words, it should be given a high-level plan or requirement for at least the rest of the first stage. This is the responsibility of the initiator together with the customer authority, and should encompass the following points:

1. *The scope of the work*. Is it to look at the whole organization or only part of it? What are the main drivers or triggers that the organization wishes to address through the use of Software Metrics? What are the links, if any, to the hardware design process or other functional groups?
2. *The requirements*. The feasibility team should be tasked to determine the needs of the organization through some initial market research. The team should also be tasked to bring knowledge of Software Metrics to the organization by familiarizing themselves with the subject, highlighting possible benefits. Finally, it should be tasked to provide a plan for the way forward, geared to the needs of the organization.
3. *The timescale*. In an ideal world, the feasibility team would be able to prepare its own low-level plan, and this should determine the time-scale. In reality, there will be time pressure on the feasibility study and on the whole implementation programme. The feasibility team will need to familiarize itself with a new subject as well as to identify the relevance of this to the organization.

The customer authority should be realistic and flexible, but should give guidance to the team about when results of this first stage will be expected.

Initial subject familiarization

Once the team is assigned, the work of the feasibility study can begin in earnest. We have to realize that we will only be able to convince the organization fully of the benefits of Software Metrics by demonstrating the successful use of those metrics within the organization itself. This activity is really piloting the use of Software Metrics rather than demonstrating their feasibility.

To demonstrate feasibility, we will need to show that Software Metrics can potentially be used by the organization, the key word being 'potentially'. The easiest way to achieve this is to show that the way in which others have successfully used metrics is applicable to our own organization. This involves three distinct tasks:

1. We have to become aware of what others have done.
2. We have to establish the needs of our own organization.
3. We will have to map what others have done to our own organization's needs and present this information in some form.

The team will almost certainly have a very limited understanding of Software Metrics when it starts the work, so it will need to gain a broader and more detailed appreciation of the subject. At the end of this book is a bibliography of selected books and papers. These will provide valuable background information about Software Metrics in theory and, to a more limited extent, in practice. The books and papers will also provide pointers to other sources of information that can be explored.

One of the best ways of learning about the practical use of Software Metrics is to talk to other practitioners. I have included in this book a list of useful European and American organizations that will help you to do this. One of the most pleasant aspects of working in this field is that people are almost invariably willing to share their knowledge and experience, even to the extent of arranging visits to their own organizations to discuss the topic. Take advantage of this, as I have, and you will have the privilege of sharing time and experiences with some of the nicest people around.

Other sources of information are certain of the so-called 'academics', who are often more practical than they are given credit for and, of course, consultants. Talking to both the academics and consultants can be a very cost-effective way of gaining an introduction to the subject area.

There are a very small number of formal training courses that have recently appeared that deal with the subject of Software Metrics. These tend to concentrate on the theory of the metrics themselves rather than the implementation of an SMP but, again, they can provide a useful introduction to the subject. The European Economic Community ESPRIT research programme does contain one project, METKIT, whose intention is to specifically produce training material in the area of Software Metrics. Contact addresses for various ESPRIT projects are given in Appendix B.

Initial market research

Having gained some understanding of Software Metrics and how they can be used, the feasibility team will need to establish the needs of the organization and the potential market for the use of metrics within that organization.

The users and customers of the metrics programme will be varied, and will impose different requirements on the programme. This is a very important point. Many SMPs concentrate on one group of these customers, and this can cause problems later on as we realize that we need the cooperation of other groups within the organization, but that we are offering them nothing in return for this.

Identifying the customers

During the initial market research activity, the first thing the team will have to do is to broadly identify the potential customers of the SMP. To do this, it is best to divide the organization into a number of functional groups. At this stage, a high-level division will be sufficient. One such grouping is:

- Senior management;
- Project managers;
- Support groups such as the planning department or the project control group;
- The quality organization if the organization operates a quality programme;
- The software engineers or programmers.

This last group is important, but is often ignored. The success of the SMP will depend, at least in part, on information supplied by 'engineers', a term I prefer to 'programmers'. If we ignore their needs, then we may well find their cooperation difficult to obtain and the data we are given suspect. After all, why should an engineer, for example, carefully record the way his or her time is spent, if there is no return from that additional work.

Another group of potential users of the SMP is the organization's own customers or the internal users of software that is produced. It can sometimes be difficult getting access to these people, but they should be added to the list above. A strategic decision must be taken by the customer authority, namely should the organization's own customers be approached at this point or not? This will depend on the relationship between the organization and the customers, but I feel that they should be approached unless there are good commercial reasons for not doing this. At the very least we can make them aware of the organization's commitment to improved service, but we must be careful not to build false expectations of rapid improvement. Change takes time.

Interviewing the SMP customers

Having identified the potential users of the SMP, the team will need to go and talk to these people. Obviously, the team will not be able to talk to every single potential customer, after all there may be 300 or more engineers alone. The team should identify a representative sample from each group, and arrange interview sessions with these individuals. The team should also concentrate on people it thinks will be receptive to new ideas, but should not totally exclude the ones that may be less positive. We might as well get an appreciation of the problems these people will raise as early as possible.

Each interview should address three areas:

1. The interviewer should be prepared to provide a brief introduction to the subject of Software Metrics, and the reasons why the organization is looking at the topic. This should not be prescriptive, because we do not want to constrain the interviewee, but we will have to provide a reason for the interview and an initial direction.
2. The problems faced by the interviewee in his or her work should be ascertained. One way to get this part of the conversation going is to ask the interviewee briefly to describe his/her role in the organization. This will usually bring up areas that can be explored in more detail, given the high level requirements placed on the SMP.
3. The interviewee should be asked what additional information they feel will be beneficial to the project. The interviewer will often need to drive this part of the session and should link the way other organizations have applied Software Metrics to the role of the interviewee.

The results of the interview should be documented. I will call the store of this, and other information, the SMP Repository. This is no more than a convenient name for what may, in reality, be no more than a filing cabinet.

The size of the market

Another area that the initial market research activity should address is the size of the potential market. How many groups or teams are involved in developing or enhancing software? Each of these groups is a potential customer. How many projects are each team involved in? How many engineers are in each group? How many senior managers or management groupings are there? How many organizations are customers for the software produced? How many support groups, for example planning departments, are there and how are these organized? How is the quality group organized and how large is it?

Surprisingly, a considerable amount of effort may be required to get this information but it will pay dividends in the future. Know your market is a good maxim that we often ignore!

Prepare and present report

Having gathered all this information and knowledge, we now need to make use of it to get authority to proceed. The information needs to be presented, at the very least, to someone with the necessary authority to sanction the future work, possibly to a group of senior managers, and this is where the customer authority can help immensely. Get access to the most senior manager you can and present the feasibility report. The more senior the recipient of this report, the briefer it should be, but it should contain:

1. Identification of the problems associated with software development in the organization. Refer to the triggers identified earlier.
2. A statement of the business priorities of the organization.
3. A definition of Software Metrics and a brief description of the scope of the subject.
4. A mapping of Software Metrics to the business priorities and the problems of software development. This states what high-level requirements it is planned to address.
5. A strategy for implementing an SMP. This can be based on the following chapters of this section.
6. A request for authority to proceed.

It is also a good idea to make a personal presentation to management. This presentation should summarize the report, and it may be that the presentation is the vehicle for getting the necessary authority. Spend time on this to make it as professional as possible. Make sure that you know your audience. Make sure it relates to the business needs of the organization. By all means include examples from other organizations, but be aware that you will only convince people, fully, when you can demonstrate success within your own organization. Make it brief! Make it a success!

One thing does need to be said. It is now quite common for the feasibility aspect of the initiation stage to be missed completely. In this sense, the metrics community is a victim of its own success. It is less difficult these days to convince people of the feasibility of measurement in a software engineering environment, but this brings other problems. The initiator, responding to a trigger or triggers, appoints a team, provides outline requirements and expects results. This is fine provided that time is given for subject familiarization, that the potential, internal market is identified and that, based on this, sensible plans are made.

The biggest dangers with this approach are that the initial requirements are so constrained to one area that they do not address the overall business needs of the organization or that, through ignorance of what is involved, impossible budget or resource constraints are imposed on the responsible team.

SUMMARY

The initiation stage of an SMP, generally speaking, is out of the control of the practitioners who will have to develop and implement that programme. It will be caused by some trigger, and it will be driven by an initiator. It is the time when the initial scope of the programme is defined. Remember that this scope will almost certainly change over time. The best advice I can give to anyone involved in the initiation stage is to listen. Listen to the various individuals in your own organization who will be on the receiving end of your programme, and listen to those outside of your organization who have been involved in measurement programmes and who have probably made many of the same mistakes that will trip you up.

10

STAGE 2 — REQUIREMENTS DEFINITION

At this point, I would like to do three things. Firstly, I want to highlight and elaborate on some key points that have been made in the previous chapters, so that you keep them very much in your mind as you read on. Secondly, I need to talk about some things that are common to each of the development and implementation lifecycle stages we will be discussing. Finally, I need to set up a fictitious organization to which I can relate elements of the lifecycle model. This fictitious organization will be as generalized as I can make it, but you will, of course, have to map elements of it to your own organizational structure.

Once we have looked at these various items, we can go on to discuss the activities and tasks that need to be carried out during this requirements definition stage of the development and implementation lifecycle.

POINTS TO REMEMBER

Software Metrics is a large, multidimensional subject. It covers management information, cost estimation and the use of metrics-based techniques to improve quality, control complexity and assist with system management. It is, and in fact must be, applicable to both new, green field developments and to enhancement or maintenance projects. It has links to project control, configuration management and customer relations.

If we consider any standard software development lifecycle, we can add an additional, parallel stream to show the relationship to software metrics as shown in Fig. 10.1. Notice how information flows to and from the project management process across the interfaces with the development process. Notice also that information is communicated between the project management process and the Software Metrics initiative, and between the Software Metrics initiative and the development process directly. There is also an interface between the customer or system user domain and the measurement programme.

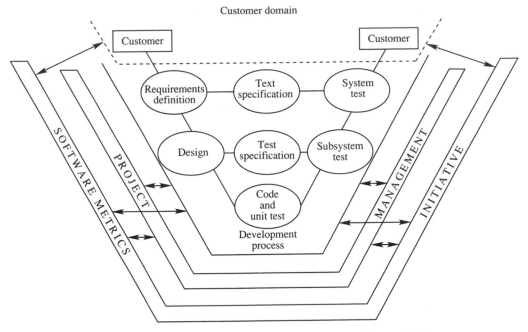

Figure 10.1 Relationship of a standard software development lifecycle to Software Metrics.

The next point to consider is that to attempt to introduce the use of Software Metrics in any kind of *ad hoc* way simply will not work. It must be handled as a project in its own right with each of the usual project stages, i.e.

- Requirements definition;
- Component design;
- Component build;
- Implementation.

One very useful concept that has been highlighted by a QA Forum working party report, *Implementing a Software Metrics Programme*, (Irvine *et al.*, 1991), is that of multiple sub-projects within such programmes. This simply states that the Requirements Definition stage may identify a number of requirements that the organization wishes the metrics programme to address. After these requirements have been identified, it is possible to establish a separate sub-project that takes each of these requirements through the design, build and implementation stages. This makes the management of the Software Metrics programme much easier, and allows an organization to concentrate on those areas where it sees a quick return, while still directing some effort towards satisfying those requirements that may provide a significant pay-back in the mid to long term.

Phasing

This idea can be further developed by introducing the idea of 'phasing'. There are a number of ways that this can be done. I have said that Software Metrics is a big subject

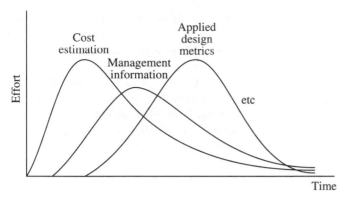

Figure 10.2 Phases of the Software Metrics programme.

area. Normally, there is another element of 'bigness' that will affect the programme, namely the size of the organization that seeks to apply metrics. Most software engineering organizations or departments consist of a number of project or product teams. Often this number is large. To target all of these at once can make the management of the Software Metrics programme a nightmare.

Phasing can help with this size problem in two ways:

1. The Software Metrics topic itself can be partitioned and these partitions addressed by different phases of the metrics programme.
2. The implementation process itself can be phased so that only a manageable number of project teams or work areas are targeted within a particular time slice.

Figure 10.2 illustrates the first type of phasing and shows effort ramping up at different times against different topic areas.

The actual partitioning can be considered right at the start of the requirements specification, provided an organization is very clear about its business objectives, and what areas will give the best short-term pay-back but, for most organizations, the detailed phasing is best left until the end of the Requirements Definition stage.

To summarize, Software Metrics covers many areas and will impinge on the total development process. It can also affect every member of the software development organization. Software Metrics is also a technical subject — because of this, the introduction of Software Metrics should be treated as a project in its own right. Finally, different types of phasing can help manage the implementation of metrication.

COMMONALITY

We are going to be discussing a number of stages of the SMP development and implementation process over the next few chapters. There are two elements of commonality across these stages.

The first relates to the normal management procedures that should be applied to any project stage. An outline plan should have been prepared during the initiation stage, and this should have been agreed as part of the decision to proceed. However, each stage will require some detailed planning. Organizations differ in when this is actually done, some preferring to carry out detailed planning for a stage as the first task within that stage, others preferring such planning to be done as the last task of the preceding stage. Provided this planning is done, I do not believe that it matters which timing option is chosen.

The second element of commonality concerns staffing. In an ideal world, a project team would be assembled, and this group of people would see all the work through to full implementation. There would be no staff turnover, and no constraint on resources, so that all team members went through the familiarization process at the same time even if this meant that some team members were then underutilized for a period of time. We live in the real world!

The reality is that, at any point in time, some staff may leave or be reassigned, as may managers. This implies that task bubbles covering staff/management appointments and subject familiarization can be added to any of the stages we will be discussing. Bear this in mind and, if you expect staff turnover, be prepared to manage this risk. One way of doing this is to ensure that the metrics team consists of at least two people, even if one of them is part-time. In this way, you can at least maintain some degree of continuity if your 'expert' leaves.

Neither of these areas will be explicitly discussed during the next few chapters, but remember that they can be present.

Some people may feel that a review task, that is the work associated with reviewing deliverables of a particular stage, should also be seen as a common element across all stages. I have deliberately left that task out of this immediate discussion, because I have found that the type of review process differs depending on the particular stage at a given time. I intend to discuss the review processes explicitly as necessary.

A COMMON FRAME OF REFERENCE

To help with our discussions over the next few chapters, I have prepared a fictitious organizational structure and business model that we can use as a common frame of reference. There are a number of reasons for doing this.

One of the major stumbling blocks when discussing software development, and it seems metrics in particular, is the use of words — terminology. I remember wasting a full day of fairly intensive effort because of a misunderstanding about the word 'interface'. More recently, I had a very interesting discussion with a colleague concerning the use of compiler preprocessors. It was just a shame that we were both discussing different things, both called preprocessors! The models discussed below will provide a common terminology for use within this book. I am not trying to impose my terminology on your organization.

While touching on the area of terminology, I will point out that I will use expressions like 'software engineering', 'product development' and 'software development' inter-changeably. In all cases, I am referring to the work that is carried out to develop new systems, to support existing systems including corrective maintenance and to enhance such systems. The context of the expression should make the meaning clear.

Model of software development lifecycle

When we get into the area of software development lifecycles, things tend to get even worse. What I call design, others may call requirements specification, what I call low-level design, others may call implementation and combine the task with coding and compilation. I offer the V model-based development lifecycle in Fig. 10.3 simply as a common frame of reference for the purposes of this book. I do not see it replacing the Waterfall (Boehm, 1981), or Spiral (Rook, 1990), models if these are what you prefer. Figure 10.3 describes the software development lifecycle model I shall use within this book. As usual, circles or bubbles indicate processes, while the connecting arrows indicate deliverables or products of those processes. Please note that each process bubble marked with an asterisk includes a review and rework cycle, and that rework, as a result of testing or proving activities, has not been shown although, of course, it will be present.

If there are many representations of the software development lifecycle, there are also

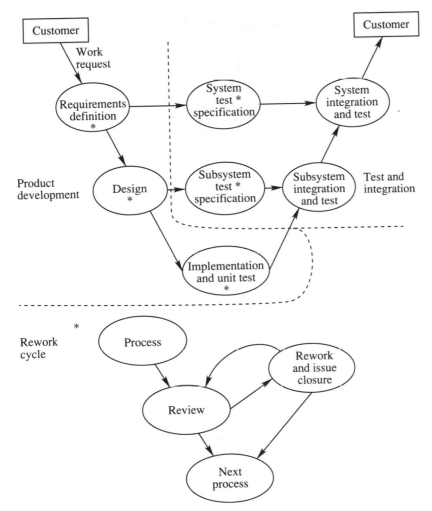

Figure 10.3 Level 1 engineering process.

many types of organizational structure and, again, terminology can be confusing. I will now suggest an organizational structure, not claiming that this is better than that employed by your own organization or even that it is a good structure, but simply to give us a common frame of reference. Let me stress that the organization I will depict is only used by me for the purpose of discussion and examples within this book.

Model of organizational structure

Figure 10.4 shows an entity relationship model for our reference organization. This is simply a diagrammatic representation of various functions, and their associations with each other within the organization. It shows *systems development* as a major function within the organization, and that this function consists of two components, *product development* and *support development,* both of which may consist of more than one established team.

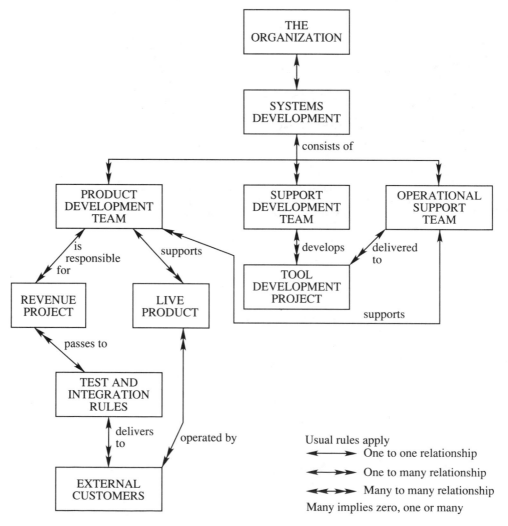

Figure 10.4 Functional linkage.

Each Support Development team is responsible for producing a tool that will only be used internally within systems development and these are delivered to the Operational Support team who will then manage its use by a number of Product Development teams.

Product development is the revenue-earning arm of Systems Development. In this case, I will assume that this revenue is earned by selling software products to external customers, although it is very possible that the organization itself may be the customer of its systems development function. I will ignore the complication of bundling software and hardware together into a product that is then sold, so as not to over complicate the model. From my experience, this does not have a major impact on the implementation of a Software Metrics programme, although there are obviously ramifications to be borne in mind.

Notice that each Product Development team can be working on a number of revenue-earning projects at one time. This reflects reality when part of the team can be working on the implementation phase of the development lifecycle, while another part of the team can be specifying requirements for another project. Please note also that I include enhancements to existing software products as revenue-earning projects in their own right. The maintenance of products currently in the field, which I have shown as also being the responsibility of the Product Development teams, I see as being the correction of faults that cannot be put off until a future, full product release, the operation of help desks, etc.

I have also separated out a Test and Integration team, who can provide this service for a number of revenue-earning projects. There may be more than one such team. Relating this back to the software development lifecycle in Fig. 10.3, the Product Development teams are responsible for all of the left-hand portion of the V model through to unit test and integration together with unit test specification. The Test and Integration team are responsible for link and system testing, system integration and the associated test specifications.

Hierarchy of organizational model

Figure 10.5 shows a traditional organization hierarchy for the model shown in Fig. 10.4. We have a Systems Development Manager operating at director level with three functional managers beneath. The Support Development Manager is responsible for a number of team leaders who will have line management responsibility for software engineers and a project management role. The Operational Support Manager is responsible for a number of functions covering the development environment.

In this organization, the Product Manager is responsible for the largest part of the systems development function. As this is the revenue-earning component within systems development, this would seem to make sense. I use the term 'Product Manager' because he or she is responsible for the development of new products, the enhancement of existing products and the maintenance of these. So he or she has two managers reporting up, one responsible for Test and Integration the other responsible for Software Development including Enhancement. Both are responsible for a number of team leaders who, again, will have project management responsibilities.

I have also introduced two additional functions, R&D and Planning. The reasons for this will become obvious later.

The models in Figs 10.4 and 10.5 are simplistic. In reality, organizations tend to be complex beasts, and the relationships between functions within the organization tend to reflect this complexity. Size alone may well add complexity, as it can introduce an

Figure 10.5 Traditional organization hierarchy.

additional level, or levels, to the organizational hierarchy. However, these two figures do give us a common frame of reference with sufficient complexity to illustrate some of the problems that will face a Software Metrics Implementation project.

The Software Metrics project

This brings us to the final component in our reference frame, the Software Metrics project itself. As we have already discussed, such a project can come about for a number of reasons, and can be actioned in a number of ways. It may be decided, as a result of the feasibility study described as Stage 1, that a pilot will be undertaken within one Product Development team and will be its responsibility; it may be that the programme will be driven by a number of external consultants reporting directly to the Systems Development Director; or it may come about as part of a Quality Programme and be the responsibility of a Quality Manager.

All of these options, and the many others that exist as a result of the diversity between organizations have an impact on exactly how the Software Metrics project is structured and operated, but the purpose of this book is, among other things, to present a generic model for the implementation of Software Metrics within organizations which can be tailored and used to help real life organizations with such an implementation.

THE REQUIREMENTS DEFINITION STAGE IN DETAIL

I am going to make certain assumptions to set up a situation within our hypothetical organization, and this will be used to illustrate such an implementation. I have chosen this model of a Software Metrics project because I believe it to be a very common approach to metrics implementation, and because it does lend itself to illustrating a range of problems that can occur with possible solutions. Where I feel it necessary, I will mention some of the situations that can arise in other styles of approach.

Obtaining authority

My first assumption is that the Stage 1 feasibility study has been carried out by an individual within the R&D group. Remember what I have said about terminology, the actual name of this group does not matter, but it is, typically, divorced from software development, and its role within systems development is to improve the software engineering process. A presentation has been given to the Systems Development Director and his first line resulting in approval to proceed with the development of a suitable SMP. Notice that, at this point, we only have authority to develop the programme, not to implement it. The reason for this is quite simple, in this hypothetical case, the other first line managers are not yet convinced that they will get a good return on the investment they see themselves having to make. Mind you, the Operational Support Manager is on our side, but that is to be understood because he or she is not really affected by this programme, not yet anyway. Notice I am assuming that the scope of the programme covers product development and support only. In fact, such a programme may well be confined to product development at first.

Now, who has responsibility for this new project? I will assume it has been placed back on the R&D Manager who, in turn, has given that responsibility to the person who did the feasibility study. Of course, there is no reason why the project could not be placed under the Product Manager, the Support Manager or even the Planning Manager. Well there are reasons, not least — given the scope of the project — the cross-functional problems that could arise. At least R&D may be seen as independent of the other functions within the organization, and may be perceived as having less of an axe to grind. There are also problems in placing the project within the R&D function. These arise from such things as a lack of credibility from which R&D staff can suffer, the ivory tower syndrome, and the 'not invented here' reaction that can occur within software development functions. There is much that can be done to overcome these problems, but not yet.

To reiterate — we have authority to develop a Software Metrics programme that will be applied, subject to authorization, to both product and support development. The high-level requirements of the project are that an SMP provides information about the software development process and its products, and that it improves that process in a cost-effective way. If we can get a tighter initial requirement so much the better, but this rather vague description of what we need to do does enable us to discuss the various aspects of a Software Metrics programme within the context of implementing that programme. We have also been given a time-scale, which no matter how long it is, will not be long enough!

At this point, the Software Metrics team may have been expanded, so that there are now more resources available than during the feasibility study. Equally, the 'team' may only consist of one person working part-time on the problem. I have already given some indications of my views on resourcing such a team. I will refer to those who have responsibility for the development and implementation of the metrics initiative as the 'metrics team'.

Having got our sanction to proceed the first thing to do is to make sure we know how to proceed. Planning is the next thing on the agenda.

Planning the work

We need a plan for the future work, but I do not intend to describe that plan at all. As stated earlier, this stage planning activity is seen as being common to all stages. Instead, I will describe the work that needs to be carried out during this and subsequent stages of metrics programme development and implementation around which you can develop your own plan. Please remember that this is not a theoretical discussion. The approach described in this book is one that has been tried in practice and is one that has proved to be successful.

Figure 10.6 summarizes the work, tasks and linkages within this stage.

Initial publicity campaign

Having prepared the project plan, we will have a good idea of what needs to be done, at least at a relatively high level. It is very tempting to get your head down and get on with it — after all you can always let the business know what is going to hit them when you are ready to hit them with it. But stop and think for a moment.

Any Software Metrics programme relies heavily on the cooperation of many individuals within the software development function. It is always a good idea to let these individuals know that such help is required as early as possible, but probably you will not know exactly from which individuals you need this help. One way to counter this problem is to inform as many people as possible of the fact that a Software Metrics programme now exists.

Apart from just raising the profile of the project, an initial publicity campaign can also be used to start the education process within software development. You may be convinced, from talking to other people outside of your own organization and from your reading during the feasibility study, that a metrics programme has a valuable contribution to make to improving the software engineering process, but you will almost certainly be in a minority. A great deal of time and effort is going to be spent convincing others of this fact.

You may also be in the fortunate position of having convinced a senior manager that the organization should adopt the use of Software Metrics immediately. This individual may also believe that mandating that use will be sufficient for it to happen. Don't believe it. A successful Software Metrics programme depends on the active participation and cooperation of the people to whom it is being applied. Time spent convincing those people that such cooperation will be worthwhile is time well spent, and will repay your efforts tenfold.

A word of warning! Beware of overselling the programme. At this point in time, you have nothing of which the development function can make use, so there is no point making exaggerated claims that you cannot back up. Also, these people have heard it all before. The IT industry does tend to suffer from 'flavour of the month syndrome'. About 20

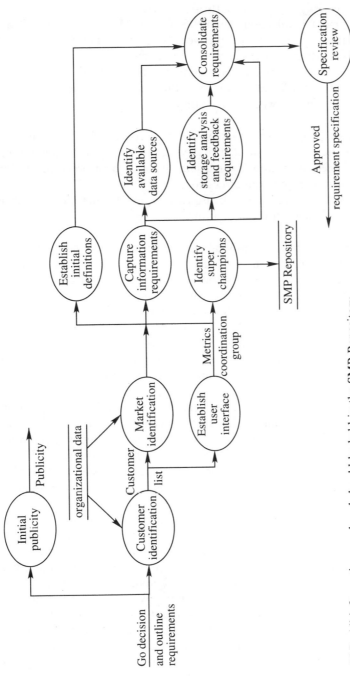

N.B. All information produced should be held in the SMP Repository

Figure 10.6 Work, tasks and linkages within the planning stage.

years ago, third-generation languages were going to solve all our problems. Then it was automatic code generators, then the ill-fated Integrated Project Support Environment. Formal methods, object-orientated design or coding and software reuse have all been hailed as the panacea to all our problems, yet the problems still exist. Do we really expect people to believe that Software Metrics will be any different? In many ways, this cynicism is justified, even when it is applied to Software Metrics.

Software development is all about people! Software Metrics *per se*, will not improve things, but the changes in the way people work and think that Software Metrics helps bring about, can generate immense savings and improvements.

So, how should such an initial publicity campaign be handled?

Firstly, another question. What do we want the campaign to achieve? There are four points that we should address with such a campaign.

1. We need to make people aware that the topic, Software Metrics itself, exists.
2. We need to tell the organization that the Systems Development function has initiated a programme aimed at monitoring and improving its own processes and products.
3. Ideally, we should also generate discussion.
4. We should alert everyone in the Software Development function that this new project may well need their help in the near future.

Does your organization have an in-house magazine? If so, you can use this as a vehicle for publicity and education. Bear in mind that you will be introducing a topic that is new to most people, and that the subject is both wide ranging and complicated by people issues. Because of this, you may wish to consider a short series of articles starting with a brief introduction to the areas that Software Metrics can address, and followed by separate articles addressing each of those areas.

Remember not to build up false hopes. There is little point in discussing, say, McCabe metrics if your programme is only addressing the measurement of productivity. Also remember not to make exaggerated claims about the benefits of using Software Metrics, as you will stretch credibility.

Another vehicle that can be used for publicity is site notice boards if your organization uses these. A simple poster, perhaps using humour, can be a good way of getting a message across. One example I have seen consists of a sword-wielding king, with a few hard-pressed knights nearby. Behind this group is a salesman holding a machine gun. The comment is: 'Don't bother me now, I've got a war to fight'. Give the king a standard labelled 'Software Development' and put the words 'Software Metrics' on the gun's ammunition box, and you have an effective advert for your work.

Perhaps your organization holds periodic, open briefing sessions. If so, you may like to consider staging such a presentation. Alternatively, you may have some sort of networked advertisement scheme on your development machines that you can utilize.

A presentation to senior management can be tempting at this point, but do beware. One of my previous managers gave me some very good advice some years ago regarding such an audience. He said: 'Keep the presentation short', which I am sure you already know, but he went on: 'tell them what the problem is, tell them the options, then tell them what they are going to do'. This is a good guideline and, while you may be able, even at this early stage, to tell them what the problem is, you are unlikely to be able to give them the options, nor are you yet in a position to tell them what to do. So, tempting though it may be, it is probably best to avoid such events at the moment, unless you need management's approval for the work, but remember, we are assuming that this has already been obtained. However, do not expect senior management to mandate every step of the metrics initiative development and implementation process.

There is another technique that can be used both to stimulate interest in a Software Metrics programme and that can provide a vehicle for education. A Software Metrics workshop can do both of these things. Please note that this is not a traditional training course. It is true that such an event will contain many similarities to a training course and it will be 'driven' by the presenter, but it is essentially a two-way exercise in communication. You, as the presenter, need to provide information about the subject, what it is and what it can achieve, but, equally, you are seeking information that will enable you to identify potential champions and that will help you focus on their needs.

A Software Metrics workshop does require a significant investment on the part of the organizer and the presenter. Also, running such an event can be very demanding, so you may feel that this is best left until you are comfortable and confident with the detailed use of metrics.

The publicity and education process within a Software Metrics programme is continuous. Use it to help maintain momentum as well as to introduce new ideas to the organization.

Finally, realize that staging a publicity campaign, even one that is only intended to introduce the topic of Software Metrics does take time, and you will need to budget for it in your plans. It does help to get rid of the 'ivory tower' syndrome that can plague Software Metrics programmes, because the key element in such a campaign should be a statement of intent saying, very clearly, that the programme will involve the people concerned with the day-to-day work of the software development function from an early stage. We will now discuss how this involvement can be achieved.

Customer identification

Internal customer identification

One element that adds complexity to a Software Metrics programme is the number of customer types that the programme must satisfy, because the various customers have different requirements.

You may still be unsure about the use of the term 'customer' in this context, so a few more words about this may be appropriate. I am convinced that all projects, be they to develop software, to introduce a new development tool or to implement Software Metrics, should have a customer or group of customers associated with them from the earliest possible stage. Now it may be that the customer is only a pseudo-customer, as in the case of a marketing group when a new software product is being developed as a speculative venture, but the customer still exists.

Why is the customer so important? Unless you recognize your customer, you cannot effectively capture the requirements for the project deliverable, and this is as true for Software Metrics as it is for anything else. The customer requirements should always drive the project, otherwise there is a very real danger that the deliverable will not have a market, and that the effort expended on the project will be wasted. Conversely, a project that recognizes its potential customers and that involves those customers has a much greater chance of success, and needs to spend less effort in marketing its products.

While the specific customers of the programme will differ between organizations, there do seem to be very definite similarities between programmes, and I have used these to develop an approach to customer identification. The first step is to model the organization that the programme will service in terms of major functional groupings.

Looking at the organizational structure of our example, we can easily see a number of clearly identifiable groups.

1. *Senior organizational management group*

This consists of the Managing Director and his or her first line including the Systems Development Manager. This group will probably possess certain characteristics that should be noted. Most senior managers view Systems Development or IT as a black hole into which they pour resources for very little quantifiable return. They also tend to view Systems Development, rightly or wrongly, as something that is very poorly managed. There are some good reasons for these views.

Historically, the drive for IT within organizations has been to put systems in place regardless of cost. Often, it has been thought that if systems were not developed, then the competition, if they developed IT systems, would gain such a competitive edge that the very survival of the organization would be in doubt. This led to a 'blank cheque' style of systems development that has cost many organizations a great deal of money, often justified by the flimsiest of cases, for little return.

In addition to this fear-driven investment, there has also been an element of 'momentum drive' acting on organizations. Momentum drive is something that has probably never been experienced before in the history of commerce, but which has typified the IT industry. Information technology has only appeared within the last 50 years, but within this relatively short period of time, it has impacted almost every walk of life and has truly brought about a second industrial revolution. We know that this is true but have we considered the effect?

The most dramatic effect has been on time. Time, unlike most physical dimensions, is not fixed. We perceive time differently in different circumstances, and the effect of the IT explosion has been to speed up our time perception dramatically. For example, acceptable time to market is now very much shorter than it was 10 years ago, product lifespan is much reduced and, even in our personal lives, we are no longer willing to accept delays in, say, transatlantic telephone calls that were previously considered normal. What all this means is that many organizations have invested in IT, at high cost, with little or no control. They have almost been pulled along by the momentum of the second revolution.

While the momentum drive is still present, most organizations have already addressed the obvious applications of IT. They have inventory control systems, payroll systems and personnel databases. Now they are taking stock and are starting to insist on greater control over their systems development functions. This is true for organizations whose systems development functions service internal requirements, and it is equally true where such functions earn the organization revenue. Senior management is demanding that greater control be applied to such divisions to reduce risk and maximize return on investment.

Another incentive to greater control is the appalling reputation that the IT industry has concerning cost and time-scale over-runs. Senior management who, previously, accepted this state of events, will accept it no longer.

So senior management at the organizational level will become important customers of the Software Metrics programme, and we can guess that they will see the programme as a vehicle by which greater control can be obtained.

2. *Systems Development senior management group*

The second customer grouping is the Systems Development Manager and his first line. Note that the Systems Development Manager is in both of the groupings identified so far. Such an overlap or intersection almost always identifies a key player.

While this identification can be trivial, such a diagram does highlight the fact that someone like the Systems Development Manager will, in fact, be relating to the programme in a more complex way than some other individuals.

The Systems Development Manager may well wish to use the Software Metrics programme to gain greater control over his own managers, especially the Product and Support Development Managers. However, the Systems Development Manager will also see the metrics programme as something that may provide a defence against the bullets other directors fire his way.

In one case, a Software Metrics programme was instigated in an organization to provide quantitative information that could be used to prevent the closure of the IT function. The proposal was that the software development function could be performed more effectively and at a lower cost by an external organization under contract than by an internal group. The Software Metrics programme was able to demonstrate that the internal group was performing as well, if not better, as others within the industry, and that the proposal to shift software development would not, in fact, generate any savings. A useful defence against some, if not all, of the bullets fired at the IT function. Identifying key players is important, because they will require special attention as the programme proceeds.

For the moment I am going to include the Software Development and the Test and Integration Managers as part of the Systems Development senior management group. This group is typified by the fact that its members are not responsible for the day-to-day activities of specific projects. They are a functional management group rather than a group focused on specific projects.

3. *Project managers*

This brings us nicely to our third customer grouping, the project managers who, in terms of our example organization are the team leaders. These individuals are right there in the firing line. They are responsible for the day-to-day working on specific software development projects. These people tend to be technically orientated and, given our industry's propensity for taking good technical staff and then putting them in positions where they have to manage people, which often demands a very different skill set, we should not be surprised to find some interesting interactions occurring between this group and the Software Metrics programme.

Project managers tend to fall into three camps. They may latch on to Software Metrics as something that can actually help them get control over their projects, and enable them to communicate facts to their own managers. Alternatively, they may be the kind of technician who insists on proving the theoretical concepts behind every idea or suggestion. This can cause problems, because of the immaturity of many Software Metrics techniques.

Finally, they may be pragmatists. Of the three camps, this is the one with whom I find it easiest to work. A pragmatic project manager knows he has problems and has tried to address these, often with limited success simply due to a lack of available time for thought let alone action. He also knows that life holds no guarantees, but because he does not have an answer to a specific problem, he is quite willing to listen and to try something new.

A pragmatic project manager will often gratefully accept a new idea, the use of a metric or metric-based technique. Typically, you, as a consultant, go back to that manager one, two or, maybe, three months later to find that he is doing things of which you never even thought. Now you become the pupil and he, or she, becomes the teacher. This is one of the most satisfying times within a Software Metrics programme. Not only have you succeeded in getting something useful in place, but you now have a practical application that can be used to convince others and, as a bonus, you probably have new ideas developed in the field.

It is often said that senior management commitment is *the* prerequisite for a successful Software Metrics programme. I disagree. It is *a* prerequisite, but I believe that identifying project managers, who are sufficiently open minded and who are prepared to work with you in implementing Software Metrics, is equally important.

4. *Support units*

Another important group is the support units. These are functional specialisms whose role is to facilitate software development within the organization. This group covers departments such as marketing, planning and project control offices. An R&D function can also be included as can the quality function within a Total Quality Management (TQM) programme. In many cases, groups like these need information like productivity and quality levels to be able to function effectively, but such information is often unavailable. Once they see that the Software Metrics programme intends to make such information available to them, support groups can become good customers of it.

In particular, it may well be that the quality function welcomes such a programme with open arms. The TQM philosophy is relatively new to western business, and especially to software development, yet it has become very popular over recent years. All implementations of such a philosophy, whether they are based on Crosby (1985), Deming (1986) or other approaches, emphasize the need for measurement, but most quality functions struggle with the application of measurement on a broad scale. This is especially true when TQM is applied to software development.

For example, the application of *statistical process control* in its traditional sense is difficult within software engineering functions, because of the general skew of data sets from that environment, and because of the need to get a reasonable data set to be able to apply this technique. However, the link between TQM and Software Metrics is obvious; Software Metrics is a specialism that can satisfy the requirement for measurement within a practical application of TQM and such a link should be exploited as much as possible.

5. *Software engineers*

And so we come to our final group of potential, internal customers of a Software Metrics programme. This group is often overlooked, yet their involvement and acceptance of a Software Metrics programme is vital to its success. The group I am talking about is the software engineers, or programmers.

I vividly remember one occasion when I spent half an hour going through my standard introduction to Software Metrics with such an engineer. He nodded in all the right places and even asked one or two pertinent questions. He saved his real bombshell until the end when he simply asked: 'what's in it for me'? This really drove home the point. Why should engineers take time to supply information, accurately, when they get nothing back in return? This important group exists and, please, do not ignore it. Simply taking the time to talk to and involve as many engineers as is practical can pay handsome dividends.

External customer identification

Having talked about internal customers, that is groups that are involved in the production of software within an organization, we really must consider external customers of the metrics programme. I mean now the actual consumers of the products of software development. In the case of our example, this means true customers, individuals or organizations that pay real money for the products of software development. But customers can also get their hands on such products without paying real money.

We all have customers even if we never speak to or see anyone who is not part of our employing organization. For example, our organization model contains a number of support development teams who generate products that are used by the product development group. These people are customers in almost every sense of the word. I consider it so important that we consider our customers as just that, be they external, paying customers or internal users of our products, that I do not intend to distinguish between them.

Customers will, generally, not be involved in the day-to-day use of Software Metrics, but they can be considered as a specific customer group for that programme. They may even be driving that programme but, more often, they will be more passive during the early stages and, depending on the commercial environment in which you work, you may have to make some assumptions about their requirements.

Once we have derived a high-level breakdown of our potential customer set we should consider this in more detail. For example, within the Systems Development senior management set, we have two levels to cater for, the Test and Integration and the Software Development managers. Also, the actual number of support groups seen as customers of the programme will be dependent on the programme's terms of reference, and the detailed organizational structure.

I do not intend to discuss the derivation of the lower-level breakdown, as it is so dependent on these factors, but please let me emphasize that performing such an analysis is worthwhile and should not be ignored. The following lists show one lower-level breakdown that could apply to our model organization.

Organizational senior management
    Managing Director
    Systems Development Director
    Finance Director
    Personnel Director

Systems Development Senior Management
    Systems Development Director
    R&D Manager
    Product Manager

Support Development Manager
Operational Support Manager

Test and Integration Manager
Software Development Manager

Support groups
R&D
Planning
Project managers
Engineers

Notice that this breakdown can include functional groups or individuals where they carry out a functional role. One way to derive this lower-level identification of customers is to merge the reporting hierarchy such as is shown in Fig. 10.5 with the functional linkage chart shown in Fig. 10.4.

Market identification

Having identified the potential customers of our programme, we should consider the potential market and the size of that market. This activity is similar in scope to the initial market research work done during the feasibility study. The difference lies in the amount of detail — this market identification being more than a sizing exercise. Surprisingly, this is an activity that is often ignored within Software Metrics programmes, yet it is important. To all intents and purposes, you are going to be establishing a business within your own software development function that will service the needs of that organization. If you were setting up an external business, one step that you would most certainly consider is to establish the potential market. There is no reason why you should not do the same for an internal business.

There are various questions that should be addressed by this activity and the answers you obtain will form the basis of a 'business plan', as opposed to a project plan, later in the programme. It can be argued that market identification does not need to be carried out until you get nearer to implementation but, from my own experience, the earlier that you start to address this problem, the better. The information you gather during this activity will also directly affect the next job, establishing a user interface.

You may be surprised how difficult it is to get some of the information you require. It never ceases to amaze me how little basic management information is available within software development functions of any size and, if nothing else, this activity will give you a better understanding of the organization in which you work.

Typical questions that should be asked during this activity include:

- How many sites is software development carried out on and where are they located?
- Is there any functional specialization between sites? For instance, does one site concentrate on integration and testing of software developed on other sites, or are different products developed on different sites?
- How many project teams are in existence at the current time?
- How many software engineers do we have?
- Do engineers work exclusively on one product/project at a time?

- Are projects grouped under functional headings? For instance, do we have a team leader managing more than one project team, each developing say a build of a current product?
- How many project teams do we plan to have at the start of the next three financial years?
- What is the relationship between the planning function and the project teams?

You may find that some of this information is readily available from organizational data. Other items of information will certainly require some digging. You may also find that these questions, in turn, raise other questions. For example, what do we mean by a project? Does the project team include the team leader? Has anyone ever defined our development process?

When in doubt, remember the first principle of Software Metrics — be pragmatic. At this stage, you are trying to get information that will allow you to proceed with the Software Metrics programme. This does not have to be correct to three decimal places, nor will it be used in any way that involves risk. Yes, you may well need to define what is meant by a project, and have that agreed by your customers, but that comes later, so use any sensible definition at this point. Having obtained this information we can now proceed to the next activity.

Establish user interface

One of the great problems with any activity aimed at changing an existing process is that the attempt can be made without the involvement of those people who will be affected. Such attempts are very prone to failure.

Software Metrics programmes are as likely to suffer from this 'ivory tower' syndrome as any other culture-changing process, and conscious steps must be taken to avoid this happening. Yet, at first glance, it is not easy to involve the process owners, especially when the team that is trying to effect the changes to that process is not directly involved in it. This is certainly the case in our model organization where the Software Metrics team is part of the R&D group, and it is also true of the vast majority of industrial Software Metrics programmes of which I am aware, both in Europe and the USA.

One of the problems is often the large number of process owners because, as I view things, anyone who is involved directly in a process has a vested interest in that process, and can be seen as an owner of it. How can we involve this large number of people in the work of changing the process, how can we ensure that the process owners own the process of process change?

One of the best pieces of advice I have ever seen regarding the implementation of Software Metrics came from the Grady and Caswell book, *Software Metrics: Establishing a Company Wide Program* (1987). They introduced the concept of a 'Metrics Council' and I have used a very similar concept when implementing metrics initiatives. Names vary, the council could be called a user group, a working party or, my own choice, a 'Metrics Coordination Group'.

The Metrics Coordination Group

The role of this group is simple — it acts as the steering committee, it guides the direction of the programme and, most importantly, it ensures that the programme does not fly off into flights of fancy that do not address the business needs of the organization.

The role of this group does depend, somewhat, on the involvement and strength of the customer authority. If the customer authority is both strong and involved, the high-level requirements for the Software Metrics programme will have been set out relatively clearly, but even these will probably benefit from having fresh minds applied to them. In most cases, the high-level requirements that will have been placed on the metrics programme will be fairly vague and, in this case, the Metrics Coordination Group will be responsible for setting the more detailed direction of the programme. The group will decide if the programme covers both productivity and quality measurement for example. Should any attention be directed towards measuring soft or environmental factors? Is there a need for more effective cost estimation techniques?

The Metrics Coordination Group is there to demonstrate that the users have been consulted from the start. Establishing and involving such a group is one step towards ensuring that the Software Metrics programme is owned by its users rather than being seen as an imposition on them. As will be seen, achieving this ownership is an important success criteria.

The group can also act as the final review body for any products from the Software Metrics programme. This is an extremely useful way of overcoming objections from the potential market for such products, be they reports, measures or a training course. It helps combat the 'not invented here' attitude of some teams. Using the phrase, 'approved by the Metrics Coordination Group' can be a powerful weapon in the war to get a Software Metrics programme accepted.

The group will also help in other ways. There is a phenomena I have labelled 'reverse synergy'. This is where the constituent parts of a group are more powerful than the group as a whole. Unlike Grady and Caswell (1987), I do not expect the Metrics Coordination Group to do 'real work' during its meetings, although I fully accept that, with the right people, a set of metrics can be defined, for example, as they describe in their book. Personally, I prefer to use the group meetings as an opportunity to share information, and a time for general discussions of strategy. However, I do use the members of the group as local champions and as doorways into different parts of the organization. They provide me, as the facilitator or the leg man, with the contacts and the introductions that are so necessary to the work of a Software Metrics programme. If you are able to get the right people on the Metrics Coordination Group, you will quickly find many centres of interest developing within your organization. All you have to do is change centres of interest into centres of working expertise. Not an easy task, but infinitely easier than trying to carve your way through the organization single handed.

So, who should be the members of the Metrics Coordination Group? There is a great temptation to insist on senior managers, from our model, for example, you may target the R&D, the Product, Support Development and Operations Support Managers. Possibly you would add in the Software Development and the Test and Integration Managers as well. Great, if you can get them all in one room for a day, but I doubt that you will. In many ways it is unfortunate that these individuals cannot form such a group, as they are the 'shakers and makers'. They have the power to take decisions and see those decisions acted upon quickly. I repeat, you will be very lucky if you get the level of representation, in terms of seniority, that you would like. The one exception to this is when you are completely external to the organization, i.e. a consultant. In this case, you may well be able to insist on access to senior management, and this is one reason why consultancy-led programmes can often move a lot faster than internal programmes. There is a down side to this. Consultants are transitory beasts, they are not there for long, and there are few consultants who can effectively accomplish the transfer of technology or knowledge that is necessary for an organization to be able to proceed under its own steam without any slowing down.

However, even if you cannot get senior managers on to the Metrics Coordination Group, all is not lost. Provided that the majority of the group members are open minded, constructively critical and believe that process improvement is both necessary and possible, the group will still be effective.

There is even an argument for establishing two groups, one consisting of more senior managers who determine strategic direction, and another made up of project managers who work on the tactical plans and oversee the introduction of operational procedures. Standard Life, a large insurance organization adopted this approach in the UK to good effect. Their experiences were reported to a QA Forum Software Metrics Special Interest Group meeting held during 1991.

Use your own and other people's knowledge of the organization to target individuals. Ensure that you have at least one representative from each of your customer groups. With luck, you should be able to get one senior manager involved. If your organization is split across sites, try to get a representative mix within the group and do not forget to include your customer authority.

Approach the targeted individuals to sound them out and, if you are happy, get their line manager's approval for attendance. This is also a good time to let senior management know that this group exists.

The first meeting is important, and will really be driven by the metrics team itself. In fact, this is going to be the case right through development to implementation. Ensure that you set out the terms of reference for the group and the individuals; remember they are to act as local champions; and use the first meeting to discuss the programme components and the strategy as it is perceived at this stage. If necessary, use the results of the feasibility study to underline the importance of Software Metrics and what can be achieved. Tell them what the organization, in this case the metrics team, is going to do, and be prepared to discuss time-scales even if you avoid the question of cost for now. Above all, get their agreement to your proposals, even if this means modifying those proposals. Remember, the involvement of many individuals means that compromise is necessary.

The first meeting of the Metrics Coordination Group can be seen as the true launch of the metrics initiative. After the initial meeting, I have found it best to hold meetings at need rather than on a regular basis, at least during the development of the metrics programme. Once you get to implementation, the role of the group changes to become more of a true user group. At this time, regular meetings, say quarterly, are probably justified.

One final point, the members of the Metrics Coordination Group will be helping you. Make sure that you thank them for that help; publicly and often. Remember it is their programme not yours, at least it will be if you succeed. If it is not, then you have failed.

Identify potential super champions

Within the Metrics Coordination Group there will be what I call potential 'super champions'. A super champion is a person who not only lends his or her name to an initiative, but who wholeheartedly adopts that initiative, becomes part of it and starts to drive it forward down new routes. Such individuals are worth their weight in gold as they become not merely centres of expertise and enthusiasm, but centres of excellence. The real beauty of it is that they are always owners of the process that is being changed, and that they are doing the changing.

Both through the Metrics Coordination Group and through other interactions with the organization as a whole, you will become aware of potential super champions. It is up to you to cultivate these people to ensure that their potential is realized.

Capture information requirements

This is the core activity of this stage. It is important because there are various techniques that can be used to derive a set of Software Metrics for use by the organization.

Data hunter's strategy

One technique is to go into a development team, a project or the data from a previous project, and then to measure everything of which we can possibly think. This is the data hunter's strategy. Having got a vast array of base data we then apply various statistical techniques to find out what all this information is telling us. Our hope is that it is telling us something useful which can then be used to improve the development process.

One problem with this approach is that the very quantity and diversity of information can produce apparently meaningful results, information that in reality is telling us very little. For example, you may find that the number of comments per thousand lines of code is running at about 30 per cent. Let us say that you are really clever and that you find the spread of this comment density ranges from 1 per cent to 75 per cent. What conclusions can you draw from this? The answer is very little.

Now it can be argued that by relating comment density to error fixing productivity, you may be able to show that high comment density relates to high productivity. In some ways this may make sense if your engineers are using the code comments as the primary source of system documentation and, before throwing your hands up in horror, go and ask them if this is the case. You may be surprised. However, the very quantity of data that you will be collecting will probably mean that you cannot form that relationship from a statistically significant number of projects or observations within a project. Essentially, the data collection costs when working under the data hunting approach are simply too high, because we do not know which base measures will be useful.

Alternatively, we may give the matter some thought and then go and measure everything that seems to make sense! Under Murphy's Law, the one thing not measured will be the one we should have measured. I state this from bitter personal experience.

In one installation, we measured every element of a system design that we felt could possibly be a valid predictor of software size. The collection and analysis took quite a while and the results were interesting. In fact, the best predictor seemed to be the number of pages in the functional specification. Try selling that one to senior management. By the by, it is worth pointing out that we were using a relatively formalized, diagrammatic documentation technique, so perhaps we should not be too surprised by this result. But the bottom line is that when we presented our results, a member of the audience asked why we had not measured a particular design attribute. The answer was that we had not thought about that one, so we agreed that we would try it out. Of course, that attribute, the number of data dictionary definitions, turned out to be the best predictor of all — at least for new systems, which was our area of interest at that time. Fortunately, there was also a need to get a size measure for enhancement work, and the data dictionary model broke down when we tried to apply it to that sphere of engineering. We managed to save face to some degree! Believe me, measuring everything in sight is fraught with difficulty and is not a cost-effective method of deriving Software Metrics.

Goal/question/metric paradigm

Luckily, there are other approaches that can be used. The most widely recognized and respected approach to metric derivation is something called the *goal/question/metric,* or GQM, paradigm, and this is discussed in some detail in Chapter 11 which describes the Component Design stage of the SMP development and implementation lifecycle.

The foundation of this approach, developed by the Software Engineering Laboratory in the USA, Rombach (1990) is aimed at making practitioners ask not so much 'what should I measure' but 'why am I measuring'? To be able to answer this question, we need to be able to answer the additional question: 'what business needs does the organization wish its measurement initiative to address'?

Systems analysis

Capturing and specifying measurement requirements uses the same procedures as classic systems analysis, i.e. interviews, workshops, prototyping, and the foundation of good systems analysis is preparation.

Taking requirements from a number of sources, we will probably identify certain similarities between requirements that will enable us to focus on those for which there is a general need. In this way, we will be able to group requirements into particular classes. The benefit of doing this is that it reduces the amount of duplicated effort that may otherwise be expended. The following list gives one possible set of headings that can be used to group metrics requirements and they can also be employed to focus an interview or workshop session:

- Project metrics
- Business entity metric
- Cost estimation
- Quality assessment (*Applied Design metrics*) and prediction
- Project Control

Project metrics I define as being any measure of a process or product attribute, where the source data and the subsequent application is confined to a single project or product and the associated team. For example, field reliability of a product. The primary customer for such metrics is almost invariably the project manager.

Business entity metrics can be defined in the same way as project metrics, except that the source data is drawn from a number of areas that, together, form a managerial unit. In terms of our example organization, a business entity could be the Test and Integration Group, the Product Division or the whole of the Systems Development area. An example of a business entity metric requirement would be of a product group manager wishing to monitor the general reliability levels of the products over time as a group rather than as a set of individual products. Another example would be where the management board wished to monitor return on investment for the whole of the IT function. In both cases, the requirement could be met by aggregating information from measures taken against individual products or product groups respectively.

These areas have been discussed in Section 1, project and business entity metrics coming under the general heading of *management information*.

Having obtained a set of requirements and grouped them into classes we may well see that we have two macro classes. The first will be requirements for information, the second will be for techniques that can be directly used to improve the development process in some form or another. Each macro class requires a slightly different approach.

Model-based approach to requirements information

Although these two approaches are really part of the design stage of our metrics programme, I will briefly introduce them here. Requirements for information will mean that we need to adopt a model, either by using one that is generally well accepted and with which we feel comfortable, because there is no reason to reinvent the wheel or, if the wheel does not exist, we will have to go through the modelling process ourselves. The model will provide us with a composite metric which, in turn, will lead to a set of base metrics.

To define these two terms, *composite* and *base* metrics:

- A composite metric is a mathematical formula, the solution of which will provide a quantitative value which, in turn, satisfies, through analysis, the initial requirement.
- Base metrics are the items of raw data that need to be collected in order that the mathematical formula within the composite metrics can be applied.

If this sounds complicated, the following may help. Imagine that the product manager has asked us, as part of the metrics programme, to supply information that will tell him or her how productive software development is within the revenue-earning part of the organization. Obviously, the source data for this requirement will be drawn from more than one project or product area, so we would seem to be talking about a business entity metric.

Productivity is a relatively well understood economic measure that is widely used within most industries and it is generally defined to be:

$$\text{Productivity} = \text{work product}/\text{cost to produce}$$

To satisfy our current requirement, this does require some additional definition. We may choose to define *work product* as *function points* or even as *lines of code*; in other words, the size of what we produce in terms of functionality or 'volume' in the same sense as a car production line output measure may be defined as the number of cars produced during one shift.

Before anyone gets too upset at this, let me stress that we need to be very careful in our definition of, say, *lines of code,* and the definition of other parameters in our model. We must also accept that productivity is not a magical, overall measure of process effectiveness. As you will have realized, we could produce lots of *lines of code,* whose quality is lousy. However, productivity can be used as a high level measure of performance, and I will have more to say about how we derive valid measures later on.

Likewise, we could define our cost parameter as 'effort' in terms of engineering days booked to a particular project. Now as this is a business entity metric, we could decide to sample a set of representative project/product teams, or we could total across all teams. I will assume the latter case for this example.

We end up with a composite productivity metric defined as:

Productivity = (total project lines of code delivered to Test and Integration during
financial year x)/(total project effort booked)

From this, we can see that our base metrics, the raw data that must be collected to be able to derive our productivity metric, are:

Project lines of code delivered to Test and Integration;
Project effort.

For now, think about the terms used and the derivation method, not about the metric itself.

Direct process improvement

For the other common macro class of requirements, direct process improvement, the technique is slightly different. Firstly we need to identify, at a conceptual level, what will be done, perhaps what we feel should be done. This is often based on examples taken from other organizations or on our own personal experience within the organization.

Conceptual models are a necessary step, but they seldom provide the answer. The elements of the conceptual model need to be grafted on to the development process within the organization. In other words, we need an application model that will describe how we will do what is described within the conceptual model.

Again an example will help. Given a requirement to improve the effectiveness, i.e. the accuracy, of our cost estimates, we may decide to use a proprietary cost estimation package. Conceptually, we should realize that the package will need to be calibrated to our own environment before we can use it properly, so our application model, based on that calibration, may say something like:

At the point when requirements analysis has been completed, use the requirements specification to complete the estimation input form. Submit the form to the estimation team who will, in turn, supply you with a modified, package-based estimate and confidence level.

Again, an over-simple example, but it illustrates that just deciding to use a cost estimation package is not enough. The application model addresses a great many issues that the conceptual model can ignore.

Obtaining requirements

Of course, all of this assumes that we are able to obtain our requirements. This is not always as easy as it may seem, so let us consider this area now in more detail.

Obtaining the set of specific requirements that will drive the Software Metrics programme is not a task that can be easily defined, because it involves interaction with people. What *can* be defined is the types of information that should be contained in such a requirement together with some approaches and techniques that can be used.

The individual, structured interview

Essentially, there are two techniques that can be used to define the specific requirements within the metrics programme. The most obvious is to adopt a systems analysis approach by identifying specific, key players within the customer set. Structured interviews are then carried out involving these individuals.

My personal preference is a two-pass approach. For each of the players, the first interview aims to identify their particular role within the organization as they see it, what processes they are personally involved in and what those processes entail, what responsibilities, in terms of deliverables, they have and, most importantly, what they perceive to be the weaknesses in the processes they operate. This can be quite a tall order!

Do not minimize the importance of this activity. Talking to people takes time, and to get the most out of the available time, there will need to be a plan and structure to the interview sessions. One plan which certainly appears to work goes as follows:

Start the session by briefly describing the purpose of the interview, which is to ensure that the deliverables of the metrics project really address the personal needs of the interviewee and the business needs of the organization. Do not try to sell metrics too hard. You are there to listen and learn, not preach. By all means explain the high-level requirements of the programme, as this will help to set the focus of the interview session.

Ask the individual to explain his or her role within the organization as he or she sees it, and be ready to spot 'key terms' such as 'project', 'build', or vagaries such as 'size', 'complexity' and 'quality'. You will see why this is important shortly. This part of the meeting is vitally important. You really need to listen to what is being said, and, perhaps more importantly, to what is not being said. Can you start to see areas that you think may benefit from measurement or from other known metrics techniques?

As the interview progresses, take notes. If you are unsure about what is being said, ask questions. Simple actions like this demonstrate interest on your part, and provide a positive stroke to the other person's ego. Don't knock it! You need this person to work with you, so you use everything you can to develop a rapport. One word of warning, a single question asked by you can drive the interview off at a tangent if you interrupt a person's flow of conversation, so perhaps you should simply note a point and return to it later.

The interviewee will be involved in processes. As the interview progresses, start to build a model of those processes on your note pad, perhaps using a *data flow diagram* notation similar to that used in this book. Look for subprocesses that do not seem to be triggered or for information that is consumed, but not used. Use points like these to drive the interview if it seems to be flagging.

Make sure that you have got it right. Play back your understanding of what has been said regarding the interviewee's work. If you have got it wrong, then do not argue, change your model. Remember, you are trying to find out how things are done. Do not try to impose textbook solutions on your interviewee. If he says that the team does not carry out any review of code designs, then feel free to query it but, if that is the case, accept it.

As you talk, note the areas where there seem to be problems. If he is involved in estimation how is it done? Can the team supply information about the last project or product delivery in terms of how big a job it was, what the quality levels were, how effective the process was at getting rid of defects?

Now we get to the difficult part. You need to find out how Software Metrics can help the interviewee, so ask him or her. Now, if you simply put the question, you will probably be met with a blank look. You will need to steer this part of the interview by suggesting ideas to the interviewee. Would some assistance with estimation be appreciated, perhaps a centralized estimation group or some training in techniques? Are there some problems because more senior managers are asking for embarrassing information such as productivity levels? Do new tools need to be justified? Explore the possibilities with your partner, and I use the word deliberately because the interviewee should now start to feel part of the metrics project, a partner in it.

Finally, try to arrange another session with your new-found friend, but also try to leave the date flexible. Why? The reason is that you will have some serious work to do now. Firstly, you have to hold similar sessions with other individuals, so that you can identify a macro set of requirements. You also need to check some of the points raised with other people. Is it really true that effort data is recorded accurately by all project team members as perhaps the manager believes, or are the engineers making a wild stab at the figures at the end of each month? You will also find, almost certainly, that your first few interviewees raise even more fundamental questions that need to be answered. Be honest, if you do not have an answer, then defer it by noting that it needs to be addressed and by telling the interviewee that various basic definitions and ground rules will be defined before the requirements are baselined. This will not be an alien concept to most people involved in software development.

Before we consider this last point, a few more words on initial requirements capture using this interview-based approach. How long should such an interview take? I seldom schedule more than two such sessions during a day, even if I can only get the interviewee to agree to give me an hour. The reason is simply that people like to talk about themselves, and it is amazing how quickly time passes in such a situation. In some cases, you may well find yourself sharing lunch and going on in the afternoon, when you originally planned to finish by ten in the morning. Do not worry, this is time well spent.

Another point about scheduling — there is always a temptation to 'start at the top'. Don't! There are two reasons for my saying this. Firstly, you will not be as well prepared as you should be when you do that first interview. In fact, it may take three or four sessions before you really start to get to grips with what you are doing, so it is best to minimize any risk at this point. Secondly, the case when this relaxed, open-format-interview technique does not work is with the very people with whom it would be most useful — senior managers! Senior managers, say the Systems Development Manager, do not have the time to chew the fat with you, and even if they do, they certainly do not want to seem as though they do.

Time with senior managers is difficult to get and is, therefore, valuable. To make the most of this time, I can only suggest that you adopt the approach mentioned earlier with one modification, i.e. tell them what you think the problems are, what the options are and what you intend to do. The modification? Ask them if they have any specific problem areas that they want addressed, or if they want any of the identified action areas given a particularly high priority?

Of course, all senior managers have already identified the immediate business requirements and their priorities for the next five years, as advised by all the management books. If you believe that, watch out for flying pigs! Even with senior managers, you will need to control the interview, but remember again, you are there to learn, not to make an impression, that comes later.

To be able to talk to senior managers sensibly using the approach outlined above means that you need to have an appreciation of the problems as perceived by the business, i.e. the very senior managers to whom you will be talking. You will need to have obtained some idea as to what areas should be addressed and to have a high-level plan, even if this is then modified by the manager. Obviously, therefore, you cannot go and talk to the senior manager first before having talked to anyone else.

One final point, do remember to use business etiquette. Within your organization, you may need to approach a senior manager before approaching any of his or her staff. From the previous stage, this permission may have been implied. It does no harm to get that permission again, politely, explicitly.

Getting the requirements through individual interview is certainly one technique that can work effectively. There is another technique that can work more quickly in terms of elapsed time but, depending on the culture of the organization, it can involve a greater risk of getting it wrong, often because you do not get the key players involved.

Brainstorming

Sometimes the approach is called brainstorming, or meta-planning or centres on a workshop. Essentially, it involves a group of people simultaneously working out a set of requirements for the metrics programme. It requires a fair amount of planning and coordination and also a strong meeting leader, who is more than a chairman, to control events as they occur. On the positive side, it can give a set of agreed requirements very quickly.

To use this approach within the type of organizational model I am using to illustrate the metrics programme development and implementation lifecycle would mean that you need to prepare some material that could be used to introduce the topic of Software Metrics. This material needs to define what is meant by the term Software Metrics; it needs to introduce the principles of measurement and relate these to a software development environment; it should show examples of the effective use of Software Metrics and, finally, it should relate the information shown to the identified business needs of your own organization which, of course, form the basic, high-level requirements of your own Software Metrics programme. Avoid the use of mathematical formula in this material as it can confuse the issue.

Once you have the material, you will need to identify the key players that you intend to use to define your specific requirements. You will need to arrange some form of management sponsorship to ensure that you can get the people you want to the workshop — ideally, the Systems Development Director would agree to attend the meeting. You will have to plan out the structure of the session in some detail to ensure that you maintain control and get from it what you want.

On the day, and you will need a full day, be up front and honest. Explain that the purpose of the workshop is to derive a specific set of requirements that will be used to drive the metrics programme. Present your introductory material in a strong way, and be prepared to handle difficult questions from the participants in a realistic and sympathetic manner. Do not be too defensive. After all, you want their participation, so be prepared to modify your own ideas and concepts in the light of their contributions. Above all, do not come across as someone who claims to have the perfect answer to all their problems. Firstly, they have heard it all before, and are probably quite rightly cynical. Secondly, you do not have all the answers. What you do have is an approach that can help them, as managers of software development work, to help themselves.

Be very sure that you steer discussion towards the requirements definition by the start of the afternoon. It is very easy to get caught up in deep discussions about, perhaps, the true meaning of system size, and to find that it is five o'clock and you have half-an-hour left to sort out the requirements. If things start to get bogged down, then try asking if they would like to try any of the approaches outlined in your examples within their own areas, or you could even ask: 'what kind of information would you like that you don't get now?'

Prototyping

Prototyping is an approach I know has been used by one US-based organization in the area of management information. The case was different from the usual situation in that the individual driving the programme had a significant amount of experience in the application of Software Metrics, was well respected in the organization and had a strong supplier/client relationship with her customer. This approach worked for her, and I could see it being very effective in phase two or three of a metrics initiative as a means of generating management commitment when expanding the programme implementation. I have some doubts about applying it during the first stage, when the metrics team itself will probably be learning about the topic.

Whatever approach we use we should end up with a set of specific requirements that have come from the business and that the business wishes the SMP to address. Looking at these we may well find that they fall into a number of categories. Firstly, we may see some to which we feel there is a reasonable answer and which will provide a quick payback for relatively little effort. We may also spot some that could be called research issues. Yes, they are important, but we know, from earlier work, that there are no immediate answers just waiting to be put into place. We will also find some requirements that are obtuse. They are either very specialized or appear so convoluted that we could spend the next ten years just getting to grips with what is wanted. These should be avoided like the plague.

In fact, we will almost certainly have too many requirements to address all at once, so we will need to prioritize. One systematic approach to this is to look at the available data sources, together with the storage, analysis and feedback requirements. We should address the areas where data is available already and where the storage, analysis and feedback requirements are clear first. How to identify what data is available is discussed shortly.

Very often, the Metrics Coordination Group is an ideal forum for determining priorities in terms of requirements to be addressed. One other thing that may well be discovered is the need to establish some initial definitions.

Establishing initial definitions

Why should we have to spend time deriving a set of initial definitions for use within the metrics programme? After all, we probably have development standards that address these very points. The answer is twofold. Firstly, standards, almost by definition, are documents that sit on shelves and that are very seldom read. Secondly, even if they are read, they seldom define basic terms in such a way that interpretation and modification do not occur. This means that when we use terms like 'fault', 'defect', 'size' and even 'project', other people will often put their own meanings on these expressions. Time and again, I have found terminology to be one of the biggest barriers to understanding.

Let me try to illustrate this by example. Consider the term 'defect'. Does this mean a perceived difficulty as reported by the user; does it mean a problem with a delivered product even if the defect has not yet been detected; or does it mean an identified problem with a product detected, verified and located? Any of these definitions are possible, but what we mean by the term 'defect' can have serious ramifications when we try to measure.

It gets even worse when we consider a term like 'fault'. Is a fault the same as a defect? Is there a relationship between faults and defects? Can we have multiple defects causing one fault, or multiple faults causing one defect? Confusing isn't it! A dictionary is not much help either. *Collins Pocket English Dictionary* defines the noun 'fault' as, 'something that mars; flaw; defect'. A defect is defined as, 'lack of something necessary for completeness' or 'an imperfection; blemish'. Now, we seem to be approaching another key problem as these defect definitions take on a similarity to definitions of quality.

If you would like to spend a fruitless, but entertaining, half hour, gather together three or four individuals who are connected with software development. Ask them to define what is meant by 'software quality', sit back and watch the fun! At the end of half-an-hour, or the day if you have that much time to waste, you will not have an agreement, but you will be very aware of the problems terminology can cause. One word of warning, do not let yourself get drawn into the argument, or you may well be surprised at the strength with which you will defend your own corner. Defining quality is like politics and religion, such discussions are best suited to late nights with good wine and trusted friends.

Just to round off this section of despair, what about the term 'project'. We all work on projects; projects have become our master in the past; we have endless meetings and reviews of the project. I will bet that even this term in your organization is not clearly defined.

So, what is the answer? Remember the first principle I discussed in Chapter 2, that of pragmatism and compromise. You will need to be able to define certain basic terms within your metrics initiative simply because you will be talking to many different people and you will be using these terms. It is important that you identify the terms that cause your organization problems, and this is one reason why I have left this activity until now within the SMP development model. By talking to your users, you will have identified the terms that you need to define. It is also important that you define them in a meaningful way, in a way that is acceptable to the organization and not as theoretical, abstract concepts. How can you obtain the necessary agreement to your definitions? I suggest that you present them to your Metrics Coordination Group and have that group ratify them.

I suppose I should practise what I preach and define some basic terms myself for use within this book. In one sense, these definitions have to be slightly theoretical because the actual definitions you use can depend upon your organization's culture and current practice. Let us return to a previous example. There is a great deal of discussion about the meaning of the terms 'fault' and 'defect'. People tend to view one as the manifestation of an error as perceived by the user of a product. The other is viewed as a flaw in the product that has caused the perceived problem. Obviously, one perceived problem can be related to a number of flaws and vice versa. The question is, which is the defect and which the fault? My answer is very pragmatic — it depends on the organization. If your user reports problems through a defect report, the defect is the perceived problem, the fault is the flaw. If the user reports through a fault report, it works the other way round.

But what if your user does not use fault or defect reports. I know one organization that uses 'incident reports'. In this case, I would suggest that you start to use one term for the flaw that causes the incident report to be raised, and stick to it. If other people use the other term, then try to educate them, gently and slowly, to use the chosen terms as agreed with the Metrics Coordination Group.

For our purposes, I will use the term *defect* as the perceived problem, so our users raise 'defect reports'. A *fault* will be the flaw that causes a defect.

Regarding size, I will use two definitions:

- *Product size* is defined as the functionality of the product currently in use and requiring support.
- *Project size* is defined as the functionality that is added, changed or deleted as the result of a software development or enhancement project.

Notice that I am not yet assigning units to our size measures, this will be done later when we select the metrics we will be using.

Now, what about the project itself? I define a *project* as a consolidated unit of work managed as a single entity. A project has a recognized start and end date, and has associated with it a project plan. The project starts when the first component of the unit is identified, it ends when the last component is delivered to the product recipient. Note that, depending on your own development lifecycle, this product recipient may be a testing team or the end user or some integration group.

This definition of a project is somewhat cumbersome, but it does allow for the case when work starts to be booked against a small work element, which then has additional elements added to it over time, during which the project team ramps up to full strength.

What about 'quality'? At a conceptual level, I prefer the idea that quality is the satisfaction of user requirements. For practical purposes, I view *quality* as a collection of characteristics that are addressed individually. Remember that the particular set of quality characteristics that you may have to address may be a subset of the totality of quality and may not be clearly specified by your users. As an example of the second point, many users do not specify requirements for maintainability when a system is being developed, but they can get very upset if a product is later found to be difficult to maintain.

Finally, remember to adopt or derive a high-level development lifecycle model for your organization.

Identify available data sources

We can think about prioritizing the various requirements we have collected essentially by how easy they will be to satisfy. Remember that business requirements and advice from the Metrics Coordination Group may take precedence over what has been considered to be important by either the organization in the past or by you, but available data sources should be identified in any case, as it is likely that they will assist you in satisfying current requirements.

The first thing to do is to look at what is currently available in terms of data, and where this data resides. To do this, you will need to talk to people yet again, and this is another case where the Metrics Coordination Group can help. You can also draw on your own experience and the experience of other contacts within the organization. Beware! It is very easy to think that the way you have done things in the past is also the way that everyone else does things, but this is not always the case. I did have one example where I built a model for capturing defect data using what I believed to be a standard tracking system used by the organization only to find that this process was used by no more than one-third of the organization. A classic case of not checking the facts thoroughly enough. Fortunately, I had only wasted a couple of days, but the situation could have been very costly and embarrassing. Imagine presenting a new system to a group of senior managers only to find that they have never heard of the process that lies at the core of your proposal.

You will find certain data collection mechanisms already in place within an organization although it must be said that the validity of this data may well be suspect. Typically an organization will collect data relating to field defects, that is as reported by the customer or the end user. This can be a useful source of information. The other most commonly collected form of data relates to time spent by development staff. Most organizations have little faith in their time-recording systems.

There are various reasons for this. Often time data is collected weekly or monthly. Personally, I find it difficult enough to remember what I was doing during the morning, if I do not record that information until the afternoon. Completing a time sheet at the end of the week or, even worse, at the end of the month, usually means that the information is very inaccurate. Having said that, things do tend to even out. I know one organization that managed to set up an experiment which compared recorded time to actual time spent on a number of specific projects. Their findings were interesting in that they did indeed verify that the recorded time was terribly inaccurate, yet it was consistently inaccurate across the sample. The recorded time was approximately 30 per cent less than the actual time for any one project.

Defect data tends to be less inaccurate in terms of absolute numbers. The problem with defect data tends to lie with inaccuracy in detail, or information that we would like to be present, simply not being collected. For instance, in one project that I looked at the number of defects that were attributed to coding faults was very high. This is a common occurrence, but equally common, and the case on this project, was the fact that, after investigating these defects more carefully, I found that coding faults only accounted for less than half those originally reported as such. The rest were design or requirements faults. This can have fairly serious consequences as the data suggested the coding phase of development should be investigated, when the reality was that the design phase was by far the more costly in terms of injected faults. This experience was duplicated by other individuals in the same and different organizations. In fact, this experience has happened so frequently that I would always be suspicious of such data.

This lack of care in recording information seems to be a direct result of the lack of feedback from these established systems. People record the information because they must, because it is part of the organizational bureaucracy. Having recorded the information, they never see or hear of it again, so why should they bother to take care? This observation led me to coin the phrase, 'write only database'. A ludicrous situation in anyone's view but one that unfortunately occurs with distressing frequency.

The problem with missing data seems to arise from design by committee, and a distinct lack of effective requirements analysis when these systems are set up. Try getting people to ask the question 'why are we collecting defect or time data' rather than 'what data should we collect?'

You may be tempted to put completely new systems in place, but take care. Developing completely new systems from the ground up for a large organization can be very costly. It is often easier to change something that already exists than to start from scratch.

At this point, you should be noting the type of information that is available, and relating this to the various requirements that you have identified. This will give you an indication of what is involved in satisfying those requirements and will help you to prioritize them. For example, it is easier to satisfy a requirement for information about productivity if you already have a reasonable, and please note the use of the word reasonable, effort recording system in place.

Identify storage, analysis and feedback requirements

Almost all requirements associated with a Software Metrics programme imply the need to store, analyse and feedback information. Taking a first stab at the scale of these tasks for each of the identified requirements is another way of determining what you will tackle in phase 1, what you will put off until phase 2, and the requirements you will do everything in your power never ever to tackle!

You need to ask questions like: 'how much data will I have to collect and from how many sources?' 'Are we talking about simple trend analysis on one independent variable or am I going to get involved in multilinear regression analysis on fifteen variables?' And if you are, then remember you will need a great deal of data and that will take time to collect. Is it really a good idea to do this during phase 1, when you need to demonstrate some quick results? Also consider: 'how many customers need to have information fed back, in what form and at what cost?' For example, if you are talking about senior management reporting, you will need to spend time ensuring that you present your results in a business-like and professional way, possibly using desk-top publishing facilities. Can you get a budget for this in phase 1, even assuming that you can get sufficient data to derive meaningful summaries?

Some people will argue that we are entering into the design stage, but we need to get some idea of what is involved in satisfying a requirement to be able to decide whether it will be satisfied immediately.

Consolidate requirements

Having got a good idea of what the requirements are, and what they may involve, you will need to pull it all together into a consolidated requirements specification.

The exact form of this will vary depending upon the culture of your organization, the profile of the Software Metrics project and your own personality. It may be that a structured, documented discussion session with your own manager, as the customer authority, will be sufficient, or you may need to prepare a full requirements specification document with, heaven help you, a cost benefit analysis that is supported by presentations at board level.

If at all possible, I would suggest that you aim for a middle ground. Going to the board of directors at this point can be dangerous, because you have really only identified the problems that need to be addressed. You do not have solutions. Simply talking things over with your manager means that the requirements may be subject to fairly dramatic changes, and this can cause serious problems later.

I would suggest that you group the various identified requirements into *goals*. For example, you may have the following set of identified requirements linked to specific customer groups:

- Improve cost estimation techniques for enhancement projects — Product Development Team Leaders;
- Improve cost estimates that feed into the planning process — Planning Manager;
- Sort out estimates (if we get hit by another fiasco like that last fixed-price contract, we won't need a metrics programme because we won't be here) — Systems Development Director.

With any luck, you have identified a common theme here. The goal or consolidated requirement becomes:

To improve the cost estimation process.

Alternatively, you may have identified requirements that go something like:

- We need some way to focus limited testing effort on the components that need testing most rigorously — Test and Integration Manager;
- We are discovering faults too late, we need to sort them out earlier — Software Development/Enhancement Manager;
- Our inspections are a joke. We need some objective criteria that will get rid of the subjectivity in deciding when a design is good enough — Senior Software Engineer;
- Why don't we use *information flow metrics* as we were taught at university? — Junior Software Engineer.

Now this one is a bit more difficult to consolidate, but it does illustrate that you should have talked to all the levels in the organization. What it boils down to is something like:

Identify and implement non-subjective techniques that can identify error-prone components at the inspection stage, or earlier, of the design phase.

You may also make a note to ask that junior engineer what these Information Flow metrics are.

A typical set of consolidated requirements, expressed very loosely, may look like this:

- Improve cost and size estimation;
- Improve project control procedures;
- Provide management information about performance, covering productivity and achieved quality;
- Address the prediction of quality attributes prior to release;
- Address the assessment of designs and requirements.

Of course, this may not be an exhaustive set, and each goal should be expressed more precisely, at least as precisely as the earlier examples. There may well be subgoals or requirements within the high-level expression, for example, management information about achieved quality may be confined to reliability and maintainability, or it may cover many more of the so called 'ities'.

You should also link each consolidated requirement to a set of primary and secondary customers. The primary customer will effectively be the individual, or functional group, that will decide whether or not you have satisfied the requirement. The secondary customers are those who have a view of what you deliver, and will be expected to provide information to help you satisfy the requirement. For example, the primary customer for productivity information may be the Product Group Manager, he or she being the person who has asked for that information. However, project managers and engineers are also customers, albeit secondary in this case, of the system that will be put in place to satisfy the primary customer's requirements. It is the project managers and the engineers who will have to supply the information that will eventually result in productivity reports to the Product Group Manager.

Specification review

Having consolidated the requirements, you will, of course, have them reviewed by your customer authority as a minimum. It is a good idea to present them to the Metrics Coordination Group as their approval will be useful later. At the very least, it means that the 'organization' has validated what you intend to do.

You have spent a considerable amount of time and effort ensuring that you know, and that the organization agrees that you know, what is required from the metrics programme. Now it is time to satisfy those requirements.

SUMMARY

This stage is all about finding out what the various parts of the organization want from a Software Metrics programme. It is about talking to people to derive these requirements and it is about establishing the foundation of an infrastructure that will be used by you, as the developer and implementor of that programme, as one vehicle for the successful satisfaction of those requirements. Finally, it is about communicating those requirements back to the organization, so that agreement about the objectives of the programme can be gained.

11

STAGE 3 — COMPONENT DESIGN

Let us recap the situation. We now know a lot more about Software Metrics than we did when we started work on the programme, we have obtained the authority to develop proposals for a metrics programme, we have identified a set of requirements against the programme linked to primary and secondary customers and we have some idea about what information the organization already collects.

You have also established a steering group, the Metrics Coordination Group. We may also have some ideas about how we intend to satisfy the various requirements we have identified. This is almost inevitable and is typical of the iteration and stage overlap that occurs in real life despite any lifecycle model that appears to impose sequential development. In fact, this overlap can be very useful as it allows us to feed back as well as forward to later stages in the development process. We must take care to control feedback, otherwise we can find that we proceed with work against a requirement only to have the requirement changed.

Control is really about baselining requirements with the agreement of the customer authority. This does not mean that a requirements change will never happen, but it does give visibility to those changes and allows their impact to be assessed. The very fact that change involves consultation and agreement to amend a baselined document often means that the need for the change is given more serious thought which, in turn, can limit the changes that occur. Like so many things, it is simply good practice and common sense.

I have called this stage 'design', and I see it as consisting of four main streams or sets of activities that will eventually come together and result in a design proposal. The first stream is the *definition of the metrics, tools and metrics-based techniques* that will form the core of our programme. Let me stress again that it is only now, after the information requirements have been defined, that we start to think about the metrics. Next we have what I call the *administration requirements*. This covers elements of the programme that are needed to use the metrics in a practical way. Another way of thinking of this is as designing the operational procedures and support mechanisms necessary for the implementation of a tactical approach. Examples of these elements include a metrics database and the data collection procedures that will be required.

The other two streams are, I believe, vital to the success of any metrics programme yet they are more to do with the organization and the people in that organization than with technical issues.

We need to consider the way the programme will be marketed and introduced to the business, so we will look at how to develop a *marketing and business plan*. It is interesting to note how often Software Metrics programmes become the responsibility of functional groups that are separate to the software development function. Effectively, the metrics team must act as internal consultants because they cannot, and indeed should not, impose their will on development teams. This implies that the metrics team must conduct itself in the same way that a small business or external consultants have to conduct themselves, namely in a professional and business-like way. I am afraid that we can have the best set of metrics ever devised, the most effective techniques for assisting development to produce high-quality software and control mechanisms that would make the harshest project coordinator smile, but if we do not market them effectively within the organization, they will never be taken up and used by the organization. This is a fact of life!

Finally, any initiative that is intended to change the way people think, act and work must address the *infrastructure* that will enable change. I found a classic case where this was not addressed in one organization which was striving to motivate its staff and to draw on their recognized ability to make things better themselves. So far so good. A huge publicity exercise was undertaken linked to a very expensive set of training courses that, together, raised people's expectancy in terms of their perception of the contribution they could make to their business. Again, so far so good. This programme had a budget of some five million pounds sterling over one financial year, so it was not a trivial exercise. And it worked! People became switched on to making the business more effective but there was a problem. One of the corner-stones of this initiative was that everyone in the business could, and indeed should, make a contribution, because the people best placed to improve things are often the ones who are already there. Unfortunately, there was no infrastructure put in place to enable this to happen. This was made painfully obvious when a secretary came to me with an idea that was beautiful in its simplicity, and that could have saved a considerable amount of money. The problem was we had no idea how to take that idea forward within the change initiative. The infrastructure had not been addressed. So, we will discuss the infrastructure necessary for a metrics programme.

I will talk about the various streams in turn, but do remember that the tasks they cover do have dependencies within the stream and on tasks within other streams. Figure 11.1 gives my interpretation of these dependencies.

However, before we talk about the four main streams, there is one set of activities that should be addressed, pilot projects.

PILOT PROJECTS

Pilot projects can occur for a number of reasons. It may be that, during the feasibility study stage, you have come across a metric-based technique that, for some reason, appears so elegant, so perfectly suited to what you know you want to do that you immediately see

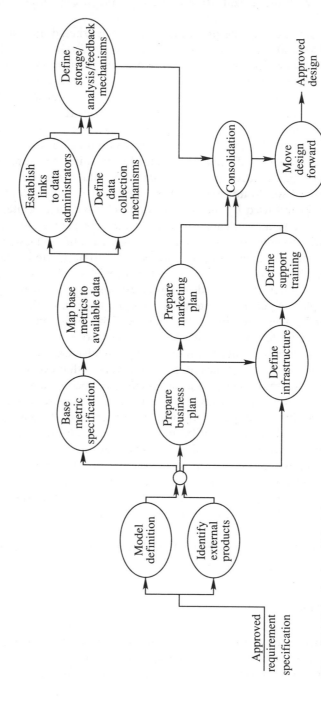

Figure 11.1 Dependencies within and among streams.

it forming part of your SMP. It may be that as you go through the design stage, you identify another metric that you wish to test out within your own environment or it may simply be that you wish to evaluate a set of tools, perhaps cost estimation packages, with a view to including one or two within the programme.

For any of these reasons, you may wish to run a pilot project at some point during the design stage. To be honest, pilot projects can be kicked off almost anytime, although it would make sense to know what requirement the pilot is supposed to satisfy before committing time and resources.

Pilots should be small, targeted and of as short a duration as possible. You should carefully consider the experimental design of your pilot to be sure that you can get the results for which you are aiming and, of course, that you are not guaranteeing the results by the design of your pilots! Experimental design is another specialism just like statistics. My feeling is that I know enough to know I need specialist help, and I try to check out the design of pilots with such a specialist, unless I have done such a pilot before. If you do not know anyone within your own organization who can help, and if you have an operational research group, I suggest it be your first port of call — then try the local educational facilities, colleges, polytechnics and universities. Academics can help in this area and usually charge consultancy at very reasonable rates. One day's consultancy could be money well spent.

Remember to review the results of your pilot, and to feed them into your design process. Very often, so-called pilots are nothing less than the first stage of implementation with no feedback loop in place to affect the design. This is fine if you are just playing word games to get things rolling, but you can find a genuine pilot becoming that implementation unless you specifically build that feedback loop. If you need convincing of this, see if you have any development teams using rapid prototyping as a development methodology. If you have, ask them how many prototypes they throw away.

Done right, pilots can provide a wealth of useful information, especially about the amount of effort that will be involved in the full-scale implementation of an aspect of a measurement initiative, and they can save considerable amounts of money. This is especially true of the pilot that appears to fail. In other words, when the results of the pilot is not what was hoped for — but is it not better to find out that something does not work in a contained, controlled experiment rather than twelve months down the line, when more money than necessary has been invested?

I would like to give two examples of pilots. In the first case, I was involved in the piloting of a specific sizing technique in a real time environment. By analysing historical data, we were able to determine that our use of the size measure in that specific environment did not work. By that, I mean that there was little correlation between size, as we were measuring it, and effort. It was much better to find this out at that point rather than to have started implementation of the sizing technique with all the training, development of storage mechanisms and the building of feedback loops that would have been involved. Such an exercise would have been costly, and would have resulted in a major embarassment if we had then found that there was no foundation for using the sizing technique.

The second pilot involved the use of a simple cost estimation strategy. By piloting the strategy within one part of the organization, we were able to develop a familiarity with the techniques involved and, most importantly, we were able to obtain in-house examples that demonstrated the successful use of those techniques.

So, bearing in mind that pilots can be taking place and feeding into the main design streams, we will now start to talk about those streams.

METRICS DEFINITION STREAM

At last, we get on to the core of the programme, the technical part, the difficult — but rewarding — part. Wrong! Let me try a bit of heresy, defining metrics for specific requirements is the easy part. Well, most of the time it is, although there are a couple of requirements that have stymied me in the past, but most of the time, the metrics are easy.

The difficult part is getting them in place, and in use, within the business. So, if it is as easy as I claim, how do we do it?

Model definition, or goals, questions, metrics

What I intend to do is discuss the derivation of metrics or measures, and then to support that discussion with a couple of examples. Remember where we are. You have identified requirements for information and metrics, based techniques linked to specific customer groupings.

These perhaps range from generalities such as 'improve the cost estimation process' to very specific requirements such as 'provide information to the Systems Development Director that quantifies the achieved productivity of all product development teams on a quarterly basis'. The related primary customers could be the project managers, because they are the people who are fed up with getting blamed for poor estimates, and the Systems Development Director respectively.

You have also been talking to people in the organization to derive these requirements, so you have a great asset available to you, personal contacts.

You have, in terms of Basili and Rombach's *goal, question, metric* (GQM) paradigm, (Rombach, 1990), the goals defined. You also have the means by which you can resolve the questions. Before you do this, do ensure that the goals you have identified are measurement goals. Individuals will often throw a general goal at you that is not suitable as a requirement within a metrics programme. For example, a manager may claim that his goal is to increase development productivity by 25 per cent within 2 years. Fine, as a strategic goal for that manager this is acceptable, but it does not help a metrics programme at all. Unfortunately, Software Metrics do not do manager's jobs for them, and they need to realize this. Acceptable measurement requirements within this manager's strategic goal may include, 'provide a mechanism by which the current and future productivity levels can be assessed', followed by 'provide metrics-based techniques that can reduce rework within development'.

This is not to say that measurement programmes will not include some direct benefits to the development process, but only some parts of a Software Metrics programme can do this. Examples include metrics-based techniques that can be used by engineers and managers on a day-by-day basis to improve intermediate or final deliverables directly and measurements which aim to identify the areas within generic products that are causing the majority of the problems, the idea being that these can be rewritten to reduce rework or testing effort. The other components of a measurement initiative, for example improving cost estimation and project control, or providing general management information, will not directly improve matters. What these components can do is enable managers to manage more effectively, and it is this which improves the process.

So be careful. Do not get forced into a situation where you have to shoulder what are essentially management responsibilities for development, you have quite enough to do just providing them with the tools they need to do their job.

Now, assuming that you have been careful about defining the requirements that have been placed against the metrics programme, we can move on to the next step in model definition, requirement classification.

Requirements classification

If we look at the various requirements you have identified, we will notice similarities between them. These similarities will enable you to classify your requirements into a small number of major categories. A typical set of such macro-requirements was given in the previous chapter and is reproduced below:

- Improve cost and size estimation;
- Improve project control procedures;
- Provide management information about performance, covering productivity and achieved quality;
- Address the prediction of quality attributes prior to release;
- Address the assessment of designs and requirements.

Generally speaking, the provision of information about achieved quality will be broken down into a number of specific 'ities'.

The reason for this grouping of requirements is to enable the satisfaction of as many individual requirements as possible in the shortest time. In almost every case that I have seen, the number of customers and individual requirements that a Software Metrics programme is expected to address far exceeds the available resources if those requirements are addressed individually. The only solution that appears to work effectively is to offer generic solutions to these requirements within the organization, which can be tailored to meet the needs of specific customers.

One question that this approach raises is related to the customer set that was identified earlier. What happens to these individuals and groups? Each customer who is linked to a generic or macro-requirement becomes a 'viewpoint authority' for that requirement.

To explain this concept, let us consider the case of cost estimation improvement. Various functional groups within the organization may have expressed this as a requirement, and these could include:

- Project managers who have to prepare estimates, and for now we will assume that this is one customer group currently using the same techniques and operating under the same constraints. While this is probably a simplification of reality, it still enables us to illustrate the point;
- Marketing who have to prepare bids for work;
- The Product Manager who wishes to see better estimation;
- The Systems Development Director who is fed up with other directors telling him that the department is costing money by failing to meet promises to customers;
- The external customers themselves.

Each of these groups has a vested interest in improving the cost estimation process and each will have input regarding the requirements for that improvement. It makes no sense at all to try to satisfy these individual requirements separately when a single, what we can call generic, solution will satisfy the majority. What we must realize is that each group will have a view of the requirement and the solution that is different to the other groups. In this sense, they all have a viewpoint on the requirement. We should also realize that each group may have subgroups within it and, to reconcile these, it is a good idea to identify or nominate a viewpoint authority. This individual is expected to express the needs of the group, and to represent its interests during the process of satisfying those requirements.

Now there may well be conflict between the various viewpoint authorities, and this can be resolved by identifying a customer authority, who is the individual with the final say in resolving such conflicts. The ideal candidate for the role of customer authority is the primary customer for the specific requirement solution you have already identified.

One other advantage that comes from requirements grouping is that we can more easily use other people's solutions. We already have the concept of tailoring solutions for the various viewpoints, but we can equally take an external solution, such as a cost estimation package that runs on a PC, and tailor its use for the organization. Requirements grouping helps because it makes the identification of external solutions easier.

Questions

Having carried out this requirements grouping, we can start to go through the question or modelling task of metrics definition.

Almost all requirements laid against a Software Metrics programme relate to attributes of the development process or its products. In fact, the recognition of this was a fundamental step forward in the use of Software Metrics. Current thinking seems to have added in attributes that also relate to *resources*. This is more a large subgroup of attributes within the process/product split, but such a view can be useful. We should not fall into the trap of thinking that this solves all our problems, or that this breakdown will automatically lead to metrics, it will not. Nor should we waste time trying to categorize metrics as product or process measures — it provides no added value.

What can be categorized is the requirement, but this is addressed by identifying the attribute of interest within that requirement, for example the productivity of the development process as a process-orientated requirement.

Now, for any attribute within a requirement, there are three items that need to be considered. The first is to determine what is meant by that attribute, in other words we will need to *define* the attribute. It may be that this has already been done when we were considering the set of initial definitions during the last stage but, if this has not been addressed, it is vital that it is done now. We need to be very clear about what is meant. The attributes that seem to typify the problem at the moment are 'maintainability', 'enhanceability' and 'extendibility'. Any of these apparently innocuous terms can be used by different people to refer to the same attribute, and individuals, including myself, will argue strongly for their own preference.

I am sure that the debate within the industry will continue for many years, and may never be resolved to the satisfaction of everyone, but we cannot afford to wait for such agreement. The approach I have adopted with a fair degree of success in the past is to define particular attributes within an organization. Even this can involve discussion and debate, but it is practical to drive definitions for attributes, perhaps agreed and endorsed by the Metrics Coordination Group, in a fairly short space of time.

As far as the various quality 'ities' are concerned, there is even a group working within the International Standards Organization (ISO) on a set of such definitions. The results of their work are currently documented in International Standard 9126, ref. IS 9126, and this can be used as the foundation for our own definitions.

Having defined the attribute, we must now realize that there are two areas of interest for such an attribute. First, we may wish to *monitor* or *assess* the attribute. Alternatively, we may wish to *apply prediction* to the attribute. An example will clarify the problem. Software system reliability is an attribute that concerns many organizations. Reliability can be defined as:

> A set of attributes that bear on the capability of software to maintain its level of performance under stated conditions for a stated period of time (IS 9126, 5 January 1990).

or my own definition, prepared before I had sight of the ISO definition:

> The capability of a software component to perform its functions to a level specified in the requirement, or defaulting to 100 per cent, within a given environment.

There may be a requirement in an organization to monitor the reliability of its software products in the field over time or across build releases. This information allows reducing reliability to be addressed before it becomes a disaster or, if reliability is increasing, it can be used to help market the revenue-earning products.

Most organizations are also interested in building reliability into their products. This implies that conditions that exist within designs, for example, have an effect on the reliability of the delivered product. So the organization may wish to measure the extent of coupling and cohesion to predict the field reliability. It may even be as simple as using faults discovered and corrected during testing as a prediction of the number of faults that will be discovered by users or customers.

The approaches used to satisfy these two demands are very different, and I suggest that you treat the 'monitoring' or 'assessment' and the 'prediction' of an attribute as separate requirements within the metrics programme.

By refining the requirements in this way, through attribute definition and determining whether you are required to monitor or predict, you will be able to identify the processes you need to consider and, hence, the process products to which you will apply measurement.

The next step is to derive a model that will satisfy the requirement. To do this, you need to identify what can be called the characteristics of the process or product that affect the attribute in which you are interested. Modelling by its very nature is a human activity and is, therefore, somewhat subjective. Again, the best advice I can give you is to talk to the people who are best placed to answer the question, 'what affects this attribute', in other words talk to the people who are involved in the process.

Identifying the characteristics of interest may cause you to do still more definition, for example, what is meant by size or complexity, but please remember to be pragmatic and to listen to what you are told. If you have doubts about presenting a definition, then call it a working definition. You are not looking for perfection, you are looking for something that will enable you to satisfy a real and important requirement.

Once you have obtained a set of characteristics, you can start to combine these in the form of a model. In this context, a model is a mathematical combination of characteristics resulting in a function for which the dependent variable provides information about the attribute of interest. The model can, and perhaps should, include a technique built around the analysis of that function.

As I have said, modelling is a human activity and also, by definition, includes an element of simplification. Do not try to form the 'perfect model' or you will be firmly on the road to frustration and despair. The metrics you end up with are unlikely to tell the whole story about any attribute, the question is do they give you more information than you have now, and is that information of practical use to the organization? This simplification may mean that you ignore some of the characteristics identified. Remember that simpler models are probably better than more complicated ones.

If you find that your models are not sufficiently sophisticated to be able to supply you with the information you require, perhaps because a characteristic is more important than you assumed, then change the model! Do not fall into the trap of believing that your models are perfect, or in some way 'right', just because you have spent time and effort developing them. The great power of models is that they can be incrementally developed and extended.

Deriving a metric from the model

Your model, or at least the component of the model that is a mathematical function, gives you the composite metric that you will use to measure a particular attribute. By looking at the components of the composite metric, you can identify the base metrics, the raw data, that you will need to collect in order to provide information about a particular attribute. All that remains is to implement the use of the base and composite metrics and then to assess the results. The implementation step is the difficult one.

So as you can see, deriving the metrics is easy! Well, perhaps you still have some doubts, so let us try it with a couple of examples.

Suppose that a product development team leader asks you for a single measure to monitor the performance of software development. I have phrased this 'to ask for a single measure, deliberately to simplify things,' as I wish to illustrate the modelling technique, not to provide you with a new metric. In fact, in this case we are going to end up with a very old metric. Such a requirement may come from a number of team leaders and similar requirements may also come from other customer groups, such as senior management, who wish to monitor performance across a number of teams. For the sake of illustration, I am going just to talk about this single requirement source, a manager responsible for a number of teams, although the steps and principles are the same as for other requirements.

This requirement can be classed as a business entity metric, because it relates to a number of projects for which the team has responsibility. All that this classification implies is that you can look at what other organizations are doing in the same area but, of course, to be able to see that, you need to have some idea of what that area is. You can also identify the customer authority and the viewpoints for this requirement. The prime candidate for the role of customer authority would seem to be the manager, as the request has come from him. Are there any other viewpoints in this rather simple example? There most certainly is at least one other viewpoint, the engineers who will be contributing to the measure. Depending on the size of the team, at least one viewpoint authority should be identified within the group. This individual will act as the spokesperson, although others should also be spoken to.

You now need to identify and define the attribute of interest. Development performance can be defined as:

'The effectiveness of carrying out software development activities within a given environment.'

Effectiveness can, in turn, be defined as the degree to which a desired effect is produced. An effect is anything brought about by a cause, a result. I think it is time to go and talk to your customer and viewpoint authorities.

You may well find that the result for which they are aiming is to deliver quality software at minimum cost. Discussion may also reveal that, of the two main elements within this target, they feel that quality is important, and that they are taking continuous steps to improve this, but what they actually want to show is that they are also improving their ability to reduce costs. This could lead to a refinement in requirement which may now become:

'Supply a single high-level indicator of development performance that describes the effectiveness of production.'

Now you are getting to the nub of the requirement We are talking about the effectiveness of production, and that sounds like productivity to me. Well, I did say it was going to be an old metric!

Productivity can be defined as *the degree to which economic value is produced.*

What we now have is an identified attribute, and a definition of what we mean by that attribute. Armed with this, we can start to look around the industry, and other industries to see how they measure 'productivity'. We can also go back and talk to the customer and viewpoint authorities again to ask the question, 'what is it that affects productivity, what do we put in and what do we get out?' In other words, what are the characteristics that affect productivity?

With many examples, there are two ways of answering this question about characteristics. One is to model them internally, the other is to find out what the 'state of the art' or 'accepted wisdom' is in other organizations and industries. For the purposes of this example, we will have a look at the first approach.

Productivity would seem to have two elements, 'what do we put in' and 'what do we get out' in terms of what does the software development process consume and what does it deliver? We put in people and time that we can call effort, equipment, managerial and organizational support covering matters like the personnel department, accommodation and travel. Of these cost elements, we will almost certainly find that the most significant is effort. We will also probably find that our accountants have techniques by which they can apportion the other cost elements down to effort costs to give a loaded salary for any individual or group. This simplifies things because we can, perhaps, just use the effort cost as the 'what do we put in' component of a productivity measure.

Now 'what do we get out' of software development? One way of looking at this is to say that we deliver a software system to the market, and what we get out is the revenue from that system. This is complicated in two ways: if the team is involved in enhancement engineering, then we may have problems determining the revenue from a particular build; and many of the factors that determine revenue are beyond the control of the software development function, falling instead to, for example, marketing. Remember that we wish to keep it as simple as possible, so take a look at the process for which software development does have responsibility. What is the product of that process? It would seem to be a software system including code, object or source, and documentation.

Now, what are the characteristics that contribute to what we get out? These could include the amount and detail of the documentation that is required; the size of the code and the complexity of that code. Talking to our engineers, we may find that the documentation is relatively standard across projects and, if this is the case, we may decide to factor out this element. What about the code? We have now got involved in looking at how we are going to combine our aspects, but this overlap between characteristic identification and combination often happens.

As far as the code is concerned, we may see the size of the system as being important and the complexity being equally important but, again, talking to the engineers and the team leaders may indicate that complexity between projects is fairly constant, especially in an enhancement situation. So in this case, can we simply use code size? We may decide to check this out by looking for a relationship between code size and development effort.

Time pressure, or more correctly varying time pressure, on projects is also seen as having a major impact on effort. If time pressure is applied, and the project must be completed by a very tight deadline then, providing scope or requirements are not reduced, the only variable that can be adjusted is effort. Despite the argument that says throwing effort at a problem will not reduce duration, the reality is that this is the only option available and that large projects can be delivered relatively quickly by using more staff. The point to remember is that the relationship is not linear, in other words if a project is required in half the time then we cannot simply double the team size, we may need to quadruple the size of the team and add further resources just to tackle the communication problem. We will probably pay for this approach to system development in terms of reduced productivity.

However, we will often find that the time pressure operating on projects is relatively constant within, and this is important, a single environment, for example a tool development group or a specific product group handling ongoing releases. Again, this effect can often be factored out. In this sense, we can justifiably simplify our productivity model.

Alternatively, we may look at what other organizations are doing and reach the same conclusion. Productivity is normally expressed as:

$$\text{Productivity} = \text{work product/product cost}$$

A ratio is used because we wish to compare 'what we get out' to 'what we put in'. Generally speaking, productivity within software development is expressed as:

$$\text{Productivity} = \text{project size/project effort}$$

This is your basic productivity model, and it is this that will be used to derive the composite and base metrics. Essentially, this means that you need to change the generalized model components, project size and effort, to specific, defined measures.

The obvious candidates for project size are lines of code or *function points*, really the unitless number that results from the application of *Function Point Analysis* to a requirement specification, high-level design or produced system.

Both of these measures can be defined in such a way as to cater for enhancement projects. For *lines of code*, you could consider the added, deleted and changed lines and the same principle can be applied to *Function Point Analysis*.

For effort you may choose engineering days, months or even years. Assume that you decide to use *lines of code* and engineering months as the components of your composite metric giving:

Productivity = lines of code/engineering months

You are almost there now. The base metrics or items of raw data that need to be collected almost drop out from this composite. There is one very important step that needs to be addressed. You have to define your base metrics in such a way as to make them meaningful, and their collection feasible, within your organization. This is true of almost every metric that you will use within the programme. Yet again, you will need to talk to the people who are or who will be involved in the programme to make sure that what you propose is practical, but once you have defined the base metrics, you have completed your metric derivation.

Well almost! You do need to ensure that what you have defined is practical, and this is another area where pilot exercises can be extremely useful. You also need to consider the analysis and feedback of the data you have collected. Do not fall into the trap of many metrics initiatives that end up with masses of data that is not being used by the organization. I will have more to say about these subjects later. You also have to consider the implementation of the processes that will facilitate the collection, analysis and feedback of data. Again we will address this topic later.

Let us try another example of the derivation technique. This time I will cut down the discussion to the bare bones. Our requirement is to provide information to senior management about the field quality of software products. Discussion indicates that our customer is the System Development Director, and he is interested in reliability as perceived by the customer. Reliability is seen as the key quality factor in this case. The requirement can be classified as a *business entity metric*.

The attribute, reliability, can be defined as before, *the capability of a software component* — in this case the delivered system within the population of products, *to perform its functions to a level specified in the requirement ... within a given environment.*

What are the characteristics that affect reliability? What is it about the product that we deliver that can affect reliability? Big systems tend to be less reliable than small ones, so product size could be considered; the complexity of the product may be important and the degree of use of the product could also be a possible attribute. Other possibilities include the time pressure applied to the development project; the degree of testing; the extent to which other verification and validation techniques were used; etc.

We also need to consider the product characteristics that indicate the level of reliability. An obvious candidate includes the time between failures, and please note that the traditional 'mean time between failures' may not be appropriate, as the use of a mean average depends upon the frequency distribution of time between failures. Another possibility is the number of system crashes over a given period of time, or the number of user raised faults. Notice that I am using faults here rather than defects. Bear in mind that the customer will raise defect reports, but that some of those defects will be duplicated or result from a lack of understanding of, say, the documentation.

This information itself can be important for other measures, for example for some usability measures, but I suggest that reliability is a function of the validated, non-duplicate defects, the faults detected by the user or customer.

Trying to combine all of these aspects would result in a very complex metric and, probably, a very frustrated metrics team member, so keep it simple. Talk to the managers and, if possible, to the users and pick on the most important aspects. I suggest that field reliability of a product can be modelled by:

$$\text{Product reliability} = \text{user detected faults}/(\text{product size} \times \text{usage})$$

What this model says is that quality or reliability is a function of the validated 'pain' being suffered by the customer to the extent that he or she will complain about it, and how big the product is, which I include so that I can make more meaningful comparisons between products and the degree to which that product is used. This may work for a single product, but the requirement is for a business entity metric that will be used by a senior manager. To meet this requirement, I suggest that an average *product reliability* be derived from a sample of product reliability figures taken over a period of months. The type of average depends on the frequency distribution. For a normal or Gaussian distribution, the mean average is the most appropriate but, for skewed distributions, median or mode averages are more appropriate. I strongly suggest that you talk to a statistician about this or at least consult statistical text books. Both sources of information can explain the reasons for this more ably than I can.

You now have your model and some components of your composite metric. I can live with user detected faults in my composite, I can define product size as *lines of code*, and usage as the number of sites on which we support the product. So my composite metric becomes:

Reliability is the average of the product reliabilities for a sample at a given time where product reliability is defined as:

$$\text{Product reliability} = \text{user detected faults}/(\text{product lines of code} \times \text{sites supported})$$

To get our base metrics, we have to define the components of field reliability in more concrete terms. In this case, I am tempted simply to amend the definitions to say that user-detected faults are accumulated over a three-month period while the other two components are 'snapshots' at the end of the three-month period.

And that is it! At this point I reach for my tin hat. Whenever we define a metric to meet a specific requirement, we can guarantee that someone, somewhere will try to shoot it full of holes. There are various reasons for this, some valid, some not so valid. Nobody with any sense would claim that any of the metrics outlined above are perfect.

I claim that they satisfy the requirements in a pragmatic way but, in all honesty, I cannot say that the field reliability measure tells me everything I want to know about the attribute. It cannot, because I have identified many characteristics that contribute to or affect field reliability, and then I have ignored some! There may be good reasons for this. For example, I may feel that I have no way of assessing the complexity of the product at the full system level. What should I do? Should I devote possibly a great deal of time trying to solve the problem of system complexity before I provide a metric, or should I be satisfied with a coarser measure that gives me a reasonable indication of field reliability?

Look at who the customer is. Will a senior manager be interested in every nuance, every aspect of the attribute? I suggest not. A senior manager requires an indication of reliability levels so that trends can be identified and, possibly, so that meaningful targets can be set. Will they be meaningful? Well, remember that you have not done this in isolation. You have been talking to engineers and project managers while you have been deriving the measures, so some degree of acceptance should be present. If you aim for perfection, you will not hit the target for many years. Satisfying the requirement is what you should aim for, and you should do this as quickly and simply as possible. Some claim that this is perfection anyway.

Now there may be valid reasons for people taking pot shots at the metrics. It may be that you have got it wrong or that you have, at least, not covered all the bases. In the case of field reliability, you are talking about faults rather than defects but, when a customer raises a defect, you may not know if it is a duplicate, or an invalid defect, or an indication of a true fault. In some ways, this is an implementation problem, but it should be given some consideration now. If you define user-detected faults to be the sum of all non-duplicated and validated defect reports raised and closed during a particular period of time together with all reports raised, but still open, you will have some that should not have been included, because they will turn out to be duplicates or invalid. You may feel that this is more acceptable than simply ignoring the open defects, because you may have some clever individuals who realize that, by never closing defect reports, they improve reliability. This is not going to please the customer. So, if you go for the first option, try it out for a couple of months to see how many of the defects actually turn out to be 'no fault' or duplicated reports. I suggest that the number will be insignificant, especially as you may be able to spot the duplicates as they are raised.

Other criticisms may be more fundamental or important. Listen! If they are valid criticisms then change the model and the metrics, but do watch out for the constant critics who will never be satisfied.

So, to summarize the steps in metric derivation as I have done it on many occasions and relating that to the GQM paradigm (Rombach, 1990), on which my approach is firmly based, the steps are as follows.

- *Goals:* Identify the initial requirement and associated customers. Refine this to a specific requirement with an identified customer set. Classify the requirement within the high-level requirements of the metrics programme.
- *Questions:* Identify the attribute that requirement addresses. Define the attribute. Find out what others are doing. Identify characteristics of the product or process that contribute or affect the attribute of interest. Derive a model by combining characteristics or through the adoption of a technique.
- *Metrics:* From the model, derive a composite metric by associating measurement units or scales with the characteristics in that model. From these scales, identify the base metrics that will need to be collected.

Then all you have to do is implement the metric. Now that is the hard part, but we will talk about that later.

Identify external products

I have used a model or technique for deriving metrics, but there is no point in reinventing the wheel. You will come across situations where there are already proprietary products available on the open market, or techniques in the public domain that you can adopt — thus circumventing the derivation process. This means that you can move on to implementing the use of those products or techniques very quickly.

This does not mean that no work will be required. You will find that many of these products and techniques need to be adapted to your own environment, but much of the hard work has been done for you. To relate the approach I have already discussed to the case where external products exist I will now consider the application of the derivation model to this process of importing products and techniques.

By far the biggest market offering in terms of proprietary products is in the area of cost estimation, so I will use these to illustrate the mechanism. Elsewhere I have discussed various software tools, and it is sufficient to say here that the list is large with new packages being added, it seems, every week. I have also discussed the value, in my view, that these products can offer, so I will confine myself to talking about the process of satisfying requirements within your own metrics initiative.

Essentially, the 'goals' step of the model needs to be addressed as before. You still need an identified requirement and an identified customer, and you should classify the requirement within the high-level metrics programme requirements. You may also find constraints creeping into your requirements. For example, you may be constrained to using PC-based software.

It is in the 'questions' area that the most significant difference is seen. What is needed is for you to investigate the market place to see what is on offer. Only you will be able to decide which of the many tools is best suited to your needs, given your requirements, any constraints and the persuasiveness of the salesman. One thing I would strongly recommend is that you get a feel for the product through hands-on experience. This is the only way that you can tell if the tool is easy to use and suitable. Ideally, you should carry out a full evaluation using historical data and comparing the results with the predictions from the tool, but this can be difficult, not least because much of the information you need may not be available. If it was, you might not need a Software Metrics programme.

The tools will tell you what information they require as input, and these are obviously the base metrics you need to collect. Another word of warning. Many of these tools ask for a great deal of information, but supplying all of these inputs can sometimes distort the accuracy of the predictions. Look instead for the key 'cost drivers' that affect the model by playing with the tool and also determine, again by talking to the people who know, the project managers and engineers, what the important drivers are.

Having made your selection, all you need do is implement the use. Yes, the hard part again!

You can also modify the derivation model to apply it to the selection of 'public domain' metrics. These include things like most variants of *Function Point Analysis*, McCabe metrics and *information flow* metrics. Many of these come complete with analysis techniques or guidelines for use, and some, such as the McCabe metrics, are also supported by proprietary products.

Again, you need to go through the 'goals' step of the derivation model, and you need to research the market to see what is on offer. A good way of doing this is to attend some of the training courses that cover the theory of metrics, and more and more of these are being staged, or you can attend some of the metrics conferences that are now regular events.

Once you have gone through the 'goals' step and identified a market offering, you are in the position of having brought in a model. Then you simply apply the derivation model in the same way as I have outlined above up to the determination of the base metrics which you need to collect.

Please remember that most 'public domain' metrics and models tend to be orientated towards code or low level designs, although the researchers are starting to push back along the development lifecycle to higher levels of design.

ADMINISTRATION DESIGN STREAM

Having defined a set of metrics, tools and metrics-based techniques that you believe will satisfy the specific requirements placed on *your* metrics programme, *we* now have to consider the more mundane, but very important, areas of collection, storage, analysis and feedback.

Mapping base metrics to available data

Defining the metrics and identifying the tools to support, say, cost estimation means that we have defined a set of base metrics and this raw data needs to be collected. Of course, we do not want to reinvent the wheel, so it makes sense if possible to use data that is already collected by the organization.

This has two distinct benefits. Firstly, it reduces the amount of work that has to be done as we do not need to design the collection system from the ground up and, secondly, it means that we reduce the amount of additional work that the data suppliers, often the engineers, have to do. This is always a good idea, because any time spent filling in data sheets is time that could have been spent on system development.

There are some problems and disadvantages in using existing mechanisms and these should not be ignored. Very often the data supplied will not be exactly what we want. For example, if you have a defect reporting system, it may not record the root cause of the defect. In this case, you are going to need management commitment to enable you to change the existing system to record that data element, but this is much less of a commitment, because of a lower cost, than that required for the development and implementation of a completely new system.

Another serious problem with existing systems is that they are often viewed as part of the unavoidable bureaucracy associated with, or perhaps more correctly hindering, 'real' work. This often means that very little care is taken over filling in the 'form' and that the data is then incorrect. The classic example of this is time-sheets, but it is often seen in defect reporting systems. In this case, the system may record the root cause of the defect, perhaps in terms of the development lifecycle stage that injected the fault, but the field that records this may be filled in with the lifecycle stage where the fix was made. After all, why worry about it, nobody does anything with the data.

As mentioned earlier, I have seen cases where defect reports have been reanalysed and I have seen the percentage split between code defects and earlier lifecycle stages change dramatically. The problem was that engineers were fixing the fault by changing the code, so that was what went into the 'cause' field — never mind that the design or the requirement specification was wrong.

If the problem with an existing system is that the specific data we require is not there, then the obvious answer is to change the system so that it will supply the required item. This is often the best option. Another option is to change the requirement on the existing system. Often there is another data item available that can almost give us what we want or, alternatively, there is another system or method by which we can obtain the data. For example, an organization with which I was involved was looking for a way of measuring software product size. The first choice was to use a tightly defined *line of code* count, but we found that this data was generally unavailable, strange as that may sound. What was available was a measure of memory required by the system, and investigation showed that there was a reasonable relationship between this and *line of code* size. Not a perfect solution by any means, but a pragmatic one given the particular circumstances.

This idea of changing the requirement can be taken one step further. Suppose we are looking for base metric data because we have identified a model-based, composite metric that will give us useful information. We could always change the composite metric or the model if the raw data is not available. This does require us to be very objective about our measures, but it is an option and should be considered. After all, these measures are not cast in stone.

If the data is being supplied, but is inaccurate, we have to deal with a more fundamental problem. We could just accept the data. From a theoretical point of view, this is not a sound approach, but it can be valid in some cases. If we consider the situation where an individual is booking time to two projects, we may not get accurate data. He or she may book more time to one project during one week based on nothing more than a guess. Rather than spending time trying to impose accuracy, we may just assume that if more time is booked to one project this week, then the reverse will be true next week, or the week after, so things will even out. Not very accurate, but it could be acceptable if coarse measures are required.

Of course, we will eventually have to bite the bullet and try to improve the accuracy of recorded data. I have more to say on this topic elsewhere.

Establish links to data administrators

Once we know, in detail, the kind of information that is available, we will need to form a link to the people who are responsible for administering the data collection systems that exist within the organization.

Obviously, you may already have been talking to these people as part of previous tasks, but this now needs to be formalized. You should document your requirements of them and have them formally agree to those requirements. There seem to be two extreme reactions to such a request for data. On the one hand, you may be seen as a major inconvenience. Some data administrators do seem to take the view that life would be wonderful if only they did not have to put up with users! Remember, it is their system and you want something from them, so be polite, be diplomatic, but be prepared to use any clout you have if necessary. On the other hand, you may find that the administrator goes into paroxysms of joy at the thought of somebody actually using the data that he or she collects and analyses. If this does happen, then build on it, do not destroy it with comments like:

'well, you obviously need some help on this!' You may laugh, but I have seen potentially fruitful relationships destroyed by a single such comment.

Above all, be generous with acknowledgement and thanks. If they help you, then say so, publicly and often!

Define data collection mechanisms

Before you even think about going live with your programme, try to have as many of the bases covered as possible. It is very tempting to instruct a project team to supply you with effort, defect and size data without spelling out how to do it.

Remember, these people are software developers. That is what they are paid to do and that is what the organization wants them to do. If you want them to do something, then help them to do it as much as you possibly can. You should define forms, with their input of course, you should tell them how often they should forward information and you should design the analysis techniques. At the very least, this means that you get a measure of consistency. It can also mean the difference between a programme that works and a programme that fails. It does not mean that you should do this definition task in isolation. On the contrary, you want them to be involved and to accept what is given to them, but do help them as much as you can.

Design storage, analysis and feedback mechanisms

Having determined where and how you are going to get your raw data, it does help if you have somewhere to put it.

Storage

Do not fall into the trap of waiting until the data starts streaming in, in the hope that you will sort it out then. You have your high-level programme requirements, you have your composite metrics and you have your base metrics definitions. These all act as inputs to the process of designing and implementing your metrics database.

Now the database may be something as simple as a spreadsheet or a personal computer (PC) database, or it can be as complex as a corporate wide Management Information System (MIS). It can be constrained by existing systems that are used by management, or it may be an area that has never been addressed by your organization. If circumstances allow, there are strong arguments for keeping the first implementation of your metrics database simple. For one thing, you will be feeling your way and, with the best will in the world, you are unlikely to get it perfectly correct first time around.

My advice is to treat the first implementation of this database as a prototype, and to use a simple spreadsheet or database application as the initial platform.

I know of one organization where a senior management decision has been taken to bring a large number of disparate, internal MIS systems together under a single system. Tempting as it is to consider this approach, it is educational to learn that the initiative is planned over 20 years, and has an engineering head count that peaks in hundreds!

The system with which you end up will depend heavily on the scope of your own metrics initiative. As I have just said, my own preferred approach is to use a form of prototype. If you adopt a phased approach to the implementation of your metrics programme, you may well be able to build a metrics database within a PC quickly and easily using resources from within the metrics team. Operating that system gives you the opportunity to learn, and then to modify, the system with relatively little cost or public loss of face. As the metrics programme expands, you can migrate the database to a larger platform within the overall MIS strategy of your organization using the operational prototype as a major input to the development of the eventual system.

Analysis and feedback

As far as analysis and feedback are concerned, you will have a problem. The specifics of your analysis may depend upon the data that you get in. For example, whether you use means or medians as the 'average' will depend upon the distribution of your observed values. While this kind of detailed question cannot be answered at this time, although you can make some educated guesses since data from software development of products is seldom 'normally' distributed, you should consider the type of analysis you will be performing. Incidentally, if the data is normally distributed, then the mean equals the median equals the mode anyway.

Within your programme design, you should consider the frequency of reports, the target audience and the style of the reports. You should also aim to store and analyse information that can be used to show the effectiveness of the programme itself. For example, if one of the high-level programme requirements is to improve the effectiveness of software estimation, then it makes sense to record and store estimates within projects and the actuals against those projects. This enables you to demonstrate the effectiveness of the programme over time.

This book is not about database design, and a great deal has been written elsewhere about this subject. I suggest that information on that subject be obtained from a better source than myself, and you should use expertise internal to your organization as a first port of call. Another subject that has had a great deal of attention over the years is the representation of information. Interestingly, most organizations totally ignore this advice.

Organizations seem to have a preferred style of graph that they feel happy with. In some, there are histograms or bar charts everywhere; in others there is hardly ever a bar chart, but there are pie charts in abundance. This is a great shame, because the different styles of pictorial or graphical representation have different purposes and are suited to different requirements.

For example, if you want to show information changing over time, you should not use a series of pie charts. It is much more effective to use a simple XY graph, perhaps with an associated rolling average.

Another major mistake is to send a senior manager a matrix of raw data. I have seen so-called reports that consist of nothing more than page after page of figures. Managers do not have time to wade through all this information, and if you want to get a point across — then get the point across — not the data.

Of course, some people go to the other extreme. No raw data is presented, but either lots of graphs suddenly land on the manager's desk or, even worse, a couple of graphs covered in bars, lines and with small tables stuck in corners. The poor manager does not know what is being said and, if the choice has been to go for lots of graphs, cannot remember what was shown on the first page when he gets to page 10, or 20 or 30. You may feel I am exaggerating, but these are real examples of reports presented to managers.

Of course, at this stage of your project, you cannot expect to design your feedback mechanisms in fine detail, but you should determine the style of your reports and, based on the metrics you will be using, you will be able to plan the type of graphical representation best suited to your requirements for information. If in doubt, ask an expert, a statistician.

My own choice for style of presentation is to mix words with simple graphs. This recognizes the fact that some people prefer to see pictures, while others prefer text. It also means that you can forge links between different sections of a report, perhaps linking productivity to your quality indicators.

You should also remember your engineers. They have supplied you with information. Can you give them anything back that they could use? If not, then can you give them information, so that they at least realize that the effort they put into giving you data is actually being used by the organization.

One way to do this is through a quarterly news sheet to all the teams contributing to the metrics programme. It is amazing how well disposed towards a metrics initiative this can make people feel.

MARKETING AND BUSINESS PLANNING STREAM

These are key non-technical areas within a metrics programme. Ignore them at your peril.

Prepare a business plan

Most organizations are large and complex beasts. Once you have gathered in the requirements for your programme, and designed specific components to satisfy those requirements, whether this involves deriving particular metrics or adopting techniques to help with, say, cost estimation, you will still have to implement the use of those components.

We have already looked at phasing within the metrics programme, and it is easy to understand how you may have to address certain requirements immediately, while others are left on the shelf until phase two or three. We also briefly mentioned the other aspect of phasing, the phased implementation across the business. This is important because of the situation outlined below, and the fact that you will probably be operating with limited resources.

It is very easy to fall into the trap of thinking that your work is complete with the issuing of instructions or standards. Please do not think that this is enough.

People need help to change. They may wish to adopt the ideas and concepts that you put forward, but they will almost certainly run into problems trying to turn the concepts into a reality, and they will need support to do this. I have come across examples of this in the areas of metrics, CASE technology and the introduction of Fagan inspections. All of these aim to improve the business efficiency of a software development organization, and all of them have the real capability of achieving this goal, but so often they fail to deliver the goods because the support function is underfunded. For evidence of the importance of the support function, I would suggest you read of the experiences of the Hughes Aircraft Software Engineering Division (Humphrey *et al.*, 1991).

If you accept the necessity for support during implementation, and this can be as little as visiting a development team once a month to check on how things are going and to, let us say, keep the plate spinning, then I suggest you do a number of things.

Support during metrics implementation

Build into your design the concept of support during the early stages of implementation. Based on experience, I believe it takes about 30 days of external support per development team to get a metrics programme up and running within that team. This does assume that the team is adopting a number of components within the Software Metrics programme. It is obviously less if you are simply, say, introducing productivity measurement.

If your organization agrees that a support team will exist for metrics implementation, then a good way of building this support strategy into the design is to treat each development, or support, team as an account or client. Within the team, you should identify a customer authority, preferably the team leader, and a facilitator. The facilitator acts as the local person on the ground who ensures that processes are put in place, data is collected and problems are identified.

The local customer authority manages the implementation of metrics within the team. It is also a good idea to draw up a contract or service level agreement between the metrics support group and the team. In this case, the metrics support group is servicing the team, but there is also an element of service from the team to the support group. The contract or service level agreement should clearly state what will be provided by each party and when it will be provided. A real life example of such a document is given below, although the names have been changed to protect the innocent. Note that the contract does not require a formal signature to work, but it does no harm at all if you *can* get it.

Service Level Agreement — Metrics Support Group and Alpha Team
As Agreed 20.11.90

1 Introduction
This document sets out the agreed level of support that will be provided to Alpha Team by the Metrics Support Group relating to Alpha Team's involvement in the metrics programme.

This Service Level Agreement (SLA) covers Alpha Team's involvement in the four components of the metrics programme, Estimation, Applied Design Metrics, Local Project Control and Management Information together with the Process Definition activities.

2 Staffing

Metrics Support Group facilitator:	Paul Goodman.
Alpha Team Customer Authority:	A N Other.
Alpha Team facilitator:	J Doe (up to 50 per cent of his time will be allowed for metrics-related activities over the next 12 months).

Viewpoint Authorities:

Estimation:	A N Other
Applied Design Metrics:	To be decided
Local Project Control:	J Smith
Management Information:	A N Other
Process Definition:	J Smith

Note that this is a large team, so I have introduced the idea of local viewpoint authorities to spread the work, and the enthusiasm across the group. I also apologize to anyone with the surnames Other, Smith or Doe!

3 Estimation

Metrics Support Group will provide:

A one-day training course on 12 December 1990.
Six days on-site support to assist in setting up Delphi sessions and the use of other estimation techniques. The dates of this support are to be agreed, but will be provided during the period January–April 1991.
Bureaux service providing off-site access to the CHECKMARK and GECOMO PLUS estimation tools.

Alpha Team will provide:

General administration for the one-day training course including organizing attendance by Alpha Team staff, provision of training room, OHP, white board and flip-chart.

4 Applied Design Metrics

To be decided.

5 Local Project Control

Metrics Support Group will provide:

A draft proposal document covering the recommended monitoring technique for submission to Alpha Team management, after modification by Alpha Team staff.*
A half-day discussion session with J Smith and other interested parties to provide sufficient information for them to set up a project control system. This is scheduled for 20 November.*
Two further half-day on-site sessions with Alpha Team to address any problems that may arise. These will be provided during January–February 1991 depending on the current Alpha Team workload.

Alpha Team will provide:

Resources from J Smith's area to establish and administer the monitoring technique.

6 Management Information

Metrics Support Group will provide:

The Software Metrics Standards together with any updates.*
One day of on-site support to discuss data collection, storage, analysis and feedback. This is scheduled for 8 January.
Further on-site support at one day per calendar month during February–June.

Alpha Team will provide:

J Doe to act as the local metrics coordinator. His role will be to establish the mechanisms for collection, storage, analysis and feedback.

The metrics that have been targeted for initial use are:

Workarea Reliability Measure   Group Reliability Measure
Local Correctness Measure   Maintainability Measure
Development Productivity Measure

7 Process Definition

Metrics Support Group will provide:

Up to two days on-site assistance to derive a DFD representation of Alpha Team's current development process. These days are scheduled for 14 and 22 of January.
A further one day is scheduled for 30 January when the derived model will be presented to various Alpha Team staff. J Smith will carry out the actual presentation.

Alpha Team will provide:

The resources outlined above.

* Already provided to date.

Notice the way in which specific responsibilities are allocated to individuals and the use of dates. As well as documenting what will be done when, this document is also a useful way of focusing the team's involvement in the programme. Basically, the team members can see what they are getting into!

Notice also that one component of the programme has been held back. In this case, it was felt that we had enough to be getting on with but, as it turned out, the development team did do a great deal of work on the Applied Design Metrics (ADM) component before it was formally adopted.

It is good to build this concept of support into your programme, but you do need to be sure that you can supply that support, so you will need to do certain other things. Look at the resources you have available, then look at the number of teams within the organization that you have to support. At this point, you should realize that other functional groups not directly involved in development may also require support.

For example, your project control office, the marketing group and the testing teams. In fact, all of your customer groupings should be treated as potential accounts with their own contract-covering implementation.

If my model is correct, one person working flat out can only support six startup accounts, allowing some time for holidays and for administration during a full financial year. Such a situation will almost certainly force you to adopt a phased implementation, and this should be reflected in your business plan. The plan should state how many teams will be addressed during each future financial year, and should express the percentage impact of the metrics programme across the organization year by year. Not only does this quantify how resources within the support group will be used, but it also gives you clearly defined targets and shows that you are approaching the implementation in a businesslike manner.

Of course, your programme may be structured in such a way as to work from the top down. It may be that you are introducing measurement initiatives across the whole organization and, in this case, your phases will concentrate more on the requirements that are being met rather than the penetration you are achieving year by year. This should also be expressed by your business plan, which will form a corner-stone of your presentation to senior management when you seek approval to proceed.

Prepare a marketing plan

We have already discussed the importance of publicity but, as you move rapidly towards implementation of the programme, this becomes vital.

You have to consider two things:

1. You need to launch the implementation phase of the programme. How will you do this in such a way as to achieve the necessary visibility and impetus? One possibility is to go 'on the road'. Perhaps a roadshow approach will work in your organization. You may consider a senior management presentation, both to seek approval to proceed, but also to act as the launch platform. The in-house magazines could be used, especially if you have been using them as a vehicle for publicity during the metrics programme development stages. Exactly how you launch the programme will depend on the culture of your organization, but please try to make it an event. Get people to notice it.

2. You will need to consider ongoing publicity for the programme targeted at both the organization in general and the participants. It is very easy to ignore this aspect of the programme believing that you can sort it out at the time, or that people 'should' be aware of what you are doing. Think about it! Do *you* know what is going on everywhere in the organization, because I certainly have never managed that feat. Planning how you will publicize the programme pays dividends in that you can plan the work involved, and this is important if you are to keep control of the programme. You can use all the vehicles we have talked about already, but I would thoroughly recommend the use of a short, periodic news-sheet for participating teams, which should also be circulated to senior managers. After all, you want them to get involved as well.

Interest and awareness needs to be turned into commitment and involvement. If you are taking a phased approach to implementation, you will need to get teams to sign up to the programme, because you will not be able to force adoption of the initiative.

There are, generally, four ways of getting groups to do what you want them to do. These four approaches are telling, selling, participating and delegating. Which approach you use depends upon the maturity of the group with which you have to interact. It would be nice to think that you could delegate the implementation of Software Metrics to the organization in general, but this is unlikely to be effective. Most organizations and groups within them operate best in a selling or participating mode, but you will often find that you first have to sell the initiative before you can be sure of participation.

So, how will you sell them the idea of measurement? By this I do not mean the technicalities of the sales pitch, but the approach you will use. I have found that the best way to deal with this is in three stages.

1. You identify a potential client. This can be done through the Metrics Coordination Group. After all, you have been working with these people for a while now and you should be aware of who the champions are, the individuals who are more keen than others. Why not target their teams first? You may also have been involved with specific teams during pilots. Do they want to carry on their involvement?
2. Having identified the potential clients, you need to use someone on the inside to get you in. Wherever possible, I use the manager who is keen to set up a meeting where I, as an external to the group — whether I am an internal or external consultant as far as the organization is concerned — come along and make a sales pitch to the management group of the team. To do this, I would use a presentation that first explains what Software Metrics are, and that provides examples of benefits realized by other organizations. As the programme develops, you can replace external examples with home-grown cases which carry much more weight.

    Very often the management group will have questions, and you need to be light on your feet to deal with these. It is very easy to get drawn into some of the office games people play in this situation, so I tend to stress the fact that the programme should be tailored to their own specific needs while still maintaining an overall conformity to the high-level requirements of the organization.

    For example, I tend to go in with about twelve management metrics that the team could adopt, but I only ever expect four or five of these to be picked up initially. Which four or five depends on the team. Nor do I go through all of the metrics at this point. Usually, I find that about 50 per cent of the audience is supportive, 30 per cent ambivalent and about 20 per cent dismissive. On a bad day, that 20 per cent could be vocally hostile. Make sure you have an idea as to who the likely champions are and who the stickers are. I reckon that such a presentation has been successful if I can get the group to agree to a second, much less formal session a week or so later. If they agree to sign up right away, then fine, but do not expect that to happen too often.

3. I tend to let the team members drive the second session, which is the final stage of sales pitch. I concentrate on answering questions in a way that makes them realize their ability to influence the programme, and I try not to dodge important issues or questions to which I do not have the answers. Being honest pays dividends provided you also come across in a positive manner. At some point during this session, I ask them if they want to sign up. Assuming the answer is *yes*, I try to get them to appoint a local customer authority and, if things have gone well, a local facilitator with effort allocated at some ballpark level. If things have gone really well, the mode of operation has changed from a sales pitch by me to joint participation in the programme. Of course, each client is different, but the use of a standardized approach means that you can concentrate on catering for those differences effectively.

All of this implies that you plan how you will sell your metrics initiative to your clients. This plan, together with plans covering ongoing publicity to the organization and feedback to participants, forms the marketing plan. Remember, if you fail to market, you will fail to sell, and you will need to sell unless you tell. Telling takes power, and never really works for metrics programmes anyway.

INFRASTRUCTURE DESIGN STREAM

Define the infrastructure

Imagine the situation; the metrics team have spent months sorting out the requirements, they have derived metrics and evaluated products such as cost estimation tools, and they have built up an awareness in the organization about Software Metrics. What happens next? Obviously, they will write a report and perhaps they will issue 'standards' explaining their metrics and how they should be used. All they have to do now is to sit back and wait for it all to happen. One year later they are still waiting!

I will say it again, generally people need help to change. Even with the best will in the world, they will revert to their normal way of working unless there is someone around to facilitate and support change. This does not just apply to SMPs. I have seen very expensive kit running CASE design tools that have been used simply as a drawing package because support was lacking.

If you need convincing that standards are rarely used in the full sense, then take a walk around your development area and ask to see the development process manual. Assuming the person you ask even knows where it is, you may like to wonder why it is in such pristine condition. Do you really think that it is because everyone knows it inside out?

Once we accept that we need to support the process of change we have to consider how that support should be provided. There are a number of options, and I will discuss some of these now.

A centralized group

An obvious choice is to retain the team that has developed your metrics programme. They assume the responsibility for implementing the programme.

The main advantage with this approach is that you do have, and can continue to develop, a centre of expertise within the organization. A centralized group can also act as a focus for the initiative ensuring that there is a single point in the organization responsible for implementation, who can ensure coordination across different groups. After all, it makes little sense for one group to measure reliability by defects per thousand lines of code, while another uses mean time to failure!

However, there are two major disadvantages with this scenario. Firstly, the group may well be external to the software development process. Ownership of the metrics initiative by those responsible for software development is very important and this approach can generate a response along the lines of 'not invented here, so it's not for us'. Secondly, if your organization is large in terms of the number of development teams, a centralized group can find it difficult to provide adequate support to all those involved. Phasing obviously helps, but this can slow down the implementation process to an unacceptable level.

Development teams

A second option is to use a centralized group to develop expertise quickly within a small number of development teams, and then to let these new experts spread the gospel to the others. This approach is very attractive to management as it costs very little. In fact, it would seem that you get the implementation for free. Believe me, there is no such thing as a free lunch.

This approach seldom works without the continued support of a central group and, unless the support is carefully planned, it often becomes engaged in fire-fighting, which demoralizes the central team, because the members know they should be out of it by now, and it demoralizes the development teams, because they never get the level of support they believe they need.

The reasons why this approach has so many problems are complex. You must remember that any metrics initiative has many customer groups within the organization, not just the development teams. This means that a large number of groups and individuals with differing requirements need to be supported. This requires some form of central coordination or you get anarchy, or worse apathy. Also, if one area does develop a level of expertise, how can you ensure that expertise is made available to other areas? Remember, there will be a great deal of pressure on individuals with expertise to get on with their real work, because metrics will almost certainly, in this scenario, be seen as an extra, lower priority task.

So how can you put in an infrastructure that will work? Let me outline an approach I believe will work for most large organizations, perhaps with some modification to suit your own specific structure. I will use the model organization described previously as the basis for this discussion.

Model for installation of infrastructure

Your starting position is this: you have a metrics programme development team in place, even if this is only one person; you have a development customer authority and, hopefully, you have a Metrics Coordination Group or the equivalent. I suggest that you should establish a centralized support group, and the obvious choice for this is to staff it from within the development team. After all, these people have spent time developing exactly the kind of metrics-related technical knowledge that will be needed. How large a group will be needed depends on the size of the organization it will service, the scope of the programme it will help implement and the speed at which the organization wishes to implement the programme. This group can also take on responsibility for the ongoing development and extension of the metrics programme. Remember, that you may need to do some centralized analysis and feedback of results. More junior staff can be used for this provided they operate with guidance from the central group.

You will also need a customer authority for the implementation. This could be the same individual who has filled the role of development customer authority, or it may make sense to target another person in the organization. The customer authority should be as senior a manager as possible provided that you can still ensure involvement. Remember, you are only designing the infrastructure at this point, so you need only target such an individual. Getting his or her commitment comes later.

The implementation customer authority should act as the chair for the MCG, and this group may well undergo some changes as you move towards implementation. These changes will relate to composition and terms of reference, but I will discuss these specifically later.

In terms of our model organization, I see the support group reporting to either the Systems Development Director, the ideal case, or to the R&D Manager. This may seem strange given what I have said about the 'not invented here' syndrome (NIH), but it does mean that the support group can be seen as being impartial. We get over the NIH syndrome another way. If you are really lucky, the Systems Development Director will take on the role of implementing customer authority.

Within each functional grouping you should identify a local metrics coordinator. This person takes on the responsibility of implementing the metrics initiative for his/her group under the guidance and direction of the centralized group. The intention is to transfer expertise from the central group to these local coordinators as quickly as possible. In terms of our model organization, I would expect to see local coordinators appointed to cover Support Development, possibly Operational Support, and Planning. You may choose to appoint a single coordinator for Product Development, or you may appoint different individuals to cover Software Development and Test and Integration.

You have to decide whether or not to appoint these local coordinators on a full-time or part-time basis. Which option you choose depends very much on the size of the function they are going to support. If you have only a couple of Product Development teams, it would be wasteful to appoint full-time staff, but you do need to be realistic. Do not fall into the trap of expecting change to happen automatically. No one can argue, for example, against the proposition that quality is the responsibility of everyone within the organization, but to generate a quality culture does demand the dedicated resources of support staff — otherwise you end up paying lip service to the ideals of quality without seeing any visible improvements. The same is true of Software Metrics.

Of course, even with local coordinators appointed to support all of your major functional groups within the organization, you are still failing to cover the needs of one very important group, senior management. Given the fact that this group is diverse in both its requirements and position within the organization, the central support group is ideally placed to supply the local coordination function for senior management. This is especially true when you realize that senior managers are the recipients rather than the suppliers of information.

Your local metrics coordinators form the foundation of the MCG for the implementation stage of the programme. During the implementation stage, the MCG should also adopt a more proactive role than it has during development of the initiative. Its terms of reference need to be very clear and should demonstrate that pro-active role. A possible set of terms of reference is listed below.

The Metrics Coordination Group should:

- Own all metrics standards used within the organization;
- Supply the requirements for additional work elements within the metrics programme;
- Prioritize those work elements;
- Act as custodian of the metrics programme plans;
- Determine the strategy of the metrics programme;
- Act as a forum for the sharing of results;
- Act as a liaison point with other organizational initiatives;
- Champion the implementation of metrics.

This set of terms of reference implies that you may need a wider membership within the MCG. As well as the local metrics coordinators, you may consider it worth having representatives of various customer groups. For example, if your organization operates a Total Quality Management programme with a separate quality function, then this group should be represented within the MCG.

Ownership of the Software Metrics programme by the engineering function is vital to its success. To generate this ownership, you may like to consider an additional level of implementation support within the metrics initiative. The concept of local facilitators is a very useful one in this context. Each development and support team will be expected to supply some information or data to the central support group, possibly through their local coordinators, but to support and police this activity can become extremely onerous if you attempt to do it from the outside. Much better to have one individual within each team charged with this responsibility. This person can also act as a focal point for metrics within the team.

The role of local facilitator is, for all but the largest teams, a part-time one. Initially, the local facilitator will need to spend some time helping to set up the necessary collection procedures and can, perhaps, assist with local process definition but, as the programme beds down, this role becomes less costly. You may well have realized that the local facilitators can also form a local MCG within each functional area.

The infrastructure that supports the implementation of the Software Metrics programme within the organization is shown in Fig. 11.2.

There are two comments that need to be made regarding this infrastructure model:

1. Such a structure may not be possible during the early implementation stage. At this time it may be a target or ideal that you move towards. How you actually support the early implementation of a metrics initiative depends very much on how you phase that implementation. If your initial implementation is more akin to a pilot, say within two or three product development teams only, then centralized support may be sufficient.

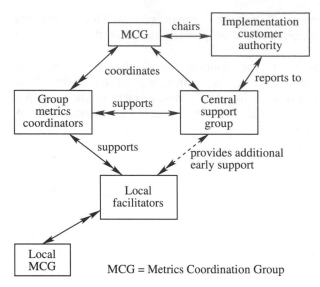

Figure 11.2 Organizational infrastructure.

Alternatively, if you are only using a small set of management statistics based on raw data taken from existing systems within your first phase implementation, then a central support group working with local coordinators will probably be enough. However, if your programme is wide ranging both in terms of what it implements and who it affects, and many successful metrics initiatives are large in both these dimensions, then please be sure that you address the question of support structure early.

2. You should not expect your local coordinators and facilitators to spring fully armed from the organization on the day that implementation starts. They will need time to develop their roles and expertise and, while this development continues, they will need a relatively high degree of support from somewhere. A central support group staffed by individuals who have gained experience of Software Metrics theory and practice, even if only from pilot work, is ideally placed to provide this. This is shown by the dotted line in Fig. 11.2 and you, as the manager of the programme, should budget accordingly.

Define support training

Which brings us nicely to the initial training that should be given to the individuals that make up the support infrastructure for the metrics initiative.

If you decide to adopt the infrastructure model described above, then you will have two specific training requirements that will need to be addressed.

Local coordinators

The local coordinators require a significant amount of training if they are to fill their roles effectively. The best training that anyone can receive comes from experience, but these individuals will need something to bring them up quickly to a level where they can, at least, operate with support. Such training needs to address the following areas:

- Motivation of the local coordinators;
- Background addressing the theory of those areas within the domain of Software Metrics that are included within your own initiative;
- General background covering other areas within Software Metrics. After all, your programme, if successful, will grow and develop;
- Practical advice regarding the analysis and representation of data;
- Training in the procedures developed within your own metrics initiative. This can include training in the provision of training.

This is a tall order, made worse when you realize how little material there is around that you can utilize directly. There are some training courses available from external sources. These do, however, tend to address the theory of metrication. For example, you will find courses that teach the use of specific techniques such as *Function Point Analysis* or McCabe metrics. You will also find some courses that cover the majority of accepted metrics techniques as a single package. There are also some courses that can help motivate individuals as to the benefits of using Software Metrics. These courses tend to be given by individuals with experience in the field, and can be very useful in providing that initial practical view of the discipline but, being given by individuals, they tend to be biased towards that individual's favoured techniques.

A newcomer to this field that seems to provide a less individualistic view of the subject while retaining the practical foundation is the material from the European Economic Community ESPRIT project, *Metkit*. This project delivers a Software Metrics Toolkit centred around training material developed by a consortium of academic and industrial partners. Initial indications are that this material will be a welcome addition to the field of Software Metrics training.

Unless some other organization starts to offer training directly geared to the needs of those people responsible for the implementation of metrics initiatives, covering the areas outlined above, you may well have to devise your own training programme that blends external offerings with internal material. I believe that it takes about 12 months to turn an individual into an effective metrics implementor just through 'on the job training' and you need to reduce this once you start implementation.

A mix of external courses to teach specific techniques that form part of your own initiative with reading material, perhaps drawn from the bibliography at the rear of this book, and a tailored course designed and built by yourselves is probably the best option at this stage. The internal course will probably need a duration of about four days to cover what needs to be addressed adequately. If you have doubts about your ability to prepare and present such a course, then you should consider making use of any internal training function that exists, or you may wish to bring in some external consultancy. If starting from scratch, such a course will probably take you about five weeks to develop, but it can be a worthwhile investment.

Local facilitators

You also need to train the local facilitators. This is less of a problem because you will be supporting these individuals directly. In fact, the main aim of the initial training is to provide the necessary motivation. It is very possible that an external course, such as that provided by the ESPRIT project, *Metkit*, will be sufficient.

Drawing the streams together or consolidation

Having designed the many facets of your Software Metrics programme, you now need to bring them together to form an integrated and complete picture. This will be taken forward to management for approval to proceed. It is possible that you already have authority to build the programme, or you may need full management approval for the next stage. If the former is the case, you still need to review your proposals with your customer authority. If the latter is the case, you will probably need to add in a cost benefit analysis.

Bearing in mind that your requirements analysis will have probably identified a number of requirements now addressed via sub-projects or component designs within your overall metrics initiatives, two elements form the basis of your design. These are the sub-project or programme component specific elements and the elements related to the overall initiative.

Sub-project

As far as the sub-projects are concerned, I would like to suggest that you view the results of each of these as a 'product'. The reasoning behind this goes back to the idea of linking each requirement to a customer within the Software Metrics programme. If you have an identified customer for each requirement, then the way in which you satisfy each requirement can be viewed by the customer as a product that is being delivered. Of course, the product will not be traditional in the sense that it is a black box but, if you think about it, most products are not 'traditional' in this sense anyway.

Assume that we have a requirement for a washing machine. More correctly, we have a requirement for some system that will clean our washable clothes. Traditionally, we satisfy this requirement by going out and purchasing a washing machine, in this case a 'white box'. However, these days we are likely to purchase a white box with an associated service package. For example, the deal we negotiate may include delivery, installation, training through documentation together with a maintenance contract or service guarantee. The 'product' is much more than just a white box.

In the same way, you can satisfy a requirement within a Software Metrics programme with a package of deliverables which the customer can view as a product. For example, there may be a requirement within your initiative for some way to monitor, control and reduce the complexity of generic software systems, that is systems that have existed for some time and undergo continual enhancement.

An obvious way to satisfy this requirement is for the development team to purchase a static analysis tool that will, perhaps, reverse-engineer code to produce semiformal documentation such as structure charts, flowgraphs, etc., and that will perhaps analyse these in terms of specific metrics, McCabe *cyclomatic* and *essential* complexity metrics being the obvious choice, although the Fenton/Whitty alternatives could also be used (Fenton, 1986).

Fine, off you go, pay the money and ship the tool out to your customers, the development teams. I believe that very little will happen as a result of this initiative. To get the most out of your solution, you need to do more than just make the tool available to users. You will need to document how the output of the tools should be analysed and used within your environment. You will also need to provide some background on the theory behind the metrics. This is especially true in a technical environment, where people do not accept things just because someone 'says' they work. You may also need to provide some training for the engineers to support your documentation. You will almost certainly have to provide some form of support or handholding to get development teams started in the use of these new techniques.

As you see, your solution now contains a number of distinct elements. You have documentation, perhaps in the form of in-house guidelines, training, ongoing support and, lest we forget, you also have the tool. This will be true for most of your requirements and is certainly true for cost estimation, Applied Design Metrics, project control and management statistics.

So, the design you take forward for review should include, against each requirement, information about the core solution, which may be a tool or a set of techniques or even a set of metrics, in-house documentation, the provision of training and ongoing support. These are the sub-project or programme component specific elements of your design.

Overall metrics programme

You will also have prepared another set of proposals relating to the overall metrics programme and how that will be implemented. These include your marketing and business plans covering internal publicity, together with high level education and the implementation strategy respectively. You also have proposals for an infrastructure to be established to support the implementation strategy. You may also have some pilot results to add credence to your claims.

These elements of your design relate to the metrics programme overall rather than to specific sub-projects within it, but please remember that they are a vital part of your proposals, at least as important as your specific 'metrics' solutions.

Presentation of design

How you actually present your design for approval will depend upon the culture of your own organization and its normal operating practices. You will almost certainly be expected to prepare your proposals as some form of document. Remember to link your solutions to requirements and business needs associated with specific customers or customer groupings within your organization. One approach that seems to be acceptable is to structure your design document as an interim report in the following way:

- *Introduction:* A high level description of why the Software Metrics programme was initiated. Keep it short.
- *Requirement identification:* What specific requirements have been identified, which are addressed by this phase of the programme, whose needs are addressed, (the link to customers).
- *Product description:* For each requirement, the core solution, in-house documentation, the provision of training and ongoing support, along with the results of any pilot work that supports your solution. Remember that you are seeking approval to build, so do not go into great detail about the pilots, simply use results to support your design solution.
- *Implementation strategy:* Covering the marketing and business plan together with your proposals for the supporting infrastructure. Do not forget to describe the training requirements for individuals involved in this infrastructure.

Cost benefit analysis

If you have to seek senior management approval and your organizational culture requires it, you may have to carry out a cost benefit analysis. This is very difficult to do for a Software Metrics programme because there is very little material available from external sources that describes the costs and benefits of a wide-ranging metrics initiative. Why is this? I believe that there are a number of answers to this question.

1. One reason must be the difficulty in quantifying the benefits that accrue from some of the traditional areas of applied Software Metrics. For example, what is the financial benefit of supplying external customers with accurate cost and duration estimates for the development of software systems? We may be able to construct a model based on assumptions of lost business that results from over-optimistic estimates, or we may operate under fixed price contracts, which certainly makes the cost of inaccurate estimates more accessible. Even in this case, we may also be operating under 'lowest tender' conditions of bidding which can distort results. The reality is that we do not know the true benefits of accurate estimation in financial terms, but we do know the cost of inaccuracy in qualitative terms.

   Basically, if we can demonstrate to end customers that our estimates are accurate, what we say it will cost is what it will cost, then that gives us a competitive edge over others in the industry. It makes us more professional, but this is difficult to model in terms of a cost benefit analysis.

2. Another problem is the differences between metrics programmes. It is very unlikely that our initiative will be sufficiently close to that of other organizations for us to be able to use their data. While we will almost certainly find similar elements between programmes that can enable us to justify parts of our own programme in terms of costs and benefits, we will find problems when you try to carry out a cost benefit analysis for the whole thing.

3. We must realize that the use of Software Metrics within the industry is in its infancy. Most organizations have only been using metrics as a practical solution to problems for a short period of time. Many of them are only beginning to realize the benefits now. But look at who is using Software Metrics. Examples include, among others, Siemens, Hewlett-Packard, parts of IBM, DEC, Toshiba, Lloyds of London and Lloyds Bank, Du Pont, NASA. All of these organizations are leaders in their field although, as with all organizations, it is never certain that they will maintain this position.

4. Finally, it may be that by looking at what organizations that are perceived to be successful are doing, we can also get ahead of the game. These organizations are realizing benefits from the practical use of Software Metrics, and they demonstrate this by their continued investment in metrics initiatives. Perhaps one of the most forceful arguments for the use of Software Metrics is not to answer the question: 'can we afford to do this?', but alternatively to ask the question 'can we afford *not* to do this?'

In many cases your cost benefit analysis can be replaced by ensuring that you have the commitment of the potential customers of metrics within your own organization. You achieve this by directing solutions towards their own specific requirements, and by making sure that they are aware of this. You talk to them!

All of which is no help if your organization demands that you still supply a traditional cost benefit analysis. If this is the case, then the following may be of some help, but I will be honest and say that this is not an easy problem to solve.

Budget

The budget necessary for the implementation of an SMP can be considered from a number of viewpoints.

1. The work to define and build the programme can be considered separately to the actual implementation.
2. Whether budgets are being considered for a particular stage or for the full programme, the person preparing the budget should always examine the likely staff and ancillary costs.

   (a) Within *staff costs* there will be two distinct elements.

       (i) There will be the staff costs of those people directly involved in defining, building and implementing the programme. We can call these people the metrics team.

       (ii) There will be staff costs associated with the additional effort required from the software production function within the organization. These costs can be consumed by pilots, reviews of the programme deliverables, such as the design document, data collection and data analysis.

   (b) *Ancillary costs* cover many items including additional hardware such as PCs, software for data storage and analysis, proprietary packages, such as cost estimation packages, consultancy for training and other purposes such as 'buying in' statistical analysis skills, and membership of external organizations such as the QA Forum or the Quality Assurance Institute. Travel and conference attendance costs may also need to be considered.

Most organizations have standards covering the presentation of budgets for management approval, and these should be used whenever they apply. A checklist of cost elements is listed below to assist with the identification of costs:

- Metrics team effort
- Engineering effort
- Hardware
- Software
- Proprietary packages
- Training
- Consultancy
- Conferences
- Special interest group membership, e.g. QA Forum (Europe) or Quality Assurance Institute (USA)
- Travel

It is always advisable to build a contingency into budgets to cover additional work that may be identified as the programme progresses.

Beware of giving 'off the cuff' budget estimates. While it is not always possible to avoid this, it is common for such estimates to become the budget for the programme. Generally, such figures are underestimates of the true cost, and can quickly become a serious constraint on the work being done.

It is tempting to think that pilot activities will provide enough evidence of the benefits of Software Metrics to enable extrapolation to model the benefits of wider implementation. Unfortunately, this is rarely the case. The reason for this is that many of the financial benefits depend on improved quality, and this may not be evident until a system has been in the field for six or even twelve months. Another reason is that pilot activities tend to address one aspect of Software Metrics, and this may only show limited benefits.

Consider a development project that pilots the use of McCabe metrics to control quality. Assume that the project lasts six months from initiation to first live use. It may take a further six months to demonstrate a lower defect level than the norm for the organization, providing that this norm is actually known.

It may take 12 months of field use, and enhancement, to demonstrate financial benefits obtained from greater maintainability. This implies that it will take 18 months to quantify the financial benefits arising from the use of McCabe metrics. It is almost certain that a cost benefit analysis will have to be produced before this.

If you cannot use pilot results to build your cost benefit analysis, then the only route left open is the use of assumption.

It should be possible to estimate the cost of the programme once the scope of the work has been defined. This is a good case for considering implementation separately, as the earlier stages contribute to the scope definition for that stage.

When considering the benefit side, it is now generally accepted, among metrics practitioners, that 'the act of measurement will improve the process or product being measured'. This is sometimes cited as the *Hawthorne effect* and this can be present. However, it is more often due to the results of the measurement activity being used to alter the process or product rather than any psychological phenomena. Beware that an alternative argument may be used against you, that 'measurement itself has no intrinsic value', and be prepared to counter this.

If the basic assumption above is accepted, it is possible to define financial benefits of a Software Metrics programme as follows:

1. You should establish an average fault rate for the organization. You will also need to derive the average cost per fault, perhaps by identifying the average effort involved to fix such a fault, and the charge-out rate used by the organization's accountants. This type of information may well be available within the organization.

2. Make an assumption that the implementation of Software Metrics will reduce the fault rate by some amount, and calculate what this will save the organization based on the amount of software produced during a given period.

Because the Software Metrics programme will probably require a relatively high investment during the first year or two, due to the purchase of software packages and perhaps a higher level of consultancy support, you may find that the programme runs at a loss for the first year or two. Because of this, it is wise to supply a cumulative cost/benefit figure to show when returns can be expected. Senior managers tend not to query the detail of a cost/benefit analysis very closely provided any assumptions are made clear. They are much more interested in the bottom line that provides evidence that the investment is justified and has been considered in 'business' terms. Be prepared to support your assumptions, possibly using evidence from other organizations.

It is also worth describing the additional benefits of the programme. The cost/benefit analysis, as described above, does not quantify the value of improved management information or more accurate cost estimates, other than to assume that these contribute to a reduced defect rate. These enabling aspects of a Software Metrics programme often carry as much, if not more weight, than the cost/benefit analysis but, as discussed earlier, this can depend on the culture of the organization.

Move the design forward

Reports tend to be weighty things and are seldom read in detail by managers. Management summaries help, but I believe that the best way to get your design proposals accepted is to make a presentation to the approvers. You can say very much more in a short space of time than you can possibly get across in a report or design document, so you should grasp this opportunity with both hands. If the opportunity is not there, then make it be there!

All the normal rules about presentations apply: keep it short, no more than 30 minutes with time for discussion afterwards; spend time planning the presentation and rehearse it beforehand; be positive. If possible, go in with organizational backing and, if you have set up an MCG you have the perfect vehicle for this by getting the Group's approval for the design proposals. You may also get organizational backing by getting prospective customers to approve your design solutions. You may even be able to get at least one senior manager so committed that he or she actually makes the presentation. This is the ideal situation, but try to make sure that you are there to provide technical support and to take the flak.

Once your design solutions have gone through the approval process, you are ready to start the build stage of the programme. Of course, operating in the real world, you may have a number of sub-projects running in parallel. You may find it easier to take the design solution for each of these through review independently and, perhaps, at different times. If this happens, then please take care to ensure that you do have designs for those parts of the programme that affect the whole initiative, for example the business plan, ready for the first review.

SUMMARY

The design stage of a Software Metrics programme can be seen as the core of that programme's development. Too often, there is a temptation to plunge into design without having done the necessary work of defining clear requirements, and this is a temptation that should be avoided. Even with clear requirements, it is very easy to concentrate upon the technical aspects of the programme, such as the metrics or measures, at the expense of the equally important streams that deal with the marketing of the programme and with its support structure. Avoid this trap as well, if you wish your programme to succeed.

12

STAGE 4 — COMPONENT BUILD

Having spent so much time and effort ensuring that we have requirements clearly specified and linked to business needs, together with the work we have put in designing solutions to meet those requirements, this stage should be easy.

Of course, anyone who has worked on building systems of any kind knows that this is true in theory, but that the build stage is, in fact, as difficult as any other stage, but in different ways. One thing that makes this stage difficult is simply the time it takes to change a design into something solid and working. Another problem is that we tend, during this stage, to be much more isolated from our customers. Breaking the stage into well-defined tasks is one way of dealing with the problems. Another is to ensure that we allow for reviews, perhaps by the Metrics Coordination Group (MCG), in the build stage.

These are two major work elements within this stage. Firstly we have to set things up so that we are in good shape to start implementation, basically laying the foundations for that stage. Secondly, we have to physically build the components of our SMP so that we have something to implement! (See Fig. 12.1.)

LAYING THE FOUNDATIONS

Select the implementation champion and group coordinators

During the design stage, you targeted a particular individual who will act as the champion, sponsor or even the customer authority for the implementation of Software Metrics within your organization. If you have not already done so, you should now obtain that individual's agreement to act in that role.

The more senior this person the better, although you should realize that simply because a manager says something will be so does not necessarily mean that it *will* be so. A high-

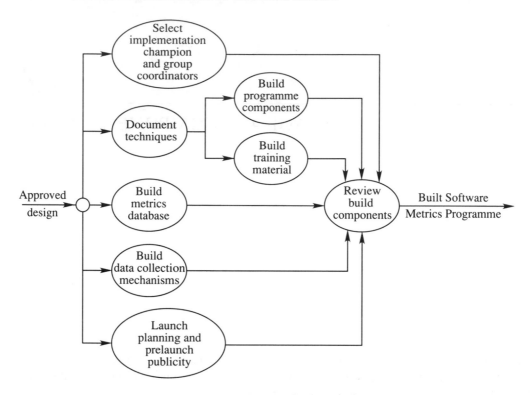

Figure 12.1 Building the components of a Software Metrics programme.

ranking, involved champion makes life easier in that others in the organization perceive that the initiative has weight, but attempting to implement an SMP through this kind of authority by association will not be enough. Successful metrics initiatives succeed because the customers of that initiative perceive benefits from involvement, not through begrudged compliance.

But there is an interesting phenomena that comes into play when you start to implement initiatives that are intended to change the organization. Whatever rank the person is who supplies the *visible* authority for the initiative, the most active collaboration will come from individuals one rank lower. The degree of collaboration decreases the lower down the power pyramid you move and, more importantly, the degree of resistance increases dramatically the further up the pyramid you go.

In other words, if the Senior Executive Officer (SEO) or Managing Director champions the initiative, board members will be, for the most part, cooperative. By the time you get to the project managers and engineers you start to run into cynicism, arguments that this is yet more bureaucracy, and simple inertia. You can overcome this problem by listening to what the more junior members of the organization have to say, by giving them solutions to their problems and, in a practical sense, ensuring that you have a good spread of seniority within your own development and implementation team. The spread of seniority within the MCG also becomes important.

This scenario is the easiest to work with because you, as the person responsible for making sure that the initiative happens and delivers results, will probably be quite senior within the organization anyway. After all, if the SEO is championing something, he or she is unlikely to give that responsibility to a junior member of staff.

More difficult is the situation where the champion is somewhere in the middle of the pecking order. In this case, the person responsible for developing and implementing the initiative will probably be equivalent to a project manager. Because of some psychological effect that seems to come into play, that individual will operate effectively within his/her own peer group and will have little trouble convincing other project managers that, for example, metrics are a good thing. The problem is that project managers seldom have the responsibility they should have considering the size of the can they may have to carry if things go wrong. Few project managers within the IT industry have true responsibility for their own project budget. Indeed, many do not even know what that budget is! Training is funded centrally as is capital investment. Staff head counts are allocated to the manager rather than being controlled by him. This means that, even when you have convinced the project manager that your proposals are sound, you have to spend time and effort convincing one, two or even more levels of higher management that even a small investment, perhaps in effort, is worthwhile. As you go up the tree, the amount of effort necessary to convince people grows. In simple terms, we seem to be suffering from a form of the 'not invented here' syndrome again.

There is no easy way around this. You need to put the effort in, but you should also start to play 'personalities'. Identify the senior managers who are willing to listen to you, who are more open to argument and who are at least willing to give your programme a chance. Be prepared to tailor your programme in the light of their comments and feelings, while still retaining the integrity of your programme. Do not waste time on the managers who are set totally against you. Finally, get yourself on an influencing skills training course and apply what you learn. After all, every little helps.

The worst case occurs when the champion of the initiative is a project manager with limited authority. The approach to metrication I have described so far will not work in this scenario. The organization lacks the necessary commitment. In this case, I can only suggest that the project manager does things in a small way and attempts to build a centre of excellence in the team. At the same time, he should try to identify and convince a more senior member of the organization to take up the banner and champion the cause. As Robert the Bruce realized after observing the spider, perseverance can pay off.

In some cases, you may be able to defer the formal selection of the implementation champion until the end of the build stage. If you have the commitment of the organization to the SMP, then the actual champion becomes less important but, in most cases, you should aim to have his or her commitment and involvement as early as possible.

Do not forget to select your local coordinators as well as the champion. After all, the local coordinators are going to be the people on the ground who will be making things happen. You need to be sure that they are the kind of people who can do this. At the risk of sounding pretentious, there are different types of people in any organization. Some are talkers, others are doers!

Talkers come in many guises, some are traditional managers who pay lip service to change, but are really too cynical to believe that an organization can change. Others are 'technicians' who will appear to support change, but whose stock phrase seems to be 'yes, but'.

Doers also come in many forms. The obvious and visible doers are often senior managers who take a completely different view of the business than that held by conventional managers. They are not willing to operate under the *status quo*, but challenge conventional wisdom at every opportunity. Often they make enemies, but are powerful enough to be able to afford to do this. An obvious example of such an individual is Margaret Thatcher. We may not agree with her, but she certainly changed things — so many things that we tend to forget that she was the first female Prime Minister in the UK. Quite a change in itself!

Of course, you are unlikely to be able to get a gang of senior 'doers' as your local coordinators, but you should aim to get the best people you can. In reality, you may have individuals nominated for you. This can cause problems as someone, somewhere will probably use this as an opportunity to get rid of some dead wood. Try to retain some power of veto and, if you have any doubts about your ability to select good staff, remembering that this is a skill that comes with experience and depends on the knack of reading people, get the assistance of someone who demonstrates skills in this area.

The centralized support group, the involved commitment of an implementation customer authority or champion and the group coordinators form the core of your metrics initiative. The importance of these individuals cannot be over-emphasized. Time spent making sure that you have the right people will pay dividends. Get this wrong, and you will be storing up future problems.

Launch planning and pre-launch publicity

Hopefully, you have been maintaining an awareness of the metrics initiative within the organization as you have gone through the previous development stages. Perhaps you have used in-house publications or staged presentations to interested groups. Whatever vehicle you have used for your publicity, you need to ramp things up as you move towards implementation. This is especially true if your first phase includes something that affects the whole organization. For example, if your organization has never used a formal defect tracking system or fault database and, if this is something you will be implementing, then you should be telling the organization why, what and when this will be happening.

I saw a good example of this in a large telecommunications equipment supplier that decided to adopt the Xerox technique of 'Competitive Benchmarking'. One of the individuals involved in this wrote many articles for in-house magazines and took every opportunity to talk to managers about this new idea. Indeed, at one point it seemed as if you could not pick up an in-house journal without there being something about Competitive Benchmarking in it. Also, it seemed as if everyone in the organization had heard of this guy's name and could link it to the technique. The result — the organization felt that it had adopted Benchmarking, it was doing things with it, it was going to get results and it was ready to use those results. This was before matters had even gone beyond the pilots. Of course, all this could have slid slowly to oblivion if there had been nothing more. Fortunately, the publicity was only a precursor to a full launch of Competitive Benchmarking, and the same is true for the metrics initiative. You need some form of launch for your programme and this should be an *event*.

It can be as simple as a statement by the Systems Development Director that Software Metrics is now an initiative supported by the organization, a part of the development strategy, or it can be as complex as a roadshow. Whatever you choose as the launch vehicle, you should aim for visibility within the organization.

An excellent method of achieving this visibility that I know has been used in both a European and an American organization is the *management workshop*. We have discussed this earlier, but now is the time it really comes into its own. Such a workshop takes a high level of commitment by the organization, but is very effective. To get this commitment, you may have to take the plan for the launch forward as part of your programme design. Essentially, you take as many senior managers as you can get off the battlefield and into a room for a day or two. Ideally, this room is off site, possibly in a hotel.

Once you have them, you take them through a guided tour of their problems, and you present them with potential solutions to those problems. This only works when you get them involved in the proceedings, so it must operate as a workshop, not simply as a series of presentations by the metrics team. In fact, the metrics team representatives will talk less and less as the event proceeds. The advantages of this approach are that it gets management involved, it confirms problems and it identifies the players who are ready to try solving those problems.

It also identifies the recalcitrant managers who may cause problems later and gives those individuals a chance to shift their stance in a face-saving manner, as they are discussing things with their peers, not with some external expert who thinks he knows their job better than they do.

Do not waste effort unless you are confident of a payback. In some organizations, too much work is needed to organize a management workshop, or you may lack the leverage to make such an event a success — then it is simply not worth it. You must judge the situation for yourself. The programme launch can help you with implementation. It should be used to its greatest advantage, but remember it is only one small step along the road to success. If the statement of intent is enough for you, or all that you feel your organization is ready for then go for that.

Target the teams for the first phase

After the launch, you must start the ball rolling, so target where you will do this first. This is important unless your first phase concerns the whole of the organization. In that case, your target is predefined, but in most cases the first phase of the metrics programme is more akin to a large pilot exercise. By this I mean that you will be putting techniques and practices in place on a finite number of development, support or testing teams. Choose the first teams well!

Throughout development of the programme, you have been interacting with the organization. You will have identified groups and individuals who are keen to see the initiative succeed, and you should use these as the foundation of your programme. The chances are that your first phase will not affect such a large segment of the organization that you have to work with the less keen elements.

A model that I find quite useful is the rolling wave put forward by Dr Hemsley, of the EEC ESPRIT research project *Pyramid*. As shown in Fig. 12.2, this highlights who should be targeted at any given time. As time goes on, the target changes.

Getting the right groups involved first means that you can use success there to convince the more sceptical groups within the organization to join you. Of course, if your initial groups are keen to see the metrics initiative succeed, then it is more likely to demonstrate that success.

A great deal can be said about the types of team you should select for the first phase. Should you go for teams working on small projects or large; should you concentrate on high profile products or the less important ones; should you only look at teams who are already using new design techniques? If you go for small projects, you have less

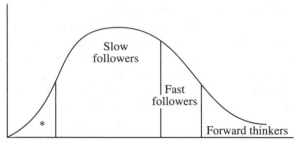

* Forget them, they will never be convinced

Figure 12.2 Targets.

communication overheads and probably a quicker payback; high profile products tend to give you more publicity, but there is a risk that they could be cancelled as they tend to be speculative ventures; new design techniques tend to lend themselves to metrication, but how far have they penetrated the organization?

Basically, it all depends. What it depends on are the people involved. There will be problems associated with any project you target, but if the team is keen to see metrics work, it will overcome most of those problems.

Whatever criterion you use, you should be very clear where your programme is going before you start implementation. Target the teams you want to see on board, but remember that you may not achieve 100 per cent success. Target a few more than you want for your first phase, so that you have a fall back position. Then go for 100 per cent hit rate on your first choice.

Build the programme components

What you have to do to build the components of your metrics programme will obviously depend on the requirements that have been placed on that programme.

For some, the first phase will consist of nothing more than, say, productivity measurement being introduced to your software development function. This may sound simple, but it can entail the introduction of a project sizing technique, maybe *lines of code* counters added to compilers or the use of *Function Point Analysis*, and a mechanism to capture project cost or effort.

For others, the programme may consist of a number of discrete components possibly covering cost estimation, project control, the use of *applied design metrics* and a range of management statistics.

Whatever the programme consists of, there will be similarities in what has to be produced to enable the effective introduction of the various components.

Document techniques

You will almost certainly have to document your design solutions for each high-level requirement in the form of a standard, a set of guidelines or a code of practice.

Such a document is a technical paper, and producing these in a way that ensures that they are usable and workable, rather than producing something that sits on a shelf, pristine and untouched by human hand, is a skill that takes time to acquire.

Of course, you may not have the time to acquire that skill, so any assistance that is offered by technical writing functions in the organization should be used. Alternatively, rigorous review procedures can help to ensure readability.

Standards that are used tend to be concise, readable and coherent. In other words, keep it short, keep it simple or as simple as possible, and keep to the point.

It is a good idea to adopt a style for standards contained within the metrics programme. You will find that spending time planning the general layout of standards will pay dividends in the future. There may be an in-house standard that is already used within your organization, and it would be foolish to make enemies by ignoring this, but you will probably find that standing instructions like this concentrate more on detail than on basic structure. For example, your document standard may insist on a scope statement, an introduction, a document body with rules for numbering sections, sub-sections and paragraphs and a summary. It is doubtful that such a standard will insist on a three-page scope statement followed by a five-page introduction. If you can get away with one line in each of these sections, then fine! After all, your potential readers are after the meat of what you have to say, rather than the waffle one often finds in standards, be they internal or external.

Talk about the style of your documents with your customer authority and the MCG. They should review any standards that you produce, so get them involved from the start. Using a general style means that your documents develop an identity. It also means that your potential readers get used to your style, and can find their way around documents more easily. Every little helps.

When it comes to the actual writing, all you can do is get your head down and get on with it, but there are some things to bear in mind. Most important is the KISS squared rule: Keep it Simple Stupid and Keep it Short Stupid! I make no apologies for saying this yet again, because it is so important that these rules are followed.

There are some traps into which it is very easy to fall when writing technical documents such as standards. I know because I have fallen into most of them at some point.

The first problem is akin to the personality change that comes over some people when they get behind the wheel of a car. Give someone a technical document to write and they seem to don a white coat, their hair becomes dishevelled, a wild look comes into their eyes; the mad professor in many of us takes over. The result is a document littered with big words or, even worse, new words that only the author has ever heard of. Software Metrics papers are very prone to this and most of the words end with 'ity'! We have maintainability, reliability, enhanceability and even diagnostability. Some times this is unavoidable, but there is no excuse for much of the jargon that litters standards. If you do have to use unusual words, words with which your audience may be unfamiliar, then please make sure that you define what you mean, preferably both in the text and in a glossary.

Another problem with descriptive standards stems from the author's familiarity with the subject matter. When the first few chapters of this book went for review, a comment that came back from more than one reviewer was that assumptions were being made about the reader's familiarity with the subject of Software Metrics. These comments were valid, and to counter this problem chapters were added to the book. This does illustrate that even the

KISS squared rule needs to be applied with care. When we say Keep it Short, we actually mean Keep it as Short as Possible.

A useful way of tackling this problem is to blend two styles in a single document. If you are describing a measure, say productivity, you can start with a brief, tight technical description of that measure. What is it intended to do? How is it defined? What raw data is required? How should results be presented? This can be followed by an elaboration of the main points that is more chatty, relaxed and that assumes no prior knowledge. If you are describing the presentation of productivity data you may concisely describe this by saying 'productivity values will be plotted over time with an associated three point rolling average'. There is no harm in describing what is meant by a 'three point rolling average' as part of the elaboration.

Supplying too much information can also be a problem. Assume that you are writing a standard to describe how your organization will use *Function Point Analysis*. Does your reader really need to know that they were devised by Alan Albrecht a good many years ago, that there are some 19 variations available and do they really need even a brief description of all 19 variants? This is a very easy trap to fall into. After all, you have spent time and a considerable amount of effort digging up all this information. You needed it to be able to make a reasoned set of recommendations to your organization. You want the organization to be aware of all your good work. Believe me, your organization will be much more appreciative if you get in something that works, and if you are able to make it work inside your organization than if you continually blow your own trumpet by telling them facts they do not need to know.

Also remember the old saw about pictures. A picture says a thousand words. In reality, some people prefer text, but others prefer pictures. You do not know the leaning of a particular reader, so whenever possible use both. KISS certainly applies to pictures. There is little merit in producing one complex picture when two, or even three simple ones, would do the same job. In fact two or three may work where one fails!

One final piece of advice. Most organizations or sites have someone who is a good technical writer. You can find such people by asking around. Who has written decent standards? Have any of your colleagues written articles on effective writing? If you can find such a person, try getting their comments on your first attempts. Then listen to what they have to say and act on their comments.

The standards that you produce are the public face of your programme. Personally, I believe that even the best standards in the world are liable to be under-used unless they are actively supported. People work best when they have a good relationship with other people, and you must be prepared to support your customers when they first start to apply the techniques you recommend. It is very tempting to believe that you will be able to do this on the hoof, to make it up as you go along. Forget it! If you are to offer a professional support service to your potential metrics users, then you need to think about how you will do that.

This support can take many forms, but one example is outlined below. If you are introducing a set of management statistics to a development team, then you may feel it necessary to model their development process first. This would seem to be a sensible approach. How will you do this? Perhaps you will apply some basic systems analysis skills to the problem, gathering information through interviews with individuals involved in the process. You need to plan those interviews. How will you start things off? How will you get your colleague talking about his or her work honestly and openly? Plan your strategy, be prepared, be flexible, but use your plan to get what you need from the interview. Document your approach so that more junior team members can benefit from your experience and, as you learn from experience, update your strategy.

This approach of planning before the event should be used whenever you interact with other people within the metrics initiative. Of course, you will suffer relapses. You will go in to a meeting unprepared or you will keep your plans to yourself, but aim to document your plans, and you will start to build a permanent foundation for the future and you will develop a professional public image. Eventually, it will become part of your make-up, you will be professional. Then you should take time out, every now and then, to examine the way you are interacting with people to see if you can make it even better. You are going to be preaching continuous improvement. Practice what you preach!

Build training material

You are introducing new concepts and techniques to the business. You will have to provide training in both the concepts and the techniques.

Many of the rules that apply to the production of standards also apply to the production of training courses. Tell your audience what they need to know, sell them the ideas, involve them in the course through the use of worked examples and exercises and, finally, delegate the responsibility for action to them. A good training course does all of these things and depends so much on the skill of the presenter that it is sometimes frightening to think about the responsibility that you take on when you first stand up to welcome the group of attendees.

Frightening — until you realize that most people are there because they want to learn, they are open-minded, they want to enjoy themselves and are willing to get involved. They want to leave the course and apply what they have learned to make things better. Of course, there is always one bad apple. Mind you, I usually find that if you give such a person enough rope, the other participants will generally hang him!

As always, planning is what makes a course work well. Plan the content, plan the timings, plan the exercises. Especially plan the exercises. These are by far the most difficult part of any course to get right. If you make them too simplistic, they will be seen as that and be devalued. If you make them realistic, they will often be too complex to manage in a course environment. I try to be honest about exercises in courses. Tell the participants that exercises are there to make a particular point more solid, to help understanding and to give them a chance to try things out. Seek their cooperation, and you will often find that it is given freely and unstintingly.

Generally, I allow five days effort to develop one day of training material. For a course on a new subject that I am less familiar with, this can double. Budget accordingly. Do not fall into the trap of thinking that a training course is a concrete entity cast in stone. Training is a two-way exercise, and I have never yet presented a course without making changes to it after the event. Some of the best parts of courses I now use have come from ideas given to me by people who have attended previous presentations.

Good training courses are well planned, but they also tend to be given by people who know their subject well. As far as Software Metrics are concerned, it is unlikely that a training department will have people who are experienced in the use of measurement techniques within software development. I have always sought to have metrics training presented by members of the metrics team. This approach has worked and I recommend it.

Once measurement-based techniques become established within the organization, the responsibility for ongoing training can be passed to the relevant support function. By this time, there will be more people available who have experience of using such techniques and who can then give effective training courses.

Build a metrics database

You are developing an SMP. You will be collecting information, data. It would be a good idea to have somewhere to store this data, facilities to analyse the information, mechanisms to feedback the results of this analysis. You need a metrics database, and preferably a simple one.

Unfortunately, you have two problems — well two major problems anyway. If you look around the market place, you are unlikely to find a metrics database package that is perfectly suited to your needs, although a couple of vendors do market offerings in this area, and there are also some research projects, such as the **ESPRIT MERMAID** project, that aim to satisfy this requirement as well. You could investigate these offerings and you may well decide that they are suitable for your requirements or that you can tailor them to your needs. The other problem, the more serious, is that you do not know your requirements at this stage.

But hold on! You have spent a considerable amount of time gathering the requirements for your programme, you have designed your programme and, surely, the results of these activities give you the requirements for your metrics database. If only it were so.

In an ideal world this would be the case, but you have still to implement even the first stage of your metrics programme. It would be foolish to think that you are not going to gain experience and knowledge from that implementation that will impact upon the structure of your programme.

The reality is that you have developed a prototype metrics programme which you are about to try out for real. It would make sense to adopt a similar strategy for your metrics database.

Of course, you can use external offerings as the basis of your prototype database, or you may decide to develop it internally. There are many database packages around that are well suited to this approach.

Whichever road you decide to travel, you should treat the development of your metrics database as a sub-project in its own right. What are your requirements as you see them now? Use these to drive your design solution and then implement that solution on your chosen platform.

Be prepared to adapt your database as your programme develops. Do not fall into the trap that one organization did. They did sterling work in developing their programme right through to implementation, and then found that some of their measures were not giving them the information they required. They sought help through a public conference asking the question: 'what should we do?' The answer was simple but surprised them — 'change your measures'! Yes, this implies that they would have to change their database. Is it really worth investing vast sums of money in an all-singing, all-dancing metrics database when fundamental changes may be necessary? Personally, I prefer a cheaper prototype that I can even throw away if necessary.

In the same vein, you may be pressured to build your database within an overall Management Information System. Perhaps you should tie into existing systems? In theory, this makes sense. In fact, it makes sense in practice, but only as a long-term objective. At this stage, the risk of change is too high unless you have a very flexible MIS with a tremendously efficient support team, who can respond to very volatile requirements. Management Information technology is still such a young area within software development that most MIS support teams are already completing the equivalent of the labours of Hercules just to satisfy basic requirements. They will not thank you if you hit them with more technical problems where even the problems change radically over time. In this case, time is on your side, use it.

So, for the first phase I suggest you aim for a prototype metrics database, possibly on a spreadsheet, that is of reasonable quality but which can be changed as you gain experience and knowledge from your implementation. If you need a politically acceptable face on this approach, you can always say that the full database implementation tied to existing systems is planned for phase two, or three — if you can get away with it.

Build the data collection mechanisms

This is an area worth some discussion in its own right. The way in which you collect this data is important to your programme, and also depends on the components of your first phase. Data collection is fraught with difficulties, but many of these can be overcome by setting reasonable expectations and applying a degree of pragmatic management. Sometimes this is known as using common sense.

Your engineers are employed to develop software, and anything else that they do is an overhead. These overheads may be very important to the business or to the development of your staff, but they all reduce the time that is available for the work that earns the organization revenue. It is sometimes instructive to add up all the time you spend during one week on activities that are not directly related to your primary work objectives.

For example, filling in expense claims, non-vocational training, team meetings or briefings, dealing with unsolicited mail from both internal and external sources. All of these things eat into your work week. Now imagine that you have a metrics programme running. Perhaps you ask your engineers to fill in time-sheets, to complete defect reports, to fill in project history files. It all takes time.

There is bound to be a reluctance on the part of project managers and others to sanction the imposition of yet more bureaucracy on their staff. You have to accept this and overcome it. Now obviously, you should never suggest that this data be collected just for the sake of it. Data collection should always be associated with benefits, even if these are only assumed at this stage. If you have applied the principles outlined in this book so far, you will only be suggesting the collection of data to satisfy the requirements of managers for information, so they should be less concerned than if you arbitrarily suggest that engineers supply you with elements of information for which there is no clear need.

The guiding principle behind data collection is that it should be non-intrusive. I guarantee that if you investigate the situation, you will be amazed at what information is already collected by the organization. Examples of this data can include problem reports, time or effort data, staffing information and financial data including IT spend and, in some cases, return. Of course, this valuable data often disappears into a black hole and is never seen again. Whenever possible, you should use these existing mechanisms as the supply source for your data requirements by breaking out of the black hole syndrome.

There are problems with this approach. Because the data is so seldom used for any obvious purpose, the people who have to supply it usually take very little care to supply accurate information. How honest are your time-sheets for example?

You have to be very clear about the validity of your currently corrected data, and you need to take steps to re-educate people about the need for accuracy. Often this involves a programme of education and close cooperation with the custodians of existing data collection systems. One thing that works in your favour is that these maligned individuals are often only too glad to have someone take an interest in what they are doing, and they will move heaven and earth to help you help them.

The other thing that helps you is that engineers would also like to see their efforts being used to benefit the business. If you can convince them that there is a need for time-sheets, they will often take the necessary care to ensure that you get reasonably accurate information. The fact that has convinced me of this is the number of project teams which I have come across who have additional data collection systems running in parallel with organizational systems. I have lost count of the number of project teams who run a separate time-recording system alongside the company system.

Why do they do it? Quite simply, they see that their own team leader is making use of the information he gets from this extra piece of bureaucracy. A feedback loop is in operation that says: 'Look, I know it's a pain, but the boss is doing something with this stuff. Decisions are made based on this information that affect me. I had better make sure that the information is correct, or I could get even less time for design (or coding or testing or training), next time.' Self interest is a great motivator.

Time-sheets

Something else that typifies these shadow collection systems is their targeted simplicity. Very often, time-recording systems, a convenient whipping horse for this type of discussion, are specified by accountants, and have little relevance to the project teams. The shadow systems are designed by the people who need to use the information, and this makes them 'fit for purpose'. They are also invariably simpler than the company system. Simple systems work!

You also need to be very careful about the level of accuracy that you ascribe to even simple systems. Do you measure effort in engineer hours? Do your engineers work a nominal seven and a half hour day? If so, you may feel that the time-sheet for any day should add up to seven and a half hours. This implies that you expect your engineers to be able to record time to half-hour accuracy. Forget it! If you can get accuracy to half a day, you will be doing well. Quarter-day accuracy is exceptional.

If you really want to get a workable time-recording system going, then you need to be clear about the requirements for that system. Having got your requirements sorted out, I suggest that you go for a two-tier system. Mandatory fields on your time-sheet should ask that time be recorded in quarter-day chunks. Time should be allocated to a small number of categories or cost buckets. You could use the following cost buckets

- Project work, perhaps linked to identifiable projects (if your people are working on more than one project at a time);
- Training, perhaps with vocational and non-vocational in separate buckets;
- Administration covering all those tasks that are not project-related, including filling out these damnable time-sheets; and, finally
- Travel, if you have multi-site projects.

Each cost bucket should have an associated booking code.

Now this is an incredibly simple time-recording system, but unless your organization is very mature in the operation of its business, and this has little to do with the age of the company, it is as much as you can reasonably expect.

The one thing about simple solutions is that they work, and as soon as people see something that works, they tend to try to make it work better. This is perhaps one reason why human beings have developed as we have, but the thing about tinkering is that you can end up with solutions that do not work. This is where the second tier comes in.

On your time-sheets you should allow for user-defined fields. This can be as simple as a two digit or character subbooking code. Of course, you need to ensure that your database can sort and total on the subbooking code. Some project teams will completely ignore the subbooking code, which is fine, but others will start to use them for all sorts of interesting purposes. Some may start to split project time between the phases of the project, others may start to record the time for planning work, still others may start to record review information such as preparation time. Really smart operators may use the first digit of the subbooking code to record the project phase and the second digit to record cost of quality information — is this work 'Price of Conformance' or 'Price of Non-Conformance', is it 'Prevention, Appraisal or Failure'?

After a while, you can survey the project teams to find out what they are doing, what benefits they are getting, and then you adopt the best and start to apply it to the whole organization. The end result is a time-recording system that is simple, effective, non-intrusive and one that has been developed by its users.

I have illustrated some of the principles of data collection using the time-recording system as an example, but the same principles apply to most, if not all, such systems.

Review built components

Within this stage of the development of your SMP you will have numerous items to review. There are standards or guideline documents, training material and process designs among other things.

Do not skimp these reviews, as they cover items that form the public face of your metrics programme. The MCG, or a subset of it, can usefully form your review group. You may decide to go for walkthroughs or you may decide to use full, formal Fagans Inspections against the design and requirements documents. In any case, it is the act of reviewing that is more important rather than the method that is used.

THE FINAL COUNTDOWN

You are almost ready to go. You have built the components of your metrics programme, the database is waiting to take data from these components, to analyse it and your feedback mechanisms are in place. You have set up the support infrastructure for your programme.

If you have decided to use local metrics coordinators or facilitators within the engineering groups and you have selected these, then you are ready to train them.

In most situations there is only one thing left to do. Management must now be committed to the implementation of the programme. If you have consulted with your potential users through the development of the programme, remembering that senior management is a very important customer of your programme, then this vital step will be much easier. If you have sat in an ivory tower, building your programme in isolation, shut off from the development and management functions of the organization, then you will probably get no further.

As always, how you gain management commitment for implementation will depend upon the culture of your organization, but I would suggest that a presentation supported by endorsements from the MCG and a detailed report is probably your best option. You will almost certainly have to present some form of cost benefit analysis at this point.

Unless you are extremely lucky, the best you will be able to do is prepare this using sensible assumptions as to the benefits. Be realistic, but also challenging. Use your business plan to present a simple cash flow analysis over, say, five years. If you can get help from the financial people, then do so. It all helps.

In the end, commitment to implementing an SMP depends on two things. You have to present a proposal to the business that is coherent, complete and that offers the business the opportunity to realize real benefits. Also, the business has to be ready for it. It is no good offering software development the capability to predict field reliability based on obscure statistical techniques, if they have never even bothered to collect defect data before. Equally, the business must be mature enough to realize that there are serious problems in trying to develop software without management control, without a sensible degree of discipline and without clear goals.

Finally, the business must realize that there is no such thing as a free lunch, and that the only certainty is uncertainty. These are clichés, but they are true. A metrics programme costs money to operate, but it can be money well spent. Organizations that use Software Metrics effectively also realize that there are few off-the-shelf solutions. Some of what they do will not pay off, but if they follow the common sense approach of gathering clear requirements and if they realize that the metrics and the techniques are only part of the problem, then they are very likely to see real benefits to the business.

Once you have everything ready, once you have management commitment, then all you have to do is implement the programme. Wave the wand and watch it all happen.

If only it were so.

SUMMARY

Building the components of your SMP should be straightforward if you have invested effort in defining clear requirements and in designing those components. Despite this, a considerable amount of effort may be required to turn clear designs into solutions that are ready to implement. This effort is necessary and the expenditure cannot be avoided.

As always, it is important to devote effort during the build stage to every component of your programme, and that includes the non-technical aspects, such as training material and documentation.

13

STAGE 5 — IMPLEMENTATION

A PEOPLE-ORIENTATED ISSUE

The problem with implementation is that it involves other people!

This is a key point to remember because a Software Metrics programme is more to do with people than about the metrics and the techniques normally associated with such initiatives. People are awkward. They come in many shapes and sizes, but more importantly they all have personalities that must be catered for and egos that must be stroked. To successfully implement a metrics programme, we must develop and apply interpersonal skills such as we never have before.

Imagine that we have senior management commitment to take our programme forward, and that this involves introducing something new to a project team. We could be talking about different ways of deriving cost estimates, we may be talking about using *applied design metrics* to get better designs. If we look at any project team, I can guarantee that we will find a broad range of personalities with which we have to interact. We have no choice about this if we are to succeed.

During the industrial revolution, a group of workers went around the country smashing the new machines because they feared they would put them out of a job. These people became known as Luddites and their genes are still with us today. Of course, we would not expect today's Luddites to attack our proposals with crowbars and hammers, although one never knows. Today's Luddite uses more subtle, but equally effective techniques of destruction.

The situation is made worse because individuals who appear to us to be Luddites are often sincere in their criticism. Put forward any new idea in any field and there will be those who balk at its introduction, people who wish to preserve the *status quo,* or those who have heard all the hype before and who genuinely believe that software development, for example, can never be managed and controlled through the use of quantified information.

As you start to work with the project team, you will see these attitudes manifest themselves in 'office games'. An individual may continually seem to agree with you, and then throw in the dreaded word 'but'. 'Yes, but we work in a different way'; 'Yes, but we do not have the resources to devote to this kind of initiative'; 'Yes, but this is just common sense.'

Of course, you can counter most of these arguments. If you look at how the team develop software, you will probably see some differences in detail or terminology, but I guarantee that software development does not differ much between teams or even organizations. Requirements, Design, Design Implementation and Testing — these basic components will be there in some form or another.

How much is being wasted within the team through delivered defects that need to be fixed or through poor maintainability? Only a small proportion of this will pay for the metrics initiative. If you never invest in the future, you will have no future.

And, of course, it is common sense! If we only applied common sense in what we did, our problems would disappear overnight. Unfortunately, common sense is like expert estimators, both are rare commodities, especially within software development. Common sense says we try out high-risk, new systems on low-key, unimportant projects.

How much has your organization invested in CASE technology based on a gut feeling that it will pay benefits? Incidentally, Software Metrics is a low-risk proposal compared to most initiatives that occur within software development. To support this statement, I would ask you to compare the cost of implementing a new design tool, project planning techniques or a *total quality management* initiative to the cost of a Software Metrics programme. I believe that you will find the cost of the measurement initiative significantly lower than the others.

My favourite 'yes, but' is the one that goes: 'yes, but we need the tools'. By tools, what is meant is: 'where are the whiz bang computer systems to support these metrics, where are the expert systems, where are the relational databases?' These questions fascinate me for two reasons. Firstly, we have managed to develop large, complex systems in both the IT world and the non-IT world with little more than pencil and paper, so why do people believe that the 'tools' are a prerequisite to improvement. Secondly, and more importantly, 'tools' can only be introduced when a process is understood to the degree that it can be de-skilled, and if the environment is amenable to the application of 'tools'. For instance, you cannot automatically collect design metric data unless your designs are held in an electronic media.

This does not mean that I am in any way 'anti-tool'. Indeed, I long for the day when every stage of software system development is supported by an effective toolset. When that day comes, Software Metrics will be part and parcel of development, always assuming that we can get the people issues right.

The 'yes, but...' game is just one of many that you may come across but, if you will excuse the pun, it is especially difficult to counteract. If you continually try to defend the programme in the face of a continued onslaught, you will eventually run out of ammunition. A question will be asked for which you do not have an effective defence. The only way to counter this ploy is to meet it head on, but to use the age-old principle of turning an opponent's energy back on himself. 'Yes, but given the current state of software development, we have to do something positive to make things better. We have to make this programme work for us. Unless you have an alternative, of course?' This approach takes confidence, but then, if you do not believe in what you are proposing, you cannot expect others to.

Office games apart, the biggest problem with the implementation stage concerns resources. Implementing a Software Metrics programme within a team does mean that the team itself must put some cash up front. This is usually in the form of resources or effort. The problem is that the amount of resources needed is very difficult to quantify until you have some experience of doing it within your environment. Here, honesty really is the best policy. You should be able to give some broad brush estimates for the amount of effort involved, and you should do so, but do tell the team manager that these are estimates. Setting yourself a limit, basically using a banded estimate, is often worthwhile. After all, software development team leaders are well used to working with rough estimates. They do it every day or they would not need Software Metrics to help improve estimation! If you do make the mistake of dodging the effort issue, you will be storing up trouble for yourself in the future.

All of this sounds rather negative, but remember that most individuals involved in software development are only too aware that they need to improve the way in which they work, manage and control software development. Most are also very willing to try pragmatic approaches to get that improvement.

In any team there will be the natural Luddites. There will also be natural champions. Concentrate your efforts on the champions, and accept that there will always be some people you will not convince.

The whole point of the implementation stage is to turn potential customers of the metrics initiative into participants in the programme. If you succeed in this, they will quickly become the owners of the programme, and you will have delegated its operation and continued enhancement to them.

Remember what you have to achieve; you will do some selling and telling to achieve participation. You and your customer will work closely together until you can pull back having delegated the programme to them. One trick is knowing when to let go, learn it.

The time to let go is when they are doing more of the positive talking and technical innovation than you are. Then you have succeeded.

THE LAUNCH

Implementation truly starts with the launch of the programme. This is the point when you use the commitment from the management for implementation, and you demonstrate to the organization that you are in a position to carry out that implementation.

You need publicity for the programme if you are to attract customers, so you should make the launch an event in some way. We have already discussed this when talking about planning the launch so all I will say at this point is that you should now put those plans into effect. We may be talking about nothing more than a memo to department heads or we may be talking about a roadshow. Whatever, make sure it happens.

The one other thing that you may need to consider relates to your Metrics Coordination Group (MCG). So far, this group has acted as the steering committee for the development of the initiative, a sounding board for possible solutions. Effectively, they have been the recipients of information and they have provided feedback on that information. They have also, hopefully, provided requirements data, but this has been prompted and driven by the metrics team. As you enter the implementation stage, this group should become much more pro-active.

The MCG now needs to own the programme. It is its custodian and should be the focal point for metrics in the organization. This is a different situation to that which has existed during the development of the programme, when you and the other members of the metrics team will have provided that focus and the drive that fuels the programme.

As part of your launch event, you may like to hold a 'final' meeting of the MCG and, during that meeting, target individuals within the organization that will form the new group. You can also draft new terms of reference for the group which will need to be ratified by it. If you have chaired the MCG during programme development, then it is now time to hand that role over to someone within the software development function. If you are very lucky, the Systems Development Director will take on that responsibility.

IMPLEMENTATION

Even if you have a clear mandate for the implementation of your metrics initiative, you depend upon cooperation from your customers. You must communicate with your customers and communication, along with all other aspects of implementation, takes effort.

And that is the key point that you must drive home to your organization. Implementation is not free, even though most of the creative work has, or at least should have been done beforehand.

Implementation is the most deceptive and risky stage of this whole lifecycle. Look, for instance, at this chapter. It is a very short chapter, and the activities it identifies are few. The reason for this is that the planning, the designing and the constructing of the metrics programme has been done during earlier stages and this, the implementation stage, is simply a question of transferring technology from a few areas to every area. This need not be difficult or complex, but it does cost.

Now imagine the following situation. You have 20 product groups within which you wish to implement Software Metrics. Even with a mandate to implement from on high, you will still need to sell metrics to those product groups and their managers. I say again, you can tell teams to measure until you are blue in the face. You have to sell them on the idea.

Having sold the concept, you have to train people, you have to support them and you have to help people make the concepts of the programme work. It all takes time. If you were to allow 30 days of internal consultancy effort per product team just to sell them the concepts and get them over the first hump of the learning curve, that would not be excessive.

This means that we are talking about 600 person days of effort across the 20 teams for initial support. You will also have to maintain contact with those teams, albeit at a much reduced rate, for some considerable time. If you do not keep this contact up, and I would recommend at least 1 day per month for 12 months, then the team will backslide and you may as well not have bothered.

Of course, these figures are generalizations, but you may be surprised at how close they are to your own particular support costs.

One final point regarding implementation. The biggest problem that you may face may be with your facilitators or support staff. Do not expect them to be able to make the transition to their new role overnight, because for most of them this will be a complete change. We must accept that we work in a technical industry. Good support staff have experience of that technical side of our work, and are possibly very good at it, because they should really have a deeper understanding of it than the average engineer. However, far beyond that in terms of importance is an ability to operate in what is basically a sales environment. Many IT people find this very difficult.

There is a very interesting book called *The Strategy of the Dolphin* (Lynch, 1990). This book has a model for classifying people as carps, sharks or dolphins. I find this a very pleasing model, and will simply say that what you want as supporters or facilitators are dolphins.

SUMMARY — CLOSING THE CIRCLE

I truly hope that you, as the reader, do not feel shortchanged by this chapter. Implementation really is easy, costly but easy, provided that you have laid the foundations properly during the earlier stages. Of course, no matter how good your preparation is, there will be problems that will have to be overcome but, if you have come this far, they should not be unsurmountable, and remember that the most difficult problems to overcome will be associated with people rather than with the technical aspects of your programme.

The circle is closed by going right back to the very beginning; by taking up some of those items that for one reason or another could not be addressed by the first implementation of your initiative or programme; by starting the second phase of your initiative even while you are implementing the first.

In other words — we do it all again!

14

SECTION 2 — A SUMMARY

As you will have gathered by now, the development and implementation of a Software Metrics programme is not something that should be undertaken lightly. Section 2 of this book has attempted to provide a guide through the complexities of such an undertaking, but it may be worth summarizing its key messages. I will endeavour to do that now.

The aim of this chapter is to summarize the messages of the preceding chapters as succinctly as possible. The question is, how can I do this? What I would like to do is present to you a set of slides (figures) that summarize the overall approach to Software Metrics programmes contained within this book. These slides have been used on real, live audiences and seem to go down quite well. In fact, they have formed the backbone of this book as I have been writing it and are as much the foundation as the summary. As to what use you make of these slides in the future, that is entirely up to you. If any of them could be used to help you get a message across, then please feel free to reproduce them as required.

We start with what this book is about. Figure 14.1 is the title slide of this show, and it says quite clearly that the implementation of Software Metrics programmes, in my

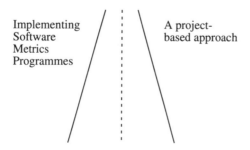

Figure 14.1 A project-based approach.

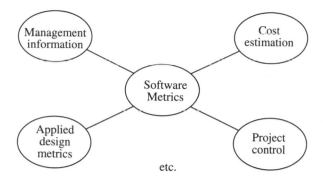

Figure 14.2 Topic scope.

opinion, relies on the use of a project-based approach. Having read Section 2, you are well aware of that already. Let us move on.

Looking at Fig. 14.2 we consider the scope of Software Metrics as a topic. As the slide shows, I consider the application of Software Metrics to fall under four main categories.

Management information is the classic approach to Software Metrics in that it gives managers the information they need to do their job. Without management information they are flying by the seat of their pants, and probably do not even know in which direction they are heading. Management information itself is a very large topic and can typically include the management of procurement as well as more commonly recognized elements, such as project productivity measurement or the prediction of quality levels for a product.

Cost estimation is an area of Software Metrics application that has been widely discussed within our industry. In fact, some people would see cost estimation as 'Software Metrics'. Cost estimation is important because it is the results that come out of this exercise that drive project planning, bidding for work and, probably, the whole environment in which our staff work for many months. Poor estimation of project cost can actually drive an organization out of existence.

Having estimated the cost of a project and used this to drive the planning of that project, it is sensible to keep track of progress against that plan. It is here that *project control* techniques come in. Will I be on time and within budget are simply two of the questions to which this area of Software Metrics seeks to supply answers.

Finally, we can consider *applied design metrics*. These are measurement-based techniques that can be used to improve the quality of intermediate deliverables produced during the development or maintenance lifecycle. Included in the applied design metrics topic are *information flow* and McCabe metrics.

Given the wide scope of the topic we call Software Metrics and the fact that most organizations are large and complex, I suggest that you apply a phasing principle to your programme. Target specific topics and specific areas of the organization at a particular time.

I also suggest that the development of a Software Metrics initiative consists of the following stages, as shown in Fig. 14.3. Adopting a project-based approach to a measurement initiative implies that certain things are considered. For example, plans for the project should exist, reviews should be recognized as necessary, resources should be allocated and management and control mechanisms should be in place.

Figure 14.3 Basic strategy.

Initiation

Looking at the Initiation stage (Fig. 14.4), there are many triggers that can start a Software Metrics initiative, and there are many individuals within an organization who can recognize such a trigger. As this is often beyond the control of the person who will be responsible for implementing the programme, we will not dwell on this. However, it is worth remembering that the more senior an initiator is, the more vague the requirements are likely to be. Vague requirements are not good news for a Software Metrics programme.

• Triggers

    Productivity/quality concerns
    Management/customer
    demands for information
    Fear
    Control = competitive edge

• Initiators

    IT management
    Senior management (non IT)
    Quality or R&D function
    A 'technocrat'

Figure 14.4 Initiation stage.

Requirements specification

Once you get past the initiation stage you can adopt a formal project approach (Fig. 14.5). Firstly, find out what is required. If at all possible, obtain a customer authority, that is someone to whom you will deliver and who will decide what is to be delivered.

Look to your customers, and these are usually internal to the organization, rarely external — although it is the business needs of the end customers that provides the context of the metrics programme.

• Obtain customer authority
• Identify customers and customer groupings
• Set up liaison mechanism – MCG
• Obtain requirements – standard systems analysis
• Group requirements – identify sub-project streams
• Prepare and review requirements specification
• SPECIFY TOR

Figure 14.5 Requirements specification.

Component design

Remember that your Metrics programme, this thing that seemed so simple and clear such a short time ago, may well consist of many sub-projects as a result of your requirements gathering work (Fig. 14.6).

'Sub-projects'

Figure 14.6 Component design 1.

Having sorted out what your programme is expected to deliver, you now have to build the components of the system that will meet those requirements. The key thing to remember during this stage is that you cannot ignore any one of three major streams (Fig. 14.7); the measures and measurement-based techniques, the marketing strategy that you will use to implement those measures and the infrastructure that you will use to support that implementation.

Notice that it is only now that you start to consider the metrics. Remember the heresy contained within this book. It is not difficult to measure — it is only difficult to convince people of the need to measure and to then get them to do something about it!

The design stage is where you start to look in more detail. As far as marketing and the business planning side of things are concerned, you need to think about education, publicity, sales strategies and rollout plans. You look at the infrastructure and you have to consider centralized versus distributed metrics functions or follow my advice, which is a compromise as shown in Fig. 14.8.

• Three major streams
    Metrics and metrics based techniques
    Marketing and business planning
    Infrastructure design
      Do not ignore any element!

Figure 14.7 Component design 2.

• Ignore the infrastructure at your peril
  Central support vs distributed functions

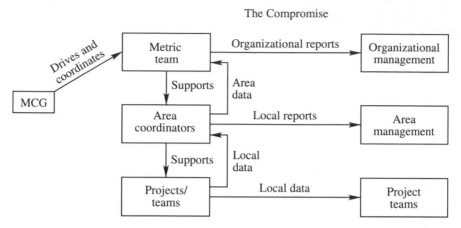

Figure 14.8 Component design 3.

Component build

Building the components of your measurement programme should be mechanistic (Fig. 14.9). This does not mean that the build process will not consume significant resources or take a considerable elapsed time to complete. It simply recognizes that most of the work should have been done during the requirements specification and the design stages.

Remember that what you should aim to deliver are complete solutions. That means training, procedures support services, etc. Having these things ready makes the next stage possible.

* Write procedures/standards — never enough

* Prepare training material

* Build prototype database

* Obtain software packages

* Train coordinators i.e. 'build' the infrastructure

Figure 14.9 Component build.

Implementation

Implementation is all about people and this brings its own class of problems. The rules for mitigating the effects of these problems are simple and are often seen as common sense. Common sense is not easy to acquire at the start of a project but these guidelines or rules may help (Fig. 14.10).

You will need to sell the metrics programme to your customers, that is to your

- Sell the programme to the projects

- Train the staff

- Provide the procedures

- Tailor to local conditions

Figure 14.10 Implementation 1.

colleagues and associates. To help these people to implement the components that form your measurement initiative, you will have to provide training and procedures or, if you prefer, written guidance addressing the application of measurement. You may well have to make changes to your generic solutions to make them valid for a specific environment. You can view this as tailoring a basic pattern to provide a bespoke service to your customers.

Having done all of this, you still cannot walk away. You must help your customers to use, on a day-to-day basis, the strategies you have provided. This means holding their hands, it means visiting them regularly, listening to concerns and, above all else, helping them to feedback the results of their efforts to their local managers and to the organization in a way that facilitates process improvement (Fig. 14.11).

Having got a part of your measurement programme running, you do it all again!

- Hold their hand!

- Visit teams regularly

- Listen to concerns

- Beware of 'other priorities'

- If you take data away

PROVIDE FEEDBACK

Figure 14.11 Implementation 2.

A RECIPE FOR SUCCESS

What do I see as the important, pervasive and fundamental points that need to guide any measurement initiative? The easy answer is to point you towards the whole of Section 2, but if I have to identify a small set of key points bearing in mind that for particular circumstances others may join the list, I would choose the following:

1. Avoid ivory towers, which means that you must know your internal market, identify your customers and listen to what they say, so that you can identify their requirements together with the business benefits that they wish to realize.
2. Software Metrics is a large topic and organizations are generally both large and complex. You cannot do everything at once, so chunk it down into phases of activity.

3. Provide solution packages. That is procedures, training and support. All three are vital.
4. Do not ignore the infrastructure. This does not just mean the fancy metrics database with all the bells and whistles which may be unnecessary at the beginning anyway. It does mean the organizational support mechanisms that facilitate or ease the use of metrics.

Finally, and very simply, treat the measurement initiative as a project in its own right.

Section 3

15

ALTERNATIVE APPROACHES TO METRICATION

This chapter does not offer any shortcuts in terms of avoiding the development and implementation lifecycle for a metrics initiative described in this book. To do that would give the impression that it is possible to succeed without, in some way, addressing the questions of requirements, component design, building and implementation. I firmly believe that this is not a feasible option for a successful, and I stress the word successful, measurement initiative.

However, I also recognize that the programme described, or implied, in the other chapters is what could be called a total metrics initiative. In other words, it recognizes that Software Metrics is a topic covering considerable scope, and it implies that the whole of that scope be addressed. Although phasing has been mentioned, it may be worth discussing this concept in a little more detail. Correctly handled, phasing can help deliver results to the organization relatively quickly, thus overcoming one of the problems with metrics initiatives, the long lead time.

PHASING OR SCOPE VARIATION

Software Metrics is a wide ranging specialism covering the whole of the software development and support lifecycle. It is likely that your organization is also large with many functional groups making it complex in structure. An obvious way to reduce costs, duration and up-front commitment is to reduce the scope of your initial programme in one or both dimensions.

Targeting one development team, for instance, can enable you to develop a centre of excellence within your organization, and you can use this to demonstrate the beneficial effects of what you wish to implement across the whole organization. Working with one team that is not too large should mean that you can get a programme running within six months. Of course, you will depend upon the willing cooperation of the development team, and you will still have to go through the various metrics programme development and implementation lifecycle stages. You benefit from having a very limited market-place for this first phase of the programme.

Of course, there are a number of problems with this approach to metrication. If there were not, then all organizations would do it this way. One problem is that really being able to demonstrate benefits will take much longer than six months. You may be able to get your programme running in six months, but genuinely to show benefits, you may have to wait for perhaps another twelve months before hard data becomes available that you can use to convince others in the organization. This is especially true if you are concentrating on things like the measurement of field reliability.

Another problem concerns the 'not invented here' syndrome. Even if you have hard data available, you may find that other teams take the attitude that just because it worked for one group does not mean that it will work for them. This is always a danger with pilots, and really we are talking about a form of pilot here. The reverse can also happen where you find it difficult to promote the use of something tried in the pilot group, because that group is seen as a centre of excellence. The feeling you then encounter is one of resistance, because the pilot group is seen as being favoured in numerous ways.

The last major problem with this approach is that you can suffer from a lack of visibility. Especially in large organizations, working with only one team may mean that your metrics initiative is unnoticed by those in the organization with real power. You need that notice if you are to affect real change. Despite all of these problems, tackling the first phase of your initiative in this way can pay off, especially if you take care to abate the risks outlined above.

Then there is the second dimension. Software Metrics is a big topic — what if we make it smaller?

This approach can work very effectively, and has been the seed from which some of the best regarded measurement initiatives, certainly in Europe, have grown. I include in these a leading UK Bank, a large government department and a leading European industrial organization. All of these organizations now have established, and it would seem effective, measurement programmes, and all of them started by concentrating on specific areas within the Software Metrics domain.

The technique is to identify a key trigger which is very important to your organization or to a specific customer. Whoever the customer, senior management must be aware of the area of concern.

Concentrating on a very specific area of Software Metrics means that you can greatly reduce the learning time for the individuals involved. If you then drive matters forwards, i.e. you essentially pilot a technique or approach, possibly under the guise of an evaluation, you can get results quite quickly, certainly within nine months providing your topic is amenable to that time-scale. Do bear in mind that you cannot expect to show benefits from the use of, for instance, design metrics in that time-scale if it takes nine months for your project simply to move from design to coding.

Provided that you are sensible in choosing a topic that can give results within a reasonable time, and that you then push those results up to senior management, you could quickly end up with a full-scale metrics initiative to manage.

As always, there are no perfect answers to life's problems, and there are some problems with this approach. Addressing one area of Software Metrics may mean that you pick the wrong one for your organization or that, for whatever reason, you do not get good results on your first attempt. Another danger is that the focus of the organization shifts, so that what was a vitally important problem yesterday is suddenly less important. In wider ranging initiatives, the occasional failure can be hidden behind successes. Of course, one way to reduce the risk is to go for two topics at a time if you have the resources.

IN BY THE BACK DOOR

If you have authority or responsibility for a metrics initiative and you sit within some functional group removed from mainstream development, perhaps as part of an R&D group, then reducing the scope of your metrics initiative may well appeal. What do you do if you do not really have management's eye or the explicit responsibility for process improvement within the organization, through metrics or through any other means?

It is possible to slide metrics into an organization through the back door, but it can take a long time and it can be quite frustrating in the short term. Let us set up a scenario, and then look at a particular solution that may work.

You are a manager. You do not report directly to the Systems Development Director, in fact, there are numerous levels of management between him or her and your lowly self. You are responsible for a particular software product, and you know that you and your team are struggling with problems. You believe that there are better ways of doing things and you have perhaps come across the idea of management through measurement at a seminar. Such a concept appeals to you, but you know that you do not have enough clout to drive such an initiative through the organization. Anyway, apart from anything else, most of your time is spent managing your own team.

Try this approach. Get your first line and any other team members whose opinion you especially respect into a room for a day. The agenda is 'process improvement'. Ask your colleagues what the major problems are today. From what they say and subsequent discussion, you should be able to arrive at a small set of key requirements that need to be addressed to improve things for your group. Obviously, you need to concentrate on items that you can affect.

Assign one individual the task of designing a solution that will satisfy the requirement. Give him or her visible support, help but do not overshadow, and aim to get a revised process in place within two months.

Run it for six months, and at the same time target the next major problem area. Do not go for sledge-hammer solutions — you are looking for levers to move things to a higher level of effectiveness. This means that you cannot put in fantastic, whiz bang, automated solutions, and that all you may end up with, apart from a better process, is a paper and pencil system supported, possibly, by a spreadsheet.

Within nine months you should be able to identify a significant improvement in the way your group operates. Of course, you will not be the only one to notice this. Management will also become aware of improvements and so will other teams. You may well find that you start to get enquiries from these other groups and from management. The problem with this is that you may end up managing the metrics initiative for the whole organization.

An excellent example of metrication came from a large European organization. One divisional manager got fed up with not being able to control software development projects, and to counter this he put in a process based on simple and regular information gathering from project managers using very straightforward metrics about progress against plans. Matters improved quickly and dramatically. The end result was the extension of the project control process to all software development divisions.

HITCHING A RIDE

Many organizations have introduced the concept of Total Quality Management (TQM) as a means of improving the processes they operate. Such a programme invariably requires a high degree of senior management commitment and obliges an organization to change its current culture.

Measurement is a fundamental part of TQM, and such a programme offers an ideal opportunity for the introduction of Software Metrics. Measurement is also implicit within Competitive Benchmarking programmes, as developed by Rank Xerox and certification to ISO 9000. Any of these types of initiative can offer a good vehicle for metrication within an organization.

The maintenance division of GAK in Holland have taken this approach of addressing metrication within their overall Quality Improvement Programme, (Dollé, 1992). Interestingly, they are using an ISO 9001 certification project as a vehicle to implement various concepts piloted within the Quality Improvement Programme. Using this approach, metrics are becoming an integral part of their process.

The key to using this approach successfully would seem to be the identification of short-term objectives that are achievable and then to use the momentum generated during one phase to fuel the next. One of the big advantages of this linking strategy is that you can use the senior management commitment to the larger programme to give authority, by association, to the metrics initiative, thus reducing the amount of effort needed to sell metrics. Do note that this effort requirement is never reduced to zero.

HARD AND FAST

This final alternative is one that demands a high degree of senior management commitment because it involves money.

One of the biggest problems with any Software Metrics programme can be the lack of in-house experience, either in terms of technical knowledge or in terms of experience relating to the management of culture change. This means that individuals who are responsible for doing the work have to spend time learning the subject. They will also spend time investigating specific techniques that turn out to be unsuitable for their particular environment. They may try things out within pilots and evaluation exercises, where somebody with experience of such techniques might be able to say, with confidence, 'this will work if we do it this way because, in a similar environment, it did last time'.

Of course, just because something worked before somewhere else does not guarantee that it will work in your environment, but there are some requirements and, more importantly, some solutions to these requirements that are common to most organizations. An expert should be aware of these, and will also be able to identify what needs to be changed to tailor a generic solution to a specific environment or organization. For example, most organizations would benefit from being able to record information about defects in their software systems as delivered to the customer. One question that must be asked is: 'what information should be recorded, and to what level should those records be kept'?

An in-house team could spend a considerable amount of time researching this concept by reading technical papers and talking to other organizations; discussing in committee what would be the best data, and finally drawing up the proposals for a defect recording system. Experience shows that the eventual system may well be difficult to operate and to use to get meaningful results, because the first attempt is often too detailed.

Any expert should also talk to potential users and operators of the system to ensure that he or she does not try to make a solution fit where it really does not. However, an expert should be able to help an organization establish a workable and useful defect recording system very quickly.

In this case, the solution may be as simple as agreeing a high-level lifecycle for software development and putting in mechanisms, often no more than simple forms and a PC database, to record point of injection and point of discovery of the defect, together with some additional information such as system name, date of discovery and date of closure. This limited amount of information can be used to provide data which, in turn, can be used to assess the effectiveness of the development process. An expert should also be able to determine quickly whether defects should be recorded at the system, programme or programme component level, so that the needs of the organization are met.

The obvious question is from where do you get this expertise? If expertise does not exist within your organization, the only solutions are to recruit it or to buy it in. In other words, I am talking about the use of external entrants or consultants. To get external entrants may not be acceptable, if it increases the permanent head count of the organization and, even if you get the go-ahead, there are not many experienced metrics practitioners in the market-place. This is slowly changing, but it will take some time before the demand for such experience is less than the supply. One reason for this shortfall is that those individuals who do have experience of implementing metrics programmes often move into consultancy anyway.

Now the big problem with consultancy, even assuming you can get the right people, is that it costs money! For this reason you can only use the strategy of a consultancy-driven programme if you have senior management commitment to spend the necessary money.

You also need to have clear objectives which you expect the consultant or consultancy team to achieve. This can be more difficult than you may think, and it often pays to set things up in three distinct stages.

1. The first stage is simply to identify suitable consultants. If you are already involved with a consultancy organization and you feel comfortable with it, then you have a good starting point, but do remember that Software Metrics is a young discipline and that, even among consultants, practical experience of the topic is scarce. How you identify suitable consultants is something that only you can determine, but the one suggestion I would make is that you do look for evidence of previous experience, preferably in the area in which you are interested. For example, someone with experience of *applied design metrics*, say the use of McCabe or *information flow metrics* may not be too knowledgeable about cost estimation models such as COCOMO.
2. The second phase is all about scoping and planning. Many organizations are reluctant

to pay consultancy fees simply to have the consultant prepare a proposal and plans for the real work. However, the advantage of such preparation is that you can get to know the consultants, and you get some indication of their effectiveness without contracting large sums of money. The consultants get the opportunity to get close to your organization and the time to properly plan the work ahead. This increases the likelihood of success so everyone wins. Of course, you must make it clear to the consultants that the proposals and plans produced must be for your organization. You do not want to pay for generic solutions lifted from textbooks.

3. Once you have an agreed proposal, you can start the third phase, the real work. You will need to consider the management of this strategy. Someone from your organization must have responsibility for the project because, at some time in the future, the consultant will walk away and you will be left to carry on. A clear customer authority and resources to review deliverables are vital components of a consultancy-driven programme.

The transfer of knowledge from the consultant to the organization is also a deliverable of the project, but only achievable when the consultant's and the organization's own staff work together. The aim is consultancy-drive with organizational ownership and involvement. To help achieve this, do not lock your consultant away in an ivory tower, instead have regular project meetings to discuss the approaches being used, progress, plans and deliverables. This may add slightly to the cost, as it all takes time, but it is money well spent.

The consultancy-driven approach to metrication depends upon senior management commitment, because it costs money, needs cooperation and, most importantly, requires trust between the consultants and the organization and vice versa.

Its disadvantage is that it costs. Its advantage is that you can have a working software measurement programme in place much more quickly than if you try to do it solely using internal resources.

These alternatives can all help with the metrication process, but underlying them all is a project-based approach that uses a lifecycle of the kind described in this book. Do not be tempted to cut corners on that, or you will significantly increase your probability of failure.

16

THE HOME STRETCH

In this chapter I would like to move away from the problem of developing and implementing a metrics initiative or programme, and close the book by discussing various topics that fall within the area of interest of anyone involved in Software Metrics. I hope to do this not from the implementation standpoint of the previous sections, but more by introducing and discussing topics that you may find interesting.

METRICATION TODAY

Firstly, I would like to look at what seem to be the key areas of interest today as far as the application of Software Metrics is concerned. This discussion will be looking at trends and at specific topics that are not covered in any detail elsewhere in this book but which, I believe, should be mentioned in a book about Software Metrics.

After looking at the world today, I would like to take a look to the future. What are the topics, areas and techniques that we will all be talking about in two, five or maybe even ten years?

The material will, I hope, be of use to some individuals, and it is offered with that intention but, obviously, the comments are a very personal view, and you may hear conflicting evidence or opinions from other sources. It is up to you to make up your own mind, but then you knew that anyway!

I have used material from many sources in both the academic and industrial environments, so specific credits are not given unless I believe it necessary for further research.

So, looking at today's world, what are the topics that come up time and again at conferences, seminars and meetings as being useful? Alternatively, what is everyone looking for, and where can we get hold of some information?

I intend to start by looking at two areas that originated in the USA, but are making greater and greater inroads in Europe. These are the *goal, question, metric* (GQM) paradigm from Basili and Rombach at the Software Engineering Laboratory (SEL) and the *process maturity model* from the Software Engineering Institute (SEI), fully described in Watts Humphrey's book, *Managing the Software Process*.

I have already discussed the GQM paradigm in other parts of this book, but I have included it here to emphasize the fact that its use is not yet widespread within the metrics community. That use is increasing, I would say, exponentially, and a great deal of credit must go to Vic Basili and Dieter Rombach for expressing, so elegantly, a process that has saved many individuals a great deal of pain.

I would also like to stress that there is a great deal more to this paradigm than is often presented at conferences and seminars. It is certainly more than setting a goal, asking a few questions and, hey look, we got ourselves a metric. The model is rich, and before you think you understand it, I suggest you read material such as Rombach (1990) and AMI (1992).

I believe that we will hear more and more about the GQM approach to metrication over the next few years. We will also hear more and more about the SEI's *process maturity model*. Like GQM, we should also realize that the *process maturity model* has more to it than may at first be obvious.

This model forms part of a technique that can be used to assess the effectiveness of a process for software development. Immediately we can think of two applications for such a technique. If I own such a process, perhaps as the manager of an IT function, then I would like to assess that process. Such information can perhaps help me to decide the best management initiatives; if the scoring mechanism is widely accepted, then a good score will do me no harm at all, and could do me a great deal of good; even a bad score is not a disaster, if I can show improvement over time.

The other application has a very different emphasis. If such a technique gives me an objective mechanism by which I can assess a software development process then I, as a purchaser of software systems, can use that process to assess potential suppliers.

These two applications have been recognized by the SEI, who have established two processes, the SEI *assessment* and the closely related *software capability evaluation*. The main differences are that an organization carries out an SEI assessment for its own benefit, but that same organization may have a software capability evaluation carried out on it, especially if it is its intention to supply a US government department. We should realize that both these techniques are essentially the same, only the emphasis being different, so I will briefly describe the process behind an SEI assessment.

The SEI assessment

The first step is a management commitment to the assessment and, most importantly, to the improvement plan that results from the assessment. Next, a small team from the organization is trained by the SEI or one of its accredited trainers. Notice that we are essentially talking about a self assessment here, but one done to a recognized and accepted formula.

Next, plans are prepared to ensure the assessment can be rapidly completed, typically within one week, and then projects or areas are selected for that assessment. The selected project or area teams then fill out a questionnaire of, currently, 101 yes/no questions.

The assessment team then corroborate the questionnaire data and delve much deeper through a series of intensive interviews and group discussions. Note that the questionnaire is not the whole assessment. These interviews actually form the key to the SEI assessment technique. Penultimately, results are presented to management, together with a set of recommendations for improvement.

The last step is for the organization to prepare and implement action plans to realize the recommendations, and that is seen as part of the assessment process, not separate to it.

The process maturity model

But what about the maturity model. This usually forms part of the management sign up discussions, and a score against it also results from the assessment. It is simply a five-level representation of the maturity of a process where these levels range from initial or *ad hoc*, through repeatable, defined, managed and optimizing (see Fig. 16.1).

It is this maturity model onto which most people have fastened although some have also latched on to the questionnaire. Most do not attempt a full understanding of the SEI assessment technique which, to judge by the experiences of part of the Hughes Aircraft organization, is a shame. Having bought into the SEI assessment mechanism and followed through on recommendations, this group moved from level 2 to level 3. It took them two years to do it, and cost about $450 000. Why bother?

Well, they estimate savings of $2 million *per annum*! Even if they have overestimated, I do not believe that they have done so by much.

How they did it is described in the IEEE Software Engineering transactions issued in July 1991 (Humphrey *et al.*). This paper, together with some of the discussion papers that follow it, both supporting and criticizing the assessment process, make interesting reading.

Related problems

We all know that there are few perfect solutions, so what are the problems with the SEI assessment process and the associated software capability evaluation? We should also ask why the maturity model has generated so much interest and how it can be used.

The first problem is an interesting one. How would you feel if your customers insisted on your development process being assessed? Obviously there has been, and continues to be, some resistance to the idea of having to suffer a software capability evaluation. However, when the organization insisting on that evaluation is the US Department of Defense, and you want a piece of their expenditure to come in your direction, you may well feel it judicious to swallow your pride. I feel that the reality is that the industry is moving, more and more, to a situation where customers will demand that the capability of their suppliers be expressed in recognizable forms, and the SEI approach is certainly a step in this direction. What we need to be very careful about is that we do not allow ill-conceived and possibly harmful initiatives to be foisted on the industry. This is more probable if suppliers of software seek to resist these initiatives. We stand a much greater chance of getting workable and helpful assessment mechanisms if suppliers and customers, professional developers and academics cooperate.

It must also be said that the SEI's two-pronged approach which, essentially, offers the same techniques for supplier evaluation and self-assessment, encourages such cooperation, and has contributed to the take-up of their mechanisms.

Level	Characteristics	Key challenges	Result
5 **Optimizing**	• Improvement fed back into process • Data gathering is automated and used to identify weakest process elements • Numerical evidence used to justify application of technology to critical tasks • Rigorous defect–cause analysis and detect prevention	• Still human-intensive process • Maintain organization at optimizing level	Productivity and quality
4 **Managed**	(Quantitative) • Measured process • Minimum set of quality and productivity measurements established • Process database established with resources to analyse its data and maintain it	• Changing technology • Problem analysis • Problem prevention	
3 **Defined**	(Qualitative) • Process defined and institutionalized • Software Engineering Process Group established to lead process improvement	• Process measurement • Process analysis • Quantitative quality plans	
2 **Repeatable**	(Intuitive) • Process dependent on individuals • Established basic project controls • Strength in doing similar work, but faces major risk when presented with new challenges • Lacks orderly framework for improvement	• Training • Technical practices (reviews, testing) • Process focus (standards, process groups)	
1 **Initial**	(Ad hoc/chaotic process) • No formal procedures, cost estimates, project plans • No management mechanism to ensure procedures are followed, tools not well integrated and change control is lax • Senior management does not understand key issues	• Project management • Project planning • Configuration management • Software quality assurance	Risk

Figure 16.1 The SEI process-maturity framework.

Another problem is a statistical one. Some doubts have been raised as to the statistical validity of the SEI approach, for example see *A Critical Look at Software Capability Evaluations* by Bollinger and McGowan (Bollinger, 1991). Watts Humphrey has written a response to this article. Now it seems to me that we can rarely get two statisticians to agree about anything. I feel we must look at the usefulness of techniques, models and approaches on their merits in terms of satisfying needs, assuming they meet basic mathematical requirements. Meanwhile, we can sit back and enjoy the statistical arguments if we wish but, personally, I would rather leave it to the Jesuits, maybe they can sort it out!

A more fundamental concern, and it is no more than a concern on my part, lies with the success of the SEI approach and the maturity model, not with the approach and the model themselves. The reason for this concern is that more and more publicity is being given to the maturity model and its five levels, but little understanding exists of the SEI assessment technique as a whole, and that whole is important if the maturity model is to be understood in context.

We have had this problem with the GQM paradigm, and I must admit I do not see an easy solution. The fundamental problem is that the maturity model is a very convenient mechanism that can be used to describe the capability of an organization. Like all models, we lose a massive amount of detail when we do this, but people can relate to that model, especially more senior managers.

Things that work, and in this context the maturity model does work, tend to get used. We, as professionals, must remember that much more lies behind the maturity model and we must use it correctly.

Certainly the GQM paradigm and the SEI assessment techniques, which incorporate the maturity model, are 'hot' topics at the moment, and they have such momentum that I feel they will be with us for some time to come.

Automation

Another topic that will still be with us for some considerable time is the question of automation. Everyone wants the data associated with a Software Metrics initiative to be collected automatically. Unfortunately, this is seldom achieved. It is true that some tools are now available which supply metrics, but these tend to be in specialized areas. For example, static and dynamic analysers such as Testbed from Program Analysers, Newbury, UK and the McCabe tool Battlemap, McCabe Associates, Columbia, Washington, USA, do provide metrics, as well as providing other functionality. The Bang or Function Weight Metric has been partially automated within the Teamwork design tool.

Unfortunately, these do not satisfy anything like the range of data collection requirements within even a simple metrics initiative. Currently, we are unable to offer a fully automated data collection mechanism within any practical measurement programme. What we can do is to ensure that automated solutions are developed where and when that approach is appropriate. For example, I do not see us being able to collect fault reports made by the user automatically. However, once that fault has been logged and entered into the system, the tracking of it and the collection of data associated with it, for example the time taken to close or resolve the fault, can be automated to a large degree. Basically, we can automate metrication only as we automate our own processes.

Research

And after that rather negative view of automation, we should look to something more positive. It is always good to hear of national institutions supporting good works; it is even more encouraging to find the international community supporting good works, in this case research into the topic of Software Metrics, and the process of technology transfer that should follow that research.

The European Community has for some years now been funding, together with industry and academia, numerous projects that address the area of software engineering. It is good to be able to say that a significant proportion of this funded research has focused on Software Metrics.

The initiative with which I am most familiar is the ESPRIT research programme. This consists of numerous projects, some of which have been completed and others which are still running. The ones I have found most useful are the MUSE project, MUSE (1992), which looked at the current state of metrication within the European arena; METKIT which has produced quite a comprehensive range of measurement training material for use by practitioners, managers and students and MUSiC which is looking at the problem of measuring 'usability'. For information regarding METKIT and MUSiC see the list of ESPRIT projects at the back of the book.

These are essentially research and development projects. Two other projects that must be mentioned are PYRAMID and AMI. These are both technology transfer projects that aim to increase the awareness and promote the use of metrics-based techniques. Further information about the EEC research programme can be obtained from various sources listed in Appendix B.

Enhanceability and user satisfaction

Other topics that seem to be generating interest today in the area of metrication are measures for enhanceability and user satisfaction. Almost all of us are living with systems that we expected to be replaced years ago, but still they go on. Not only do they still exist, but they are also continually enhanced. I do not believe that anyone has got to a system in the same state as the axe that had three new heads and four new shafts and was still as good as the day it was bought, but who knows? If, as we now realize is possible, systems can have vastly extended lifespans, then being able to control and manage the enhanceability of that system is important. Elsewhere in this book a simple model of an enhanceability measure is proposed, i.e. number of system components affected divided by size of enhancement in LOC or Function Point Score but this topic is one that merits more discussion within our community.

As far as user satisfaction is concerned, it should come as no surprise that this is seen as important. Satisfied users provide repeat business, they tell other potential customers and they can generate new business; and a satisfied customer is much less likely to cause us pain on a daily basis. But how do we know if our customer is satisfied? The obvious answer is to ask them, but ask them in a way that enables an objective answer to be obtained rather than by means of a quick phone call.

There are two points to bear in mind about user satisfaction assessment. Firstly, our business environment will impact heavily on how we address this problem. For instance, if we are cooperating closely with a client on a large project, we can build user satisfaction evaluations into our project control mechanisms so that the user has a chance to express any concerns there may be. Remember, we must drive this because many problems are not large enough to make the user or customer actively complain, but it only takes a few of these 'little' problems to leave a nasty taste in the user's mouth. Alternatively, we may be maintaining a system for a user. In this case an annual meeting with a structured format can work in assessing user/customer satisfaction. Finally, we may be selling a product to many customers. In this situation, we cannot ask all our customers how they feel, but we can sample.

The second point to remember is that user satisfaction does not depend solely on satisfying expressed requirements. A classic example of this could be the organization that has a service level agreement with a client which requires an engineer being on site within one hour of a problem being reported, and that 99 per cent of all problems be resolved within one day. If a supplier organization achieved this tight constraint, they would be surprised if the customer cancelled the contract. What if the engineers always arrived within an hour, but were surly and condescending when on the client's site; what if the client had trouble reporting faults, because the idiots on the switchboard always routed the call to the wrong department, and what if every time a fault was fixed, it seemed to trigger ten more? The only way we will become aware of these problems is when the client walks away from us, unless we regularly make sure that the client is satisfied. Useful information on measuring user satisfaction can be found in Rodgers (1990).

THE FUTURE OF METRICATION

Quality management

The most interesting trend from my point of view is a move away from measurement *per se*. This, I feel, is a real indication that we are maturing as an industry. More and more organizations are realizing that measurement for its own sake will do little to solve their problems. Only a quality management, and notice I say management not improvement, approach towards process optimization will do this. Of course, measurement is a cornerstone of this approach. This shift of emphasis opens up a whole new topic and this, I believe, will be one of the most interesting areas to be involved in over the next few years. The leaders, of course, will be the ones who get on and do it. They will reap the benefits.

Even with this trend towards the implementation of truly total quality management, there will still be areas of particular interest to the Software Metrics community, and I would like to consider some of those now. We can take this opportunity to look at some techniques that are perhaps less well known than they should be, and to consider their possible impact on the area we call Software Metrics.

Formalization within Software Metrics

The first area I would like to consider is that of formalization within Software Metrics. I remember teaching an evening class of students some years ago. The idea was to introduce this group of students, who ranged from storemen to army officers, to the intricacies of computers. My starting point was to explain that most individuals are, in effect, lazy, and that the use of the term 'computer' was actually incorrect. What we should talk about is the computer system. This gave me a good lead into an explanation of operating systems, programs, hardware, and how these various elements hang together to make up something that can do useful work.

The point of this example is to illustrate our misuse of words. This misuse continues with the use of the term 'Software Metrics'. Technically speaking, a metric is a unit of measure such as the amp, a nautical mile or a parsec. In software terms, an example of a metric would be a *line of code*, provided it were clearly defined, or the McCabe metric known as *cyclomatic complexity*. And that is it, a metric is no more and no less than that unit of measure, and there is a discipline concerned with the definition and use of such metrics. That discipline is *not* what we know today as Software Metrics.

It is interesting to note that at least one ESPRIT project, METKIT, now discourages the use of the terms Software Metrics, preferring Software Measurement. Now we may ask: 'what's in a name?' I must admit that I have some sympathy for this view believing that, if we want to call our area of interest Software Metrics then, provided it is seeking to promote best practice, we call it Software Metrics. We can call it statistics if we want! However, I do recognize that laziness in the use of terms can be symptomatic of a deeper malaise. There is a tendency within Software Metrics, and I will continue to use that term for this book to avoid any more confusion, to lean too heavily towards pragmatism.

Now, bearing in mind one of the main themes of this book, that pragmatic solutions are often perfectly acceptable, that last statement may come as a surprise. Pragmatism is all very well, but we must always remember that there are certain rules which we do not buck. For example, there is a great tendency to add simple measures together to produce a more 'complete' indicator of some characteristic. Let us say that we recognize that the simple line of code (LOC) measure does not totally reflect the effort needed to make an enhancement to a section of code. Furthermore, assume that we consider the McCabe cyclomatic complexity measure a valid measure of complexity. So the model says that, by combining LOC with cyclomatic complexity, we will have a better measure of enhancement effort — so add them. However, the two basic measures use different scales, and cannot be added in this way. It is simply against the rules of mathematics.

I once had the great pleasure of attending a 'mathematical nightclub'. This was an event staged by a group of tutors for the benefit of newcomers to the world of mathematics. It was here that I saw it 'proved' that 2 equals 3 — if you miss the sleight of hand that makes you skim over the line in the proof that says divide by zero! Equally, excuse the pun, if we 'add' LOC and cyclomatic complexity, then we are performing a sleight of hand, because we cannot add quantities of different units together. The reason I have taken so long over this story is that this addition of cyclomatic complexity and LOC is one that I come across about every 12 months! The point is that we can only get away with this type of thing if we do not apply any formalism in our definition and use of Software Metrics.

Three individuals in the UK stand out in my mind as being strong proponents of this formalism: Barbara Kitchenham (1991), Martin Shepperd (Ince and Shepperd, 1989) and Norman Fenton (1991). It is also good to see that more and more people are starting to take note of the points made by these, and other, individuals. The only thing that we have to be aware of is that formalism does not become an excuse for élitism, which the three individuals I have mentioned would wish to avoid. There is a good balance between pragmatism and formalism, the trick is finding it.

International standards

Continuing with the concept of formalism brings us, quite naturally, to the question of International Standards. There are two main centres of activity in this area, the first being the impact of ISO 9000.

ISO 9000 and 9001 This is an International Standard that defines procedure requirements for the management of the customer/supplier relationship. Its impact on the software engineering industry has been significant with numerous organizations seeking and achieving certification to ISO 9001, the 9000 series standard that applies to this industrial sector.

There seem to be two reasons for this preoccupation with certification. The first concerns business strategy. It is a strong sales aid when an organization is chasing work to be able to quote ISO 9001 certification. In fact, for some areas it is becoming a prerequisite. British Telecom, the largest commercial organization in the UK, has made a policy decision that all its suppliers will have to be certified, or at least actively seeking certification, by 1995.

The second reason behind the interest in certification is more of a sociological one. When attempting to instigate a Total Quality Management (TQM) culture, many organizations find it relatively easy to move management and staff towards an acceptance of the need for TQM. This may have something to do with the inherent professionalism of most IT staff. The problem facing these organizations is how to achieve the implementation of the necessary procedures to support TQM, and it is here that a drive towards ISO 9000 can provide the implementation vehicle giving, as it does, a clear goal at which to aim. Although ISO 9000 is not directly related to Software Metrics, it does contain a number of references to measurement, and I see its influence continuing to grow in the future.

IS 9126 The second area of activity in the International Standard's arena is directly related to Software Metrics. In the mid-1980s the two main international standardization bodies, ISO and IEC, formed a Joint Technical Committee to deal with standards for Information Technology. The JTC subcommittee No. 7 deals with software engineering and has identified metrics as a key area. A special working group has been established to address this area. The working group is chaired by Professor Azuma, previously with NEC for some 20 years.

The result of this work has been the definition of a standard, IS 9126, that describes a number of quality characteristics or attributes. These include a number of the well-worn 'ities' such as reliability and maintainability. Such definitions, whether taken from an ISO standard or derived locally, seem to me to be fundamental when one seeks to measure quality characteristics. Of course, the definitions in IS 9126 may be seen as simply one set of such definitions, but they do provide an adequate foundation for local use, and they reduce the amount of work necessary within a measurement initiative.

Having established the feasibility of at least defining International Standards in the area of Software Metrics against, it must be said, a background of some individuals who claimed it could not be done, the JTC working group has now expanded its problem domain beyond the question of quality characteristics. Currently, they are seeking to define standards in the areas of Metrication Methodologies, Process, Product and Resource metrics. As this larger initiative gathers momentum, the impact on the Software Metrics community could be great, as several large and important organizations are already involved in this work.

The challenge facing the software engineering sector of industry is to adapt to this greater degree of formality in a positive way. One concern that is sometimes expressed is that standards may not be workable within particular organizations or areas, but it should be noted that the current trend, at least as far as Software Metrics is concerned, is towards guideline standards rather than prescriptive mechanisms. Having said that, the realities of business, and particularly the demands of customers, may force us to accept standardization more readily than we might otherwise.

Recognizing that the current chairman of the JTC Metrics Workgroup is a Japanese professor provides a nice link to the next area I would like to discuss, namely the Japanese phenomena.

Total quality management and the Japanese

Looking first at Japan, it is interesting to find that a Westerner has greatly contributed to the establishment of a modern quality culture in that country. At the end of the Second World War a gentleman by the name of Deming, having had limited success in getting his ideas accepted in America, was invited by General MacArthur to help in the restructuring of post-war Japan. Deming's philosophy of quality management, with its emphasis on measurement and the use of statistical process control, found fertile ground in this oriental culture which already had an historical acceptance of the principles of continuous improvement. The difference between oriental and occidental culture, where in the East the journey is seen as so important while Westerners tend to be more goal-orientated, obviously contributed to Deming's success. However, we cannot deny the contribution of this man to the whole concept of TQM worldwide, and specifically in Japan — his provision of a philosophy, a route, that enabled the Japanese journey.

We are well aware of the results. Japan is now seen as a major industrial power that has an enviable reputation for supplying the right goods, of high quality at the right price. Now, even the Japanese recognize that this reputation has something to do with the way in which the Japanese phenomena has been hyped (Matsubara, 1991). None the less, the proof of the pudding is in the eating, and numerous industrial sectors have felt the impact of that phenomena. We now see Japanese companies dominating an ever-growing list of markets from motor cycles to televisions. Software engineering is another likely candidate. A recent report, prepared for a specific US-based organization, concluded that the main threat to that organization's market share during the next ten years would come not from Europe, even with the single market economy scheduled for 1993, but from Japan.

Other Far Eastern countries have not been slow to learn from Japan. Singapore and Korea are both examples of countries that are gaining a larger slice of the IT market. It would seem that the foundations for this rapid development of both an IT capability and a reputation for quality is the use of TQM principles, the use of measurement to guide process improvement and individual commitment. So often I feel that we have individual commitment from our IT professionals, what we lack is the ability to apply TQM, and the willingness to use pragmatic measures.

Techniques for the future

Having looked at some relatively large-scale trends, I now intend to shift the focus to look at some specific techniques that have not yet caught the attention of the metrics community in general but which, in my view, have considerable potential for the future. Within this chapter, it will not be possible to describe these measurement-based techniques in full, and I see these summaries as more of a taster. If further information is required, references are provided within the bibliography.

Data Envelopment Analysis

I would first like to look at a technique known as Data Envelopment Analysis (DEA), an extremely intimidating name for something that is inherently elegant and practical. It is a development of the mathematical technique known as *linear programming*, and it is used in the following way:

> Imagine a situation where you have identified two characteristics of your process or products that are common across the organization, for example you may consider productivity and reliability. Further imagine that you have measures associated with these characteristics, and you have collected data from a number of projects. Now, what many managers want to know is how these different projects have performed in terms of these two characteristics.
>
> One thing that you may consider doing is to present a graph with productivity as the x axis and reliability as the y axis. So the performance of each project can be described in terms of two-dimensional vector coordinates. This is all very well, but managers often want information in non-graphical form. They also like comparisons against 'best in class'. Within the DEA technique, these requirements are met by identifying the boundary cases and using these to describe an envelope around the set of observations. For any particular project, its performance can then be represented by drawing a vector from the origin, through the project point to the boundary.
>
> Performance is then expressed as a ratio of the distance from the origin to the project point compared to the total length of the vector to the boundary. This is shown in Fig. 16.2.

The great beauty of DEA is that the technique can be applied to more dimensions than two, in fact any number, subject to the computation capabilities available. DEA has been used in the USA to compare educational establishments, and is also being used now within the IT industry. Tool support is also available. For more information about DEA, see Elam (1989) and Charnes (1978).

Soft factors

I would like to close this chapter by considering an aspect of Software Metrics that is often considered, but seldom actioned, which is a great pity because its impact could be huge. The area I refer to is that known as the soft, or environmental, factors.

Soft factors are all to do with the people aspects of software engineering — in fact, another way of referring to this topic is 'peopleware', and there is an excellent book by Tom DeMarco and Tim Lister (1987), that bears this title. One reason that this topic gets such little attention is because of managers' reactions to it. So often we find that managers see any

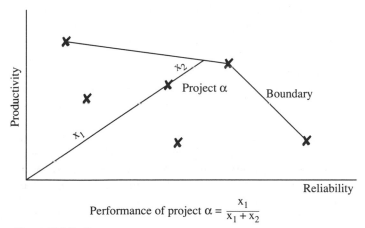

Performance of project $\alpha = \dfrac{x_1}{x_1 + x_2}$

Figure 16.2 Performance.

initiative in this area as one that will lead to demands for more money, bigger offices, more desk space, etc., yet soft factors go much further than this.

There is, of course, another point to consider. If you were a manager and it was proved, beyond reasonable doubt, that giving your staff more of something would increase quality and productivity to such an extent that the cost of giving would be more than outweighed by the return, what would you do?

The sad situation in the vast majority of organizations today is that the information to assess the payback from improved environments is not even collected. Even worse, we know that some teams perform well in adverse conditions, while others cannot perform adequately even when everything is going right. Why is this? What, for example, is the effect of team composition in terms of experience, age, even sex. What size of team is the optimum within your environment? When did you last attempt to discover the morale level of your team other than by listening in on the grapevine?

And yet there are organizations which do apply management principles to the soft factors, although they are few and far between, who seem to be getting good results. IBM did invest heavily in one installation specifically designing it to provide an office environment that was wanted by the workforce. Perhaps it is too early for them to be able to report the result of that experiment formally, but I have seen one reference that claimed a 30 per cent higher productivity rate than that found in other sites doing similar work (McCue, 1978).

A problem with soft factors is the question of data collection, so I would like to describe one experiment in which I was involved that gave limited, but promising, results in that area. The purpose of our experiment was really to see if data could be collected, rather than to try to assess specific soft factor impact, but we did get some interesting results, as you will see.

Feasibility exercise in data collection

Our first problem, of course, was actually what to collect. There are very many potential soft factors about which data could be collected, but this leads to a classic 'data hunter' scenario, and we felt that should be avoided. The approach adopted was quite simplistic, but seemed to work. I and a colleague sat down together and, over the course of a day, brainstormed out a whole raft of potential factors. All the classics were in there, such as experience of team, availability of terminals, and compiler speeds. There were a few others that crept in from the dark, for example, the sex mix of the team. Is this a valid soft factor? In other words, could the sex mix within a team affect performance in any way? When venturing into this area, one can only depend upon personal experience, so I can only talk for all male teams and the mixed variety. What I have found is that mixed-sex teams tend to work better than single-sex teams, although I freely admit that this is a subjective opinion. However, why might that be the case?

Firstly, I believe that the broader range of interests commonly found in mixed-sex teams acts to increase team cohesion. An all-male team can easily get caught up in, say, the world cup to the extent that work suffers. Secondly, I have found that more lunchtime drinking takes place in all-male teams than mixed, although some of the mixed-sex teams I have worked in take some beating! Thirdly, and perhaps this is the real reason such teams work, I find that people in mixed-sex teams are more polite to each other than in all male teams. This is merely an observation, but I will also state that politeness is, in my opinion, the oil that lubricates the social machine. Perhaps such lubrication helps to improve performance in teams as well as in engines.

I include the discussion on mixed-sex teams to show that we did give some thought to the various factors that we were considering at that point — we really had some fun with some! But we then had a problem in that we were suffering from an over-plenitude of riches! We had some 60 or 70 soft factors identified, and we knew that we could not collect, or use, data on so many. To reduce the set, we ran a limited survey. We circulated our list of soft factors to a number of experienced software engineers and managers, and we asked them to score the factors in terms of impact on performance. This was a subjective assessment based on their experience. This was where we had our first interesting result. Because of the way the organization was structured at the time, we were able to include representatives from an American plant in the survey as well as individuals from the UK.

Not only did the two groups identify the same set of factors as most important, but the importance given to each critical factor, judged by the percentage ranking it as critical rather than merely important, were also almost identical. This went against the perceived wisdom that said there were significant differences between the US and UK environment, and came as a surprise to us. Basically, it seemed to suggest that we were operating the same value system. An interesting result, but not one that would 'stand up in court'. Our sample size was too small, our analysis fairly simplistic. We got what we wanted from the exercise, but we did not believe that it could go any further at that time. The sex mix in teams did not survive either.

By means of this survey we were able to reduce our initial set of factors down to about 30. The next step was to come up with some way of measuring those factors. Now I wish that I could tell you that we evolved some wonderful new measurement technique, but the reality is that we gathered data on almost all of those factors by means of a good old-fashioned questionnaire. There were only two factors about which we could collect data from some other source, and they were the experience in the industry and the experience of the organization of team members. This data was available from the personnel department but, in the end, we asked the pilot group directly anyway.

This brings us to the next part of the exercise, the pilot. We were lucky enough to have the cooperation of a very helpful group within the organization, and they had a six-month enhancement project starting at just about the right time. We spent some time with this team explaining what we were after and why. We identified a specific individual as coordinator within that team, and off we went.

The approach was relatively straightforward. Some of the factors we had identified as potentially critical to performance lay within the domain of the project manager, for example, information regarding promotions was most easily obtained from the project manager, while some concerned the whole team. A third subset of factors also lay with the project manager, and were unlikely to change much over short periods of time. To cover these three areas, we set up the following mechanisms:

1. The project manager completed a questionnaire at the end of each month.
2. All team members completed a different questionnaire monthly. These were anonymous.
3. The project manager was interviewed at the beginning, the mid-point and the end of the project.

We completed the experiment by reporting to our own management, by analysing the collected data and by feeding back to the pilot group. What did we find out?

Remember that the purpose of the experiment was to test the feasibility of such a data collection exercise, and we were pleased to learn that nobody in the pilot group felt that it was intrusive. The actual cost for the team questionnaires was about ten minutes per person per month. An extremely satisfying result was that the project team response to the exercise was very positive. They felt that such a mechanism gave them a chance to influence their own environment, which does not simply mean bigger desks, and also gave them a chance to report things that were good as well as drawing attention to things that were bad. Certain changes were needed to the questionnaires, and we realized that the administration of the exercise would need to be improved but, overall, the results were positive. We could collect that kind of data.

We also got a couple more interesting results. One of the soft factors identified was awareness of the local development process, so we asked our team members whether or not they felt familiar with that process. Almost invariably the answer was 'yes'. At the end of the pilot, we introduced the team members to process modelling notations, such as those used elsewhere in this book, and asked them to draw out their own view of the development process. The results were interesting, and varied! Even allowing for the fact that different team members were involved with different viewpoints, different processes were described there.

The other interesting result was that during the course of our pilot, a number of individuals were made redundant in a completely different part of the organization. While this did not directly affect our group, one would expect morale to be affected. The interesting thing was that our morale indicators did register a significant drop for that month. The surprising thing, if our indicators could be believed and we would not claim that they were anything but coarse, was that morale returned to its normal level by the end of the next month.

We found the results of this experiment very encouraging. What was not so encouraging was the brick wall we then ran into. It was obvious to us, and to our immediate management team, that there was merit in establishing mechanisms to collect this type of data across a large part of the organization, but it was also a political bombshell and would have to be handled with great care. We did map out a strategy for achieving implementation of our proposals — the politicking, marketing and effort involved would have cost multiples of the original experiment. Sadly, we had other priorities.

It is typical of many areas in Software Metrics, and in Process Improvement in general, that simple techniques which could genuinely be used to make things better for all concerned, including managers, become political footballs within the organization. Fortunately, there are some individuals working within these organizations who can and do play the political game and who also recognize the worth of techniques, such as those mentioned in this chapter. Very occasionally, such individuals reach the upper echelons of power. When that happens, the impact is large and far-reaching.

SUMMARY

I hope that this chapter has introduced some different and, perhaps, new ideas that you may not have come across before. Of course, it is a very personal view of which topics are receiving attention in terms of applied research today, and which will be important in the near future. There are many things happening today in the broad spectrum of activity covered by the term Software Metrics, and even if only some of them impact on our engineering discipline, then the face of that discipline will undergo major changes over the next few years.

17

CLOSING THOUGHTS

This book has dealt with the development and implementation of a Software Metrics programme. Hopefully, it has done so in a practical way, and you will have gained some appreciation of the work involved and the type of tasks that need to be addressed. Perhaps you have been surprised by the relatively small part that 'metrics' have to play in this work, and how much the involvement of people can affect the success or failure of such a programme.

If you follow the lifecycle laid out in Section 2 of this book, you will stand a relatively good chance of implementing your programme but, in the end, it all comes down to you.

There is one final point that I would like to make. Software Metrics are a very 'hot topic' in our industry today. Every conference and seminar that you attend will have some mention of metrics, and it is seen more and more as a topic in the trade press. People are even writing books about metrics!

The point is that *Software Metrics in isolation are useless*. Only when they form part of the enabling function within an organization's will to improve its process and its products can Software Metrics deliver their full potential.

Measurement simply puts you in a position where you have the chance to solve problems. Let's face it, before you started measuring, you probably did not know what your problems were, you just knew they existed. As for solving them without any form of measurement, forget it. If you don't measure, how will you know when the problem has been solved. Think about it.

Do not fall into the trap of thinking that measurement will solve all your problems — it will not. Only you can solve your problems. Measurement, though, does help. The other thing that helps is to share your problems and concerns with others who face similar circumstances. By far the best advice I can give to close this book is that you take the trouble to attend conferences and seminars that address the problem of measurement in a software engineering environment. I hope I have provided plenty of ideas for such venues.

Talk to people who have faced, or who are facing, the same situation you face, and you will be happy to find that many people have found solutions.

Appendices

Appendix A

USEFUL ORGANIZATIONS

In this appendix I have listed organizations that I or my associates have found to be useful during our work in the area of Software Metrics. I do not claim that the list is complete or even exhaustive, but I do believe that you will find these organizations helpful.

IFPUG
The International Function Point User Group
5008 Pine Creek Drive
Blendonview Office Park
Westerville
Ohio, 43081 4899
USA
Tel: + 1 614 895 7130

EFPUG
European Function Point User Group
2 Park Place
North Road
Poole, Dorset BH14 0HP
UK
Tel: + 44 (0)202 739 533

Netherlands Function Point User Group
Mr E Koneng, Secretary
Postbus 23030
1100 DM Amsterdam
Netherlands
Tel: +31 (0)20 691 0871

European COCOMO User Group
Mr Paul Rook, Secretary
65 Terrington Hill
Marlow, Bucks SL7 2RE
UK
Tel: +44 (0)628 485853

Quality Assurance Forum
17 St Catherines Road
Ruislip, Middx HA4 7RX
UK
Tel: +44 (0)895 635222

Quality Assurance Institute
7575 Dr Phillips Blvd.
Orlando
Florida, 32819
USA
Tel: +1 407 363 1111

Centre for Software Reliability
City University
Northampton Square
London, EC1V 0HB
UK
Tel: +44 (0)71 477 8000

Institute of Electrical and Electronic Engineering
Software Engineering Standards
Service Centre
445 Hoes Lane
PO Box 1331
Piscataway
NJ 08855 13
USA
Tel: +1 908 981 0060

Institute of Electrical Engineering
Savoy Place
London, WC2R 0BL
UK

Tel: +44 (0)71 240 1871

International Standards Organization
1 rue de Varenbe
Case Postale 56
Ch-IZ11
Geneva 20
Switzerland

Tel: +41 22 749 0111

British Standards Institute
2 Park Street
London, W1A 2BS
UK

Tel: +44 (0)71 629 9000

Appendix B

A LIST OF SELECTED **ESPRIT** PROJECTS AND CONTACTS

This appendix lists a set of ESPRIT projects together with a brief description of what they are intended to achieve, and a contact point for further information. The list is in no way exhaustive, it simply provides information relating to those projects about which I have knowledge or in which I have been involved. Hopefully, the results of these projects will be of use.

MUSE
A survey of the state of the art as far as the use of Software Metrics is concerned in Europe.
Contact: M Kelly
            BRAMEUR Ltd
            237 High Street
            Aldershot, Hants GU11 1TJ
            UK
            Tel: +44 (0)252 313437

METKIT
A range of training materials that are intended to promote the use of Software Metrics
Contact: Dr N Ashley
            BRAMEUR Ltd
            Address as for MUSE

MERMAID
This project addresses various approaches to the use of cost estimation strategies, and the more general application of Software Metrics.

224

Contact: Dr B Kitchenham
National Computer Centre
Oxford Road
Manchester M1 7ED
United Kingdom
Tel: +44 (0)61 228 6333

MUSiC

This project addresses the problems associated with the measurement of usability of software systems.

Contact: Mr M Kelly
BRAMEUR Ltd
Address as for MUSE

PYRAMID

A technology transfer project responsible for motivating the users and suppliers of software systems in the use of Software Metrics.

Contact: Monsieur F Copigneaux
VERIDATAS
Aeroploe Batiment A
20 Avenue Didier DAURAT
F31700 Blagnac
France
Tel: +33 61 71 1177

AMI

Again, a technology transfer project, but one that is using a handbook to disseminate much of the knowledge acquired during other ESPRIT projects and from the experiences of the consortium members.

Contact: Mr K Pulford
GEC Marconi Software Systems
Elstree Way
Borehamwood, Herts
UK
Tel: +44 (0)81 906 6705

BIBLIOGRAPHY

Ahlgren, M. and Wohlin, C. (1992) 'Lead Times and Soft Factors' in *Proceedings Eurometrics '92,* April 1992.
Albrecht, A. J. (1979) 'Measuring Application Development Productivity' in *Proceedings Joint SHARE/GUIDE Symposium.*
AMI, (1992) The AMI Handbook, GEC Marconi Software Systems, Borehamwood, UK.
Boehm, B. (1981) *Software Engineering Economics*, Prentice-Hall, Englewood Cliffs, NJ.
Bollinger, T. B. and McGowan, C. (1991) 'A Critical Look at Software Capability Evaluation', *IEEE Transactions on Software Engineering*, July 1991.
Charnes, A. and Cooper, W. (1978) 'Measuring the Efficiency of Decision Making Units', *European Journal of Operational Research*, **2** (6), November 1978.
Crosby, P. (1985) *Quality Improvement through Defect Prevention*, Training Materials, Philip Crosby Associates Inc.
DeMarco, T. and Lister, T. (1987) *Peopleware*, Dorset House, US.
Deming, W. E. (1986) *Out of the Crisis*, MIT Centre for Advanced Engineering Study, Cambridge, Mass.
Dollé, P. and Jackson, K. (1992) *Experiences of Software Quality Management in Software Maintenance — A Case Study*, UK Computer Measurement Group Conference, Session 145, May 1992.
Elam, J. J. and Thomas, J. B. (1989) 'Evaluating Productivity of Information Systems Organisations in State Government', *Public Productivity Review*, (USA), **12** (3), Spring 1989.
Fenton, N. E. (1991) *Software Metrics — A Rigorous Approach*, Chapman and Hall, London.
Fenton, N. E. and Whitty, R. (1986) 'An Axiomatic Approach to Software Metrication through Program Decomposition', *Computer Journal* **29**, (4).
Grady, R. B. and Caswell, D. L. (1987) *Software Metrics: Establishing a Company Wide Program*, Prentice-Hall, Englewood Cliffs, NJ.
Henry, S. and Kafura, D. (1981) 'Software Structure Metrics — Based on Information Flow', *IEEE Transactions on Software Engineering*, **7** (5).
Humphrey, W. S., Snyder, T. R. and Willis, R. R. (1991) 'Software Process Improvement at Hughes Aircraft', *IEEE Transactions on Software Engineering*, July 1991.
Humphrey, W. S. (1989) *Managing the Software Process*, Addison-Wesley, Wokingham, UK.
IFPUG, (1990a) *Function Point Counting Practices Manual Release 3.1*, IFPUG, Westerville, Ohio.
IFPUG, (1990b) 'Counting Practices Manual' in *IFPUG Conference Proceedings*, J. C. Penney Inc. Presentation, Autumn 1990.
Ince, D. and Shepperd, M. 'An Empirical and Theoretical Analysis of an Information Flow-based System Design Metric', in *ESPRIT Project 1, MUSE Report Paper*, 1989.

Irvine, G., Downs, D., Eden, N., Goodman, P., Hemens, A., Shepperd, M., Stanbridge, T., Wall, R. and Woods, J. (1991) 'Implementing a Software Programme', in *Working Party Report*, QA Forum, UK.

IS 9126 (1990) *Software Product Evaluation, Quality Characteristics and Guidelines for their Use*, International Standard 9126, International Standards Organisation, Canada.

Jones, C. (1988) 'A Short History of Function Points and Feature Points', *Software Productivity Research Inc Technical Paper*, Cambridge, Mass.

Kitchenham, B. (1991) 'Empirical Studies of the Assumptions Underlying Software Cost Estimation Models', *Proceedings of European COCOMO User Group*.

Kitchenham, B., Pickard, L. and Linkman, S. J. (1990) 'An Evaluation of Some Design Metrics', *Software Engineering Journal*, January 1990.

Lehman, M. M. and Parr, F. M. (1976) 'Program Evaluation and its Impact on Software', in *Proceedings of 2nd International Conference on Software Engineering*.

Littlewood, B. (1990) 'Software Reliability Measurement', in *Proceedings IEE Colloquium on Software Metrics*.

Lynch, D. and Kordis, P. L. (1990) *Strategy of the Dolphin*, Arrow Business Books, London.

Matsubara, T. (1991) 'Ten Myths of Japanese Software Development', in *Proceedings Joint EOQ/Software Management Circle Meeting*.

McCabe, T. J. (1990) 'Reverse Engineering, Reusability, Redundancy — The Connection', in *American Programmer*, October 1990.

McCue, G. (1978) 'Architectural Design for Program Development', *IBM Systems Journal*, **17**, (1).

Mermaid, (1989) *The Mermaid Project — A Status Report*, issued at ESPRIT Technical Week, November 1989.

Muse, (1979) The MUSE Consortium, *The MUSE Handbook*, Brameur Ltd., Aldershot.

Putnam, L. H. (1979) 'Software Costing and Lifecycle Control', *Proceedings IEEE Workshop on Software Quantitative Models*.

Reifer, D. J. (1989) 'Asset-R: A Function Point Sizing Tool for Scientific and Real Time Systems' in *Marketing Paper*, Reifer Consultants Inc.

Rodgers, P. (1990) 'Customer Satisfaction Metrics' in *QA Formum Presentation*, Leeds University, January 1990.

Rombach, D. and Basili, V. (1990) 'Benefits of Goal-orientated Measurement', in *Tutorial, CSR 7th Annual Conference on Software Reliability and Metrics*, September 1990.

Rook, P. (1990) *Software Reliability Handbook*, Elsevier, Amsterdam.

Rubin, H. (1990) 'Keynote Presentation', in *Proceedings EFPUG Conference*.

Swanson, E. B. (1976) 'The Dimensions of Maintenance' in *Proceedings, IEE/ACM, 2nd International Conference on Software Engineering*, October 1976.

Symons, C. R. (1991) *Software Sizing and Estimating, MkII FPA*, John Wiley, New York.

INDEX